THE
WESTERN
WAY
OF
WAR

THE
WESTERN
WAY
OF
WAR

Infantry Battle in Classical Greece

VICTOR DAVIS HANSON

WITH AN INTRODUCTION BY JOHN KEEGAN
AND A NEW PREFACE BY THE AUTHOR

UNIVERSITY OF CALIFORNIA PRESS
Berkeley · Los Angeles · London

University of California Press, one of the most distinguished university presses
in the United States, enriches lives around the world by advancing scholarship in
the humanities, social sciences, and natural sciences. Its activities are supported
by the UC Press Foundation and by philanthropic contributions from individuals
and institutions. For more information, visit www.ucpress.edu.

University of California Press
Berkeley and Los Angeles, California

University of California Press, Ltd.
London, England

ISBN 978-0-520-26009-2 (pbk. : alk. paper)

The Library of Congress has cataloged an earlier edition
of this book as follows:

Library of Congress Cataloging-in-Publication Data

Hanson, Victor Davis.
  The Western way of war : infantry battle in classical Greece /
Victor Davis Hanson ; with an introduction by John Keegan. — 2nd ed.
    p.   cm.
  Includes bibliographical references and index.
  ISBN 978-0-520-21911-3 (pbk. : alk. paper)
    1. Military art and science—Greece—History.
  2. Infantry drill and tactics—History.   I. Title.

U33.H36   2000
355'.00938—dc21   99-29002

Manufactured in the United States of America

18   17   16   15   14   13   12   11   10   09
10   9   8   7   6   5   4   3   2   1

This book is printed on Natures Book, which contains 30% post-consumer
waste and meets the minimum requirements of ANSI/NISO Z39.48-1992
(R 1997) (*Permanence of Paper*).

FOR

William Frank Hanson

Justice Pauline Davis Hanson

Contents

Introduction

by John Keegan

This is a fascinating, wholly original, and deeply important book. Before I try to explain why—though any reader, expert or lay, who takes it up will need no explanation of its fascination or importance—let me say how I come to be writing this introduction, which I feel privileged to do. Some five years ago the author, Victor Hanson, whom I then did not know—and we know each other so far only through correspondence—sent me the manuscript of his doctoral thesis, called "Warfare and Agriculture in Classical Greece." I, like many established authors, often receive unsolicited manuscripts and find most of them embarrassments. One lacks the time to read them and one lacks the nerve to tell the authors frankly, from such reading as one does, that one's attention has not been engaged.

Victor Hanson's manuscript was different. In the first place, it addressed a genuinely interesting question: What was the real extent of that "laying waste" of crops, vines, and fruit-bearing trees so frequently mentioned by ancient historians in their accounts of warfare between the city-states? The question was interesting because the worst damage one city could do to another, after the killing of its citizen-soldiers on the battlefield, was to devastate its agriculture. But in the second place, Victor Hanson advanced a convincing answer to the question he asked. And he was able to do so not only because he was a systematic classical scholar with a sound knowledge of the appropriate texts, but also because he knew about his subject in the best of all ways—the practical way. As the son of a California grape-growing family, he had tended, pruned, and harvested vines.

As a result, he was rightly doubtful of claims that the outcome of this war or that between city-states was to leave the defeated party supine and impoverished. For he knew that the vine is a

sort of weed that flourishes all the more strongly from savage cutting. And, with that in mind, he took the trouble to discover that
olives—hard, scrawny, and resistant to flame—defy rapid defor-
estation. "Devastation," he concluded, must usually have been
quite limited in its effect. A defeated state, though it probably
lost its grain crop and so passed a hungry winter, would not have
lost its agricultural capital stock—vines and olives—because the
vines regenerated in one season; the victors could not, for both
economic and military reasons, afford the time necessary to hack
down the olive groves to stumps.

Had Victor Hanson left his investigation of the nature of classical warfare there, I think he would still deserve the title of a
creative scholar. However, he did not. "Devastation" was not the
central act of classical warfare. Battle was. Victor Hanson recognized that, but he found himself dissatisfied—rightly so—by the
analysis that modern historians advanced of the nature of battle
between the ancients. They told the reader a great deal about
the archaeology and iconography of battle—the weapons that
excavation has found, the warrior postures that vase paintings
depict—but they seemed reluctant to marry artifact with testimony, the testimony of the ancient historians themselves of the
battles they had seen and sometimes fought in, to produce a picture of what ancient battle was like and, more important still, what
ancient battle was *for*.

Some have proved more than reluctant. Numbers of Victor
Hanson's scholarly colleagues showed themselves downright
hostile to the eventual result of his inquiry into the nature of "infantry battle in classical Greece." They reacted to the chapters
he circulated with the judgment that his thesis fell outside the
accepted and orthodox reconstructions of Greek warfare; that it
ran counter to the theories of scholarly grandees; that it did not
abide safely within the confines of archaeology, iconography, and
textural exegesis; that it drew upon concepts and ideas from
which conventional classical scholarship held itself aloof; and
that the publication of his manuscript could, therefore, only
harm his professional reputation, perhaps—since he was young

and junior in the academic world—with permanently damaging effect.

A less imaginative writer might have been deterred. Fortunately, Victor Hanson's imagination had led him to perceive that at the root of infantry battle in classical Greece lay the value of personal courage. Courageously, therefore, he set aside the warnings of blinkered and timorous classicists and decided to publish all the same. Elisabeth Sifton, herself a scholar as well as a publisher, needed no persuasion from me, as soon as I asked her to read the manuscript, that it was a work of the highest quality. It is here presented to the general reader—and the specialist—so that they may come to a similar conclusion about its worth.

I delight in Victor Hanson's book for two principal reasons. The first is that it is written with the greatest imagination. That is not to say the picture of Greek warfare he offers is an imaginary one. On the contrary, everything he writes is founded upon strict examination of the evidence—textual, iconographic, or archaeological. But his examination is formed by the same powers of imagination, now focused on the human side of warfare, that in his earlier book he brought from his practical experience as a viniculturist to its material aspects. Thus, while he thinks it important to tell us a great deal about the form and construction of Greek armor, he does not think that form and construction exhaust the subject. As he points out, armor was not a thing in itself; it was an appurtenance of the human body. And there are limits to the weight and discomfort of appurtenances that a human body can bear—limits to be measured not only by the index of immediate physical strength but also by that of stamina and endurance. Thus, for example, when we calculate the weight of a hoplite's shield, we must think of how much muscular effort he had to put forth to support it, and for how long he could sustain that muscular effort. In doing so we begin to be able to estimate the duration of those clashes between phalanxes of hoplites that figure so frequently in the histories of Thucydides and Xenophon. And as soon as we can begin to impose a dimension of time upon the accounts of ancient historians, we prepare ourselves also to make calculations about the speed at which phalanxes moved, the distances they covered in maneuver, and all the other factors that transform an ancient source from a literary record to a scientific text.

The second reason for which I delight in Victor Hanson's book is that it does not seek merely to define and calibrate the acts of Greek warfare. It goes further, much further. It seeks to show that Greek warfare was different in kind from the warfare that preceded it; that it was different not merely in technique but in ethos; and that its ethos pervaded Greek life, culture, and politics—and thus our own, too. What Hanson suggests—utterly convincingly, to my view—is that the Greeks of the city-states were the first people on earth to contract between themselves, as equals, to fight the enemy shoulder to shoulder, without flinching from wounds, and not to yield the ground on which they fought until either the enemy had broken or they themselves lay dead where they had stood.

Fifth-century Greeks, in short, invented not only the central idea of Western politics—that power in a state should reside in the vote of the majority—but also the central act of Western warfare, the "decisive battle." For ambush, skirmish, ritual conflict, and single combat between heroes, the types of warfare that had preceded their own—and which M. I. Finley analyzes so brilliantly in *The World of Odysseus,* a book beside which I believe Hanson's will take its place—the Greeks of the city-states substituted the all-or-nothing of pitched battle.

Democracy and pitched battle were, of course, two sides of the same coin. The connection between democracy and the militia principle has long been recognized; it takes little insight to perceive that those who vote for war also commit themselves to fight in it. What had not been perceived, until Victor Hanson lifted the veil, is that the Greek militiamen were also voting for a new kind of warfare dedicated to the same outcome as democratic process—an unequivocal and instantaneous result. Democracy and decisive battle differ, of course, in quality: the first is unviolent, the second unavoidably—and, indeed, necessarily—brutal and destructive. But the logic of the second resides in the first. A man whose life is rooted in that of his city, his farm, and his family cannot, unlike the footloose and the unpropertied, undertake commitment to an open-ended campaign. Better the risk of death tomorrow, but the chance of a victorious return home the day after, than the interminable, deracinating, and wealth-draining uncertainties of guerrilla warfare. A free man—this is Victor Hanson's central point—has mortgaged his life to his liberty, and must be ready to risk his life on the battlefield if the mortgage is to be redeemed.

It was the readiness of free Greeks to die on the battlefield that invested their political life with its heroic quality. Victor Hanson's concluding (and depressing) point is that the modern world retains the ideas both of democracy and of decisive battle, but that while it has not improved upon the former, it has grossly perverted the latter. For the Greeks, battle was a brief and direct encounter between bodies politic, the point of which was to spare families and property from destructive involvement in the brutal decision-making. The modern world, by its efforts to make decisive battle ever more instantaneous in its outcome and conclusive in its result—through the application to warfare of human wealth and ingenuity rather than the commitment of courage and muscular strength—has had exactly the opposite effect. It now demands more of man than any Greek was ever asked to give and threatens the devastation of all he loves and possesses. The Western way of war, conceived by the Greeks as trial by ordeal, leads their descendants into the pit of the holocaust. Victor Hanson's brilliant and moving meditation on the fatal steps along that path may, let it be hoped, help to draw us back from the brink.

Preface

In this account of the fighting between infantry soldiers during the classical age in Greece, I have tried to suggest the environment of that battle experience and the unusual hardship and difficulty for the men who fought. I hope also to offer something more than a narrative description of blows given and received. For it is my belief that the Greeks' stark way of battle left us with what is now a burdensome legacy in the West: a presumption that battle under any guise other than a no-nonsense, head-to-head confrontation between sober enemies is or should be unpalatable. The Greek way of war has developed in us a distaste for what we call the terrorist, guerrilla, or irregular who chooses to wage war differently, and is unwilling to die on the battlefield in order to kill his enemy. We feel no fondness either for the religious or political extremist, the suicidal fanatic who wishes to perish rather than live on through an ordeal of battle. So accepting in the past 2,500 years have we been to the Greek model of pitched battle that we have scarcely noted that in fact Western war has not resembled it for a very long time, nor have we noted its demise in the wars of the latter twentieth century.

No North American or European army can fight a Greek-style battle of mutual consent any longer unless, ironically, war were to break out among "ourselves." That could only occur if there were to be the most fundamental social and political upheavals in Western Europe or North America, or a head-on collision of East and West Europeans, which grows more unlikely each year, especially as it might involve ultimately the use of nuclear weapons, not to mention the less publicized, but even more deadly biological and chemical arsenal. In the Middle East, the peculiar nature of on-again, off-again battle in this century reveals something altogether different from the classical model. So it is certainly unlikely that the crack infantry divisions of Europe and America, for all their expensive firepower, will march out like the Greeks to seek a decisive confrontation. With whom might they now fight in such an engagement? Who would face us across that plain of battle?

Secondhand experience of warfare has become universally popular during the past four decades, a period of relative calm in the West, both for the veteran and—more ominously—for the uninitiated. Lately in England and France, a variety of well-written, nicely illustrated, and seriously scholarly books on Greek and Roman warfare have appeared that successfully meet the general enthusiasm for military history. I have tried to make this study accessible and also interesting to the same general reader; has not the legacy of the Greek manner of combat affected millions of lives in the West even in our century? It is taken for granted in our culture—more or less—that men and women, like their Greek predecessors, do not have to be told by their governments that the only way to defeat an enemy is to find and engage him in order to end the entire business as quickly and directly as possible; and so they have entered upon that crowning absurdity of warfare, the pitched battle.

A word of warning is needed to classical scholars who may be disappointed by my selection of material. I have included no information, for example, on casualty ratios, burial practices, provisioning, and the like; there is also no picture of the tactical (much less strategic) situation on the battlefield. Most of these topics are fully discussed in articles in learned journals and especially in Kendrick Pritchett's recent volumes on Greek warfare. My vision is deliberately focused, instead, on the infantryman in the phalanx at the moment he fought. I provide only a few speculative glimpses, rather than a comprehensive account, of what classical Greek soldiers saw and did during those very few minutes of hard fighting, but at least I hope I have succeeded in renewing some interest in the long-forgotten world of the Greek fighter. For too long he has been seen only as citizen, soldier, marcher, recruit—not as warrior, killer, and victim. My citations to literature and vase painting are mostly representative rather than comprehensive. I have left out a great deal both for the sake of brevity and, to speak honestly, out of fear of boring the reader with a compilation of references he may well never consult. But I hope my evidence is presented fairly and that additional information discovered by other scholars will support my general conclusions about the nature of hoplite battle. Obviously, this is not the place to discuss any of the major controversies concerning Greek warfare—the nature of Homeric fighting, the hoplite reform, or the battle of Leuktra. But I should confess that recent attempts to prove some idea of widespread fluidity in the phalanx, to envision individual skirmishing rather than collective pushing, make no sense at all; the image is not based, it seems to me, on a fair reading of the ancient evidence.

Greek hoplite battle coincides with the rise of the city-state itself, and I have tried to draw most of my evidence from the period 650–338 B.C. However, much of both the literary and pictorial evidence is fragmentary, and it must be augmented at times with information from later Hellenistic and occasionally even Roman times. I believe that some issues, such as panic in columnar formation or battle wounds, can be illustrated quite well in that wider context.

An explanation is also needed concerning the form and organization of this study. The book is divided into five parts. Part 1, "The Greeks and Modern Warfare" (chaps. 1–5), discusses the traditional lack of interest shown by scholars in the actual conditions of Greek battle and suggests that more than tactics and strategy must be studied if we are to learn why the Greek manner of fighting has been so influential in the West. Two general chapters of review are included: a historical account of the evolution of warfare among the agrarian societies of the Greek city-states, and a discussion of our sources of knowledge about Greek battle, which, I hope, will provide the reader with a general idea of the Greek authors and works that are cited in parentheses throughout. In part 2 (chaps. 6–8), I describe the physical and psychological challenges that each man faced before the battle had even begun. In part 3, "The Triumph of Will," I discuss the presence of the general beside his men, the close family and kin relationships among Greek soldiers in the formation, and the use and abuse of alcohol—all to explain why in the last seconds before the charge these men usually chose to fight rather than to flee. Some comparative material from much later periods is included here, not merely to illustrate the universality of the experience of battle, but also to demonstrate how closely most subsequent infantry fighting in the West has followed the Greek model. Part 4, "Battle!" (chaps. 12–16), follows the sequence of events from the moment the men of the phalanx began to move out until the defeated were cleared from the battlefield. At this point I narrow my focus dramatically and try to discuss from the soldier's viewpoint the mechanics of fighting with spear and shield, in an attempt to explain the process through which one phalanx engineered the defeat of its counterpart. My hope here is that the reader will find the narrative exciting, while classical scholars will see new questions raised about phalanx battle and old assumptions questioned. I conclude ("Aftermath," chaps. 17–19) with a reminder that the experience of Greek battle did not end with cessation of the fighting: days or even weeks and months later the wounded continued to die, while the sheer carnage of smashed bodies and equipment on the small area of the battlefield left a powerful, haunting image in the minds of both soldier and civilian onlookers for years to come. In a brief epilogue, I return to the larger questions addressed in chapters 1 and 2 in an effort to relate the graphic details of ancient Greek battle to the problems of conflict in our own society.

In the past twenty years there has emerged, at least in the United States, a rather haphazard practice of spelling Greek names that has nevertheless worked remarkably well. Only a few personal and place names, ones not well known to the general audience, are transliterated in this book directly from the Greek (such as Karneios or Amyklai). More recognizable proper nouns are left in their well-known anglicized forms to prevent needless confusion—for example, Cyprus, Corinth, and Socrates. Let us hope that this successful nonsystem, which relies on our good sense, will not soon be labeled arbitrary and therefore replaced by a complexity of guidelines.

I have translated nearly all the Greek and Latin quotations in the text myself, to be free of the chore of constantly citing existing translations, though most modern published versions are usually reliable and may well read better than my own; the most notable exceptions to this procedure are Homer and the Greek Lyric poets, where I have used Lattimore's translations throughout. In hopes that those outside the university will read this book, I have not written any Greek words in Greek script, and generally have avoided their transliterated forms as well. In a few cases that has been impossible, obviously, for example, "hoplite," "phalanx." References to primary works of classical literature cited in parentheses in the text usually follow the chapter and section numbers found in the Oxford series of Greek and Latin texts: a list of these abbreviations is at the end of the book. There are no footnotes, and references to secondary works in modern languages have been kept purposely to a bare minimum. (These are cited in the text by the author's last name and page number of the work; a fuller citation of each source may be found in the bibliography.) Vase paintings are listed by author's name and plate number of the book in which reproductions of them may be found. (I have not cited these representations, as is properly done, by the standard abbreviations and numbers in Beazley's red- and black-figure lists or those of other major catalogs. I have chosen the book references on two grounds: their accessibility to the general reader and the quality of the reproductions.)

Because ancient Greek battle, as opposed to both strategy and tactics, has not been studied so frequently by classical scholars, I have relied almost exclusively on the ancient evidence, as the references make clear. Yet, that should not suggest that I have collated all of these citations myself. I went through nearly all the major Greek literary and historical texts, but I would have missed much had I not been constantly surprised by relevant passages which became known to me only through the works of other scholars. The bibliography of ancient warfare is immense, as the select list at the end of this book suggests, but here I would like to draw attention to two unique works: Kendrick Pritchett's four-volume "encyclopedia" of Greek warfare, and J. K. Anderson's sensible account of fourth century B.C. Greek battle tactics. It is no exaggeration to confess that this present study simply could not have been written without the work of both these men. Obviously, John Keegan's *The Face of Battle* has been both a model and inspiration for my treatment of Greek battle, the ideas of which came to me nearly ten years ago when I first read, but did not fully appreciate, that most unusual book—a book so fresh in spirit that it has changed forever our very notions of what military history should be.

Finally, I thank those few classicists who wrote to or visited me in Selma, California, during the four years after I finished graduate school and began farming. Professors Leslie Threatte of the University of California at Berkeley, John Lynch of the University of California at Santa Cruz (who first introduced me to the ancient world in a series of unusual Greek and Latin classes as an undergraduate some fifteen years ago), and Michael Jameson, my former thesis adviser at Stanford University, all taught me much of what I know about the Greeks. If it were not for Professors Steven Oberhelman, Josiah Ober, and Deborah Kazazis (former colleagues at the American School of Classical Studies, Athens), I might have forsaken an interest in classical scholarship altogether. Once more Edward Spoffordand especially Mark Edwards, faculty of the Classics Department at Stanford, have saved me from repeated blunders in both research and teaching through especially sound advice. Both Professor Edwards and Dr. Lawrence Woodlock of Stanford—as classicist, lawyer, and oldest friend—read the entire manuscript, and their blunt criticism improved it a great deal. Three classical-language graduate students at California State University, Fresno—Nancy Thompson (currently of Stanford University), Susan Kirby, and Megan Bushman—checked an early draft in its initial form, and have given me insights about the ancient and modern world as well. Jennifer Heyne typed and edited various and often garbled drafts; my thanks are due to her and to the chairman of the Department of Foreign Languages, California State University, Fresno, who ensured that she could devote such diligence to this book. Elisabeth Sifton, my editor at Alfred A. Knopf, through her unchecked enthusiasm, gave me the confidence to keep thinking and trying. My brother Alfred and cousin Rees took over many of my own responsibilities on our family's ranch at a most desperate, discouraging, and forgotten time in American agriculture, and so enabled my research for this book to continue. During the past two years, my wife Cara has aided those efforts on the farm, but she also did much more—in reading the final draft and in supervising our three small children, Pauline, William, and Susannah, who for so many hours were without their father. I have dedicated this book to my parents, for all that they have done.

V. D. H.

May 1987
Selma, California

Preface to the 2009 Edition

The Argument

The Western Way of War appeared nearly twenty years ago and was published in several editions, both in the United States and abroad. Since the volume's initial publication, some elements of its argument have been questioned, as has the accepted notion of ancient Greek hoplite warfare in general.

Before addressing these revisionary views of Greek infantry practice, I remind the reader, as the subtitle suggests, that the book is not intended as a systematic history of Western warfare from the classical period to the present. Although it ends with worry about the Western preference for decisive battle in the nuclear age, the book is hardly a pacifistic warning about the destructiveness of present-day Western war. And it surely is not a celebration of the lethal dynamism of Western military practice in general.

Despite the title, *The Western Way of War* does not discuss all the unique elements of Western warfare. I have outlined those themes more comprehensively in *The Other Greeks: The Agrarian Roots of Western Civilization* (Berkeley and Los Angeles: University of California Press, 1999), *The Wars of the Ancient Greeks* (New York: Collins, 2006), and, at length, in *Carnage and Culture: Landmark Battles in the Rise of Western Power* (New York: Anchor, 2002).

Instead, *The Western Way of War* had three aims: to reconstruct what it was like to be a hoplite soldier in classical Greece, to argue that the peculiarities of hoplite equipment and the tactics of phalanx war make sense once we understand the emergence of the ancient Greek landowning citizen of the polis, and to suggest that the Hellenic desire for decisive infantry battle waged by means of shock and direct assault has had lasting consequences in the West.

Decisive Battle

Western warfare could be defined in a variety of other ways—for example, the European embrace of superior technology that is the dividend of Western rationalism and science. Western armies repeatedly showed a singular ability to welcome and incorporate change, often from outside the West itself. They often were better financed and integrated within the general landscape of free markets than other militaries. And because civilians frequently oversaw the practice of Western armies, the result was often an army of consensual soldiers—a nation in arms that itself voted to go to war. This unique tradition of having civilians, not professional military men, oversee and audit the conduct of war—along with the give-and-take of a free society that embraces self-critique and reflection—has enhanced, rather than retarded, the effectiveness of European armies. All these elements in various ages since the ancient Greeks have made Western armies especially effective.

The Western Way of War focused on a particular preeminent characteristic, however: decisive battle. The term *decisive battle* is somewhat hazy. All cultures, after all, fight at times horrifically and often in mass confrontations. Near Easterners and Egyptians, to take one example, had waged such wars long before the Greeks. But were their battles truly shock collisions of free citizens? That is, were infantrymen elsewhere willing and able to meet head-on, en masse, against like bodies of spearmen as part of citizens' overall effort to conduct war in an open, quick, and decisive manner? I argue that they were not.

In contrast, Egyptians, Hittites, Persians, or tribal forces from central and northern Europe were not heavily armed and armored by Greek standards. The bow, the javelin, and the sling were usually the preeminent offensive weapons of such forces. Accordingly, contingents of horsemen and chariots often ensured victory or defeat. Even the foot soldiers who charged one another did so in small groups and often in uncoordinated attacks. None were free citizens; none could vote. Rarely could they as citizen-soldiers freely buy, own, or pass on private property. The fifth-century B.C. historian Herodotus felt that no other armies fought in the "absurd" way of the Greeks—heavily armored militiamen crashing together on flat plains during the long days of summer, each side seeking, after the initial collision, quite literally to push the other off the battlefield through a combination of spear thrusting and body shoving.

The Singularity of Hoplite Warfare

Why did the Greeks craft a method of infantry battle so brutal, yet, at least in spirit, guided by rules of engagement that often discouraged and deprecated ruse, ambush, night attack, and long, extended campaigns?

The answer perhaps is to be found in part in the peculiar nature of the Greek city-states, the first consensual governments in the history of civilization that often fielded soldiers who were free and independent property owners—militiamen, family farmers, and voters all in one. Such men not only found it in their own economic and political interests to fight decisively—they had no wish to be absent from their farms on long campaigns and no desire to pay taxes or spend money to hire others to do so—but also accepted fighting as a reaffirmation of the free farmers' preeminence in Hellenic culture at large.

In Greek art, literature, and popular culture the free landowning citizen—the hoplite—was willing and able to endure the spear carnage of phalanx warfare, and thus deserved the prestige and honors of his polis at large. The public imagery of polis society—the graphic killing on the friezes of the Treasury of the Siphnians at Delphi and the Temple of Aphaia at Aigina are good examples—was mostly hoplitic. Gods, demigods, and larger-than-life ancestors were portrayed gloriously as contemporary heavily armed infantrymen of the city-state.

Geography played a role as well. Before we use the nomenclature of social science to characterize hoplite war as "socially constructed" or "ritualized," a type of artificial fighting intended to "valorize" a particular landowning class in the polis, we should remember, as Plato reminds us (*Laws* 625c–d), that the manner of Hellenic fighting also mirrored the physical landscape of Greece itself. Flat plains such as those found in Thessaly and coastal Macedon favored the raising of horses and the military culture of cavalry. In more mountainous areas such as Aetolia, Acarnania, and Crete—the ideal enclaves of livestock and herdsmen—skirmishing and missile attack were more the norm.

In contrast, most of the major city-states—Argos, Athens, Corinth, Mantineia, Sparta, and Thebes—were situated amid valleys surrounded and divided by nearby mountain ranges. Such rolling plains not only favored the culture of small farming but also allowed heavy infantry to march unencumbered for short distances to flat battlefields. They gave little natural shelter for the less well armored. The nearby hills also protected the flanks of infantry columns from horsemen.

Hoplite battles did not remain the only way of fighting Greek wars. By the fifth century there were sizable navies, and these maritime forces were to grow dramatically in the centuries that followed. The costly hoplite panoply became too cumbersome and expensive for larger armies—often mercenary forces—which marched greater distances in the Mediterranean summer and therefore adopted lighter models of armor.

Over the course of polis evolution, skirmishers augmented by missile troops would also come to play critical roles in all major engagements. Cavalry, artillery, and sieges were integral to Greek warfare by the fifth century as well. But for at least the two centuries between 700 and 500 B.C., and perhaps for much of the early fifth century as well, hoplite infantry battle was at the symbolic center of Greek warfare. It proved the most decisive means to settle disputes—instantaneously, economically, and ethically.

Much of the phenomenal growth of the poleis between the eighth and the fifth centuries B.C. perhaps reflects this Greek genius for accepting warfare as omnipresent—what the philosophers considered a "natural" state of affairs—and yet crafting protocols to ensure the prompt and decisive settlement of disputes.

The Persian and Peloponnesian wars called into question elements of the hoplitic code—not by demonstrating that hoplites we rean outdated asset in pitched battles, but by proving that they were also matchless troops in terrain other than the small valleys of Greece if augmented by auxiliary forces not drawn from the middling stratum of Greek society. In short, the Greeks were to discover that armored spearmen in phalanxes, albeit with greatly reduced armor and longer pikes, were even deadlier when protected by horsemen and lightly armed troops and used against nonhoplite forces. The Greeks gradually learned, as we have, how to transfer the idea of decisive infantry battle to an environment of total war never dreamed of by the hardy yeomen of the eighth and seventh centuries B.C.

This new edition of *The Western Way of War* retains the supplementary bibliography (added in the 2000 paperback edition), in which I referred the reader to further discussions and controversies that had arisen since the original 1989 publication. Here I add some further observations on more recent scholarly revisionism relevant to the book's arguments.

A Middle Class?

Some critics have suggested that the notion of classical Greek hoplites as a middling class—known in our sources as *hoi mesoi*—is most likely a myth. Infantry warfare, they argue, was mostly the domain of the upper classes, who alone could afford armor. That the Greeks themselves did not always recognize hoplite infantry as a clearly conceptualized "class"—or that the middling status of the *mesoi* at times was loose and fluid—does not negate its existence. Three major points support the connection between moderate landowners and hoplite infantry.

First, the arguments for and against the presence of middling hoplites sometimes hinge on interpreting Aristotle's famous description of the rise of the city-state and its connection with its hoplite citizenry:

Indeed the earliest form of government among the Greeks after monarchy was composed of those who actually fought. In the beginning that meant cavalry, since without cohesive arrangement, heavy armament is useless; and experience and tactical knowledge of these hoplite systems did not exist in ancient times, and so power again lay with mounted horsemen. But once the poleis grew and those with hoplite armor became stronger, more people shared in government. (*Politics* 4.1297.16–24)

Note Aristotle's impression that the city-states were at first dominated by horsemen, since hoplites were few and did not fully employ the tactics of the phalanx ("cohesive arrangement"). But as the population grew and those who used heavy equipment found its optimal employment on the battlefield, government incorporated this new group ("more people") of citizen-soldiers.

Aristotle's sociology of classes is not systematic or even consistent. And he is often imprecise (as are moderns who evoke a simplistic rich-poor political dichotomy in casual political discourse) about the rich, poor, and middle classes. Nevertheless, he is mostly unambiguous elsewhere in the *Politics* when talking about the relationship of hoplites to farming (e.g., 4.1291a.31–33; 4.1297b.15–28), a connection that echoes through Greek literature in authors as diverse as Aristophanes, Plato, and Xenophon, in implicit references as well as frequent metaphors and similes.

More important, middleness is a ubiquitous sociological ideal in Greek literature (e.g., Phocylides frag. 7.1–2: "Much good is there to the middle ones; I wish to be midmost in a city"). Such preference for the in-between is often connected to the hoplite ranks, who are framed on the battlefield by the mounted wealthy and the poorer lightly armed troops. And in the rural sociology of the polis, they remain distinct from both the horse-owning wealthy and the landless poor.

Second, farmland is sometimes assessed in Greek history and philosophical writings by its potential to produce hoplites, emphasizing the connection between those citizens who farm and those who fight as hoplites. Passages in Euripides, Aristotle, and Xenophon, moreover, equate farmers with hoplites and define them as the true measure of the city-state.

Third, there is also the more practical argument of demography and landscape. Take Athens—generally not thought of as a preeminent hoplite power—where rough estimates of the citizen population, average farm size, and total arable land make it likely that middling farm owners there numbered roughly fifteen to twenty thousand, roughly the same as the customary number of Athenian hoplites. Other surveys in Boiotia and the Argolid suggest the ubiquity of moderate-size plots of land that would support these city-states' large hoplite infantry forces.

Was Greek War Rare?

The Western Way of War assumes that the Greeks believed that war was innate in humans and so ubiquitous as to be a "normal" phenomenon—perhaps because wars of annihilation in the pregunpowder age analogous to the devastating wars of the nineteenth and twentieth centuries were rare.

This assumption has been challenged recently on the basis that it is a fallacy hinging on a misreading of a single, though famous, passage in Plato's *Laws* to the effect that all Greek city-states are by nature engaged in a relentless war against all others. At one point in the dialogue, Cleinias, a Cretan, quotes an anonymous Cretan lawgiver: "What most people call 'peace' is nothing but a word, and in fact every city-state is at all times, by nature, in a condition of undeclared war (*akêrutos polemos*) with every other city-state" (*Laws* 626a).

Orthodox interpreters usually cite this passage as evidence that the Greeks philosophically accepted that periodic outbreaks of hostility were more likely than long periods of peace. Here the Athenian stranger and Cleinias are discussing the Cretan constitution, why the custom of group messes and communal dining arose, and the need for constant preparedness given the perception of near-constant war. The explanation of a constant condition of undeclared war is not, as revisionists sometimes argue, followed by a sneer against the masses who are unaware of it, or an implication that this explanation was only a rarified theory. Instead the concept clarifies why the anonymous Cretan lawgiver—as an authority responsible for the safety of the Cretan community—"established every one of our institutions, both in the public sphere and private, with an eye on war."

More important, other abstract observations across a wide chronological spectrum reflect a similar Hellenic view of war as a near-constant and natural state of affairs. Most famously, Heraclitus remarked, "War is both father and king of all; some he has shown forth as gods and others as men, some he has made slaves and others free" (frag. 53). And in another fragment, he reiterated the view that war is a natural state of affairs: "It should be understood that war is the common condition, that strife is justice, and that all things come to pass through the compulsion of strife" (frag. 80).

The point of these observations is that abstract Greek thinkers saw generic conflict as almost natural—a ceaseless, omnipresent state that at any time can alter even the status of the citizen and the slave. In Xenophon's *Hellenica* (6.3.15), the Athenian envoy Callistratus matter-of-factly remarked to his Spartan audience, "We all know that wars are forever breaking out and being concluded, and that we—if not now, still at some future time—shall desire peace again."

The Acceptance of War

There is a certain Hellenic resignation to, and perhaps even cynicism about, the state of war as so common among city-states that men should accept it as inevitable. The particular allegiances between the city-states that for a time might deter a war pale in comparison with the larger bellicosity of the poleis, and of human nature itself, that ensures nearly constant wars of some sort. War was seen as a natural state or an undeclared reality, or as a king or a father, or, in Thucydides' words, as a "violent teacher" (5.82).

These reflections seem natural given the sheer number of city-states, the limited amount of arable land in Greece, and the geography of small enclaves set off from one another by hills and mountains that form convenient borders between relatively small populations—and especially a pretechnological age in which wars of massive annihilation were unknown.

Although it is easy to suggest that the experience of nearly constant warring by classical Athens is atypical of its own history and that of other poleis, it is nonetheless true that Athens warred for three out of every four years in the fifth century, and perhaps two out of three over a longer period. Likewise, the fourth-century Spartan state suffered severe social dislocations given its almost nonstop deployment of its officers abroad in the aftermath of the Peloponnesian War. The ubiquity of martial scenes in ceramic art and on temple friezes and pediments emphasizes the Greek sense that war was almost a natural state of affairs—which is borne out in literary genres from Homeric epics to the Greek histories that are devoted to explications of war.

The Greeks accepted the notion that although it was impossible to ban war, outlaw it, or ensure that it would never break out again, there were nonetheless ways to prevent individual wars and to mitigate their severity—through deterrence, a balance of power, the creation of coalitions, constant preparedness, and eternal vigilance. This way of thinking is well illustrated in the speech of the Theban general Pagondas before the battle of Delium (Thucydides 4.92), in which he outlined the need for constant vigilance against his Athenian neighbors, who were likely to be aggressive when they sensed weakness. "As between neighbors generally, freedom means simply a determination to hold one's own," he said, adding, "people who, like the Athenians in the present instance, are tempted by pride of strength to attack their neighbors, usually march most confidently against those who keep still, and only defend themselves in their own country, but think twice before they grapple with those who meet them outside their f rontier and strike the first blow if opportunity offers." This tragic acceptance of war is not an endorsement of its utility, but it is antithetical to the modernist notion that human nature can be altered sufficiently—through education, training, and freedom from want—to eliminate war entirely.

Fluid Fighting?

Since the publication of *The Western Way of War,* others have suggested a different scenario, in which hoplites along the battle line fought more fluidly at some distance from one another, with neither an initial collision nor a subsequent push to achieve a breakthrough.

But once again there is reason to doubt this revisionism. A variety of Greek authors use a rich vocabulary to describe battles in which a "breaking" of the ranks, a "storm" of spears, and a literal "push" take place. It is hard to accept that the repeated references to the *ôthismos* (the "push") are merely figurative. In a war of shock and pushing, one would expect hoplite battles to involve running and the breaking of spears—and often that is just what we read in extant descriptions. Indeed, at most major battles—such as Marathon, Delium, Mantinea, Coronea, and Nemea—hoplites a re specifically mentioned as approaching at a run or trot. In general, the need to keep close in rank and protect the man to the left is emphasized and alone rewarded with formal commemoration. The shield is frequently praised as a defensive weapon used in unison along the battle line and as the most common measurement of phalanx depth.

If phalanx warfare were not a matter of shock and pushing, as historians believed until recently, why would hoplites in a Mediterranean climate carry spears and large shields and wear such heavy bronze armor—an ensemble not particularly suited to fluid individual combat and not replicated elsewhere in similar climates?

Analogies to Macedonian phalangites, Roman soldiers, or contemporary tribesmen who mass in formation only to advance in smaller groups and fight with greater fluidity are not convincing: Hellenistic phalangites, with much smaller shields on their necks or arms, used both hands to carry long pikes; Roman legionaries relied on the short *gladius;* and modern tribesmen with long spears who fought fluidly usually did so nearly naked. In contrast, I imagine that if anthropologists had discovered indigenous tribes with full suits of bronze armor, large willow shields, and thrusting spears, they would have described shock tactics similar to those of hoplite warfare.

In addition, battle narratives in Thucydides and Xenophon often concentrate on entire contingents that advance or retreat collectively and either are annihilated or escape casualties as a whole. At Delium, the Thespians are encircled and wiped out. At Nemea, the Thespians meet the men from Pellene and both sides die in their places. In the same battle, the Spartans let entire contingents of the Athenians go by and then collide with the Argives. At Coronea, the Argives run away en masse and the Thebans and Spartans collide as two identifiable contingents. At Tegyra, the startled Spartans let the Thebans come through and then they collectively are broken apart. The accounts of these battles give a sense not of fluid stages, with fatalities evenly divided on both sides in individual hand-to-hand combat, but of collisions, collective retreats, and synchronized advances, in which entire columns of men suffer terribly or escape losses altogether.

A Late Phalanx?

The orthodox view allowed that the phalanx evolved in a more complex fashion from the seventh century to the fourth, in the same manner that the Corinthian helmet and the solid bronze breastplate gave way to lighter models. But current revisionism claiming that the phalanx of the fifth century was largely a new phenomenon seems altogether mistaken. Greater population, more state control, and accumulated battle experience made clas-

sical phalanxes larger and more sophisticated than earlier phalanxes. And fifth-century warfare took advantage of the synergy
of specialized light and mounted troops and more elaborate tactics of advance and concentration of force than had been used
previously. But there is no reason to think that the classical phalanx ipso facto was so very different from its archaic origins, much
less that it was altogether novel. Instead, it was a product of the
natural evolution of those antecedents.

A number of pragmatic considerations explain perceived differences in early and late formations. First, whereas archaic hoplites at war are known largely from vase paintings and poetry, their
classical counterparts are known from prose accounts in
H e rodotus, Thucydides, Xenophon, and the later historians and
biographers. Historians could present more detail, both of battle and tactics, than earlier epic and lyric poetry and vase painting. That said, it is remarkable that both the poet Tyrtaeus and
the historian Xenophon, three centuries apart, speak of an *ôthis -
mos.* The scene of hoplites portrayed on the Proto-Corinthian
Chigi vase of about 650 B.C. differs little from a similar battle line
sculpted on the Nereid monument at Xanthos about 400 B.C.

Second, there is little logical connection between the known
evolution of hoplite weaponry and the hypothesis that the phalanx first appeared in the fifth century. Traditionally, the introduction of heavy weaponry is thought to have refined and improved
fighting in dense mass. As the polis grew larger and richer, phalanxes incorporated more hoplites; and in response to these
changes, warfare became more complex, with greater use of
maneuvers, as armament, often produced in "factories" by the
state, grew somewhat lighter and thus perhaps cheaper as well.

But if phalanx warfare—that is, fighting in close rank and dense
formation—was a phenomenon of the late fifth century, followed
by the even more compact formations of the Macedonians, are
we then to believe that archaic hoplites with cumbersome arm
and thigh guards, wearing the obtrusive Corinthian helmet and
bronze bell-corselet, fought fluidly as skirmishers, whereas their
more mobile successors belatedly discovered the advantages of

battle line solidarity and shock? The opposite sequence seems more credible—that as the phalanx coalesced, grew denser and less fluid, and began to rely on shock, the crowded hoplites in the ranks would adopt heavier, not lighter, arms and armor.

Finally, why would eighth- and seventh-century Greeks fabricate heavy infantry arms and armor whose optimal use was discovered more than two centuries later? The hoplite panoply was unlike any other set of arms and armament seen before or since. The notion that citizens would craft such armor without knowing its uses is unbelievable and unsupported by literary descriptions and artistic renditions.

A Century-Long Orthodoxy

Recent questions about hoplite warfare that have followed the publication of *The Western Way of War* are often framed as a revisionist questioning of an orthodoxy that grew up in the past twenty years among a "face-of-battle" group of scholars influenced by John Keegan and others. In fact, the orthodoxy of eighth- to seventh-century hoplites as a middling group of citizens, neither rich nor poor, pushing and spearing en masse in frequent wars fought over disputed land, was established over a century of scholarship by historians as diverse as F. E. Adcock, J. K. Anderson, G. Busolt, H. Delbrück, Y. Garlan, A. W. Gomme, G. B. Grundy, J. Kromayer, W. K. Pritchett, A. Snodgrass, and dozens of others who had no allegiance to a particular ideology, approach, methodology, or politics but drew conclusions from their close reading of Greek texts, inscriptions, and representations on vase paintings and in stone.

V. D. H.

September 2008
Selma, California

Chronological Table

Relevant Dates of Some Important Greek Hoplite Battles (All dates B.C.)

1200	Collapse of Mycenaean Greece
1200–800	Greek Dark Ages
750–700	Composition of Homeric poems
700–650	Introduction of hoplites and the tactics of the phalanx; beginning of Greek Lyric poetry
560	Spartan War with Tegea
494	Spartan victory over Argos at Sepeia
490	Battle of Marathon
480–479	Conclusion of the Persian War at Thermopylai, Salamis, and Plataia
471	Collapse of Arcadians at Dipaia
457	Athenian defeat at Tanagra but subsequent victory over Boiotians at Oinophyta
447	Victory of Thebes over Athens at the first battle of Koroneia
431	Outbreak of the Peloponnesian War; first Spartan invasion of Attica
424	Athenian disaster at Delion
422	Death of Brasidas and Kleon at Amphipolis
418	First battle of Mantineia
415	Athenian victory at Syracuse
413	Athenian disaster on the heights of Epipolai and final Athenian defeat in Sicily
403	Thrasyboulos' victory at the Piraieus
401	Kunaxa and retreat of Xenophon's Ten Thousand
395	Death of Lysander at Haliartos

I

The Greeks
and Modern Warfare

1   *Ordinary Things, Ordinary People*

> He talked to me at club one day concerning Catiline's
> conspiracy—so I withdrew my attention, and thought
> about Tom Thumb.
>
>   —*Samuel Johnson*

More than five years ago I wrote in a small monograph, *Warfare and Agriculture in Classical Greece,* that the favored way of initiating infantry battle between classical Greek city-states at war, which was to devastate farmland, was a paradox of the highest order. Nearly all of our ancient literary sources make it clear that the Greeks themselves believed that the ravaging of grainfields, orchards, and vineyards was a serious affair. And we have traditionally assumed that the entire premise of Greek warfare was that the belligerents mutually assumed that further attacks by invaders against farmland must be checked by decisive infantry battle on the plains of Greece in order to save the livelihood of the defenders. Yet upon closer scrutiny a variety of disturbing indications from Greek literature, archaeology, and epigraphy suggested that, in fact, nearly the opposite seemed to be true: the sheer difficulty of destroying trees, vines, and acres of grain virtually ensured that comprehensive destruction was unlikely. Instead, farming continued immediately after the departure of the invaders, or in the very midst of their occupation, times when we might have imagined that destroyed farmhouses, ruined grainfields, and stumps in place of orchards and vineyards made such an enterprise impossible for an entire generation to come. For example, despite the shrill complaints of Attic farmers portrayed in Aristophanes' comedies concerning their losses to Spartan ravagers, elsewhere in those very plays (first produced during the

Peloponnesian War) there are plenty of references both to farm produce and to being able freely to move about in the countryside. Even the somber historian Thucydides, who presents the most detailed narrative of Spartan ravaging during the Archidamian (431–425) and Dekeleian (413–403) phases of the Peloponnesian War, presumes that the actual long-term losses to Athenian agriculture were not great. Why then did men march out to fight when the enemy entered their farms?

The rationale of Greek battle between heavy infantry of the classical period cannot be that it was a preventative to agricultural catastrophe but, rather, we must consider that it arose as a provocation or reaction to the mere *threat* of farm attack. The mere sight of enemy ravagers running loose across the lands of the invaded was alone considered a violation of both individual privacy and municipal pride. Usually a quick response was considered necessary, in the form of heavily armed and armored farmers filing into a suitable small plain—the usual peacetime workplace of all involved—where brief but brutal battle resulted either in concessions granted to the army of invasion, or a humiliating, forced retreat back home for the defeated. Ultimate victory in the modern sense and enslavement of the conquered were not considered an option by either side. Greek hoplite battles were struggles between small landholders who by mutual consent sought to limit warfare (and hence killing) to a single, brief, nightmarish occasion.

Ironically, most city-states (Athens of the late fifth century B.C. being the notable exception) never questioned the effectiveness of enemy ravaging of croplands, which continued before and after these ritualized set battles; yet we can be sure that the greater danger to any landholding infantryman was painful death on the battlefield, not slow starvation brought on through loss of his farm. The Greek manner of fighting must be explained as an evolving idea, a perception in the minds of small farmers that their ancestral land should remain at all costs inviolate—*aporthetos*—not to be trodden over by any other than themselves, land whose integrity all citizens of the polis were willing to fight over on a moment's notice. At the end of the fifth century B.C., after two hundred years of hoplite warfare, Athens and other communities learned that it might be more advantageous to remain inside the city walls and dare the enemy to ruin their farm estates; the formalized ritual of pitched hoplite battle was then questioned and thus jeopardized. The rapid growth of auxiliary troops and siegecraft in the ensuing fourth century accompanied these new ideas and ensured that battle thereafter would be relentless rather than episodic, expanded rather than confined, a new opportunity for the victor to seek not a benign humiliation but often the unconditional surrender and subjugation of the defeated. In short, the entire notion that infantry battle was integrated irrevocably with agriculture was cast aside.

In my earlier work I felt that a proper understanding of agricultural devastation was significant chiefly in economic terms: we should not attribute civic upheaval during periods following even lengthy hoplite wars to wartime farming losses since so little actual damage was done in the countryside. However, there were, I realize, military implications as well that concerned the very nature of Greek battle. Infantrymen marched out not to save their livelihoods nor even their ancestral homes, but rather for an *idea:* that no enemy march uncontested through the plains of Greece, that, in Themistocles' words, "no man become inferior to, or give way, before another." (Ael. *VH* 2.28)

The initial ideas which led to that study a few years ago did not, I must confess, originate solely from a close reading of Greek literary and historical texts, or walks in the Attic countryside, or examination of epigraphical collections—although I argued such sources do confirm the general outlines of my thesis. Instead, it was my practical interest in the difficulty and frustration of removing fruit trees and vines on a small farm in the San Joaquin Valley of California that suggested that these problems could only have been magnified (as they had been in my grandfather's time on farms without tractors and chain saws) where the process was not an occasional, bothersome task for a forgotten fraction of the population, but a real worry in the mind of every citizen of the classical polis. I was struck also by how overly sensitive, how irrational, were our present-day neighbors (and myself) to the slightest incursion of their farms by troops of urban young hunters or the weekend horsemen who trespassed so freely. Convinced that our electrical pumps, sheds, irrigation pipes, and orchards had been ruined or at least "tampered with" by these invaders, on inspection we rarely found anything other than the occasional bullet hole or manured alleyway.

Obviously, then, I do not believe that we should imagine classical Greek society frozen in time and space, as a cultural standard maintained over the millennia, for a small elite. Humanists in our universities who look back to the fifth century B.C. to find solace in the excellence of Greek literature, art, or philosophy, all too often conceive of an image of a society that never existed. They picture writers, artists, philosophers, and other men of genius, but they do not picture them as related to the vast majority of Greek people and their "petty" concerns and, worse yet, they divorce them from the very physical landscape they inhabited. In their hands classical studies has grown only more rarefied and isolated from those who surely need its guidance now more than ever: all serious and hardworking citizens of *our* polis. All too many scholars—as any visitor to the learned societies' conventions can attest—have somehow convinced themselves that classical Athens was a community similar to their own universities, a notion that is not only demonstrably false but also dangerous: this attitude has virtually ensured that only scarce resources are invested in their own limited interests, which in turn casts a further veil over the Greeks and removes them yet a further generation away from the rest of us. A good example is found in the relative neglect by classicists of ancient Greek agriculture. Nearly eighty percent of the citizens of most ancient city-states were employed in farming, and questions of food supply affected nearly all their economical or political discussions. Yet, until recently not more than a half-dozen books were devoted to the subject. Modern scholars have been far more interested, ironically, in "pastoralism," the artificial and detached view of the countryside created by just a few ancient escapists, who like their modern admirers were often far removed from the concerns of contemporary society. Nor do the social scientists do us any better if they investigate the role of labor, slavery, women, family, and kin relationships in order to discover some structure in classical society that validates their ideas about contemporary politics—for inevitably they have a political agenda.

Rather, classical Greece still offers us the best—perhaps the only intellectual—explanation for how the pragmatic concerns of our own daily existence in Western society have been addressed and solved. If we concentrate on mundane and ordinary activities—the mechanics of ancient farming or fighting, to take a small example—we can discover in a well-documented, brief period in history that honesty and clarity of expression in all types of inquiry were of vital concern to the pragmatic Greeks of the fifth century B.C., to the men like Socrates, Sophocles, and Pericles who were stonemasons, soldiers, farmers, and businessmen. This process is inevitably a circular one: contemporary issues of vital concern, which we began by thinking so simple, inevitably become complex when we discover the unexpected ways in which Greek experience shared them, which in turn brings us a renewed appreciation for the versatility and novelty of the Greek legacy.

Of course, one naturally sees the ancient Greece one wants to see. For example, if there is a dangerous tendency among contemporary military strategists to make the experience (and thus misery) of soldiers in battle forever of only secondary concern, whether at the tactical level on the battlefield or in the global vision of the nuclear planner, Greek history can, I suppose, provide the supporting intellectual framework: strategy and tactics in the abstract sense are, after all, Greek words for generalship and troop arrangement. Yet the architects of the Somme, Schweinfurt, Vietnam, and other misadventures to come draw on the experience of their own counterparts, the fourth-century B.C. armchair tacticians or the Hellenistic pedant, not on the world of Aeschylus and Socrates, who knew the Greek battlefield as ordinary hoplites in the Athenian phalanx. The example of classical Greece insists that there was, is, and always must be a connection between the adolescent unshaven men who kill and either those who order or we who ignore them.

The only prerequisite in any investigation of classical Greece is that we must always consider the seemingly ordinary as well as the extraordinary if we are to understand and thus learn from the most profound lessons of these most practical of men. And while today the university is the last island in America where we can learn the necessary philological skills to study ancient Greece, the university surely has not taught us—nor will it or can it teach us—how to use the knowledge we acquire. That task is an individual affair, unwelcomed by many classical scholars. But the rewards of turning to classical Greece to investigate the ordinary are great, for the ultimate answers are always of a moral nature, and have a far greater likelihood to be applicable and comprehensible to nearly every one of us.

2   *A Western Way of War*

Therefore, though the best is bad,
Stand and do the best, my lad;
Stand and fight and see your slain,
And take the bullet in your brain.

—*A. E. Housman*

War which was cruel and glorious has become cruel and sordid.

—*Winston Churchill*

Firepower and heavy defensive armament—not merely the ability but also the desire to deliver fatal blows and then steadfastly to endure, without retreat, any counterresponse—have always been the trademark of Western armies. It was through "hammer blows," thought Clausewitz, that the real purpose of any conflict could be achieved: the absolute destruction of the enemy's armed forces in the field. Here, too, can be found the genius of Napoleon, who saw, as Jomini conceded, "that the first means of effecting great results was to concentrate above all on cutting up and destroying the enemy army, being certain that states or provinces fall of themselves when they no longer have organized forces to defend them." (Earle 88) It is this Western desire for a single, magnificent collision of infantry, for brutal killing with edged weapons on a battlefield between free men, that has baffled and terrified our adversaries from the non-Western world for more than 2,500 years: "these Greeks are accustomed to wage their wars among each other in the most senseless way," remarked Mardonios in 490. According to Herodotus, Mardonios was the nephew of Darius and commander of Xerxes' armada on the eve of the great Persian invasion of Europe. "For as soon as they declare war on each other, they seek out the fairest and most level ground, and then go down there to do battle on it. Consequently, even the winners leave with extreme losses; I need not mention the conquered, since they are annihilated. Clearly, since they all speak Greek, they should rather exchange herald and negotiators and thereby settle differences by any mean rather than battle." (7.9.2) Herodotus' account suggests awe, or perhaps fear, in this man's dismissal of the Greek manner of battle and the Greek desire to inflict damage whatever the costs. Perhaps he is suggesting that Mardonios knew well that these men of the West, for all their ordered squares, careful armament, and deliberate drill, were really quite irrational and therefore quite dangerous. All the various contingents of the Grand Army of Persia, with their threatening looks and noise, had a very different and predictable outlook on battle. In Herodotus' view here, the Persians suffered from that most dangerous tendency in war: a wish to kill but not to die in the process.

Americans, despite their Revolutionary tradition of surprise attacks and ambushes by a motley collection of guerrilla frontiersmen, are the most recent captives of this classical legacy. American armed forces in recent wars have sacrificed mobility, maneuver, grace, if you will, on the battlefield in exchange for the chance of stark, direct assault, of frontal attack against the main forces of the enemy and the opportunity to strike him down—all in the hope of decisive military victory on the battlefield. "When war comes," reasoned twentieth-century American infantry strategists, "there should only be one question that is ever asked of a commander as to a battle and that one is not what flank did he attack, nor how did he use his reserves, nor how did he protect his flanks, but did he fight?" (Weigley 6) Like the classical Greeks, who employed no reserves, flank attacks, or rear guard, American thinkers have given more importance to the immediate application of power against the enemy than to the arts of maneuver and envelopment. We have at least professed that victory was achieved solely by frontal assault until one side cracked. "Maneuvering in itself will not gain victories," declared the Americans. "The combat is the scene of the greatest violence in war. As it is the only set act in war from which victory flows, we should be prepared to achieve victory at any cost no less than the price of blood. All preparations in war must aim at victory in battle." (Weigley 7)

In this last generation, however, it has become popular (like Mardonios in Herodotus' history) to dismiss if not ridicule this manner of warfare, this legacy of single, head-on battle bequeathed to us by the Greeks. The heavy infantry, the tactics of direct assault, and the very firepower of American and European armies, which once captured the public imagination as somehow "heroic," have proven embarrassingly ineffective in the postcolonial conflicts and terrorist outbreaks of the era since the Second World War, as the men of the West have become bogged down in the jungle and the mountainous terrains of Africa, Latin America, and Southeast Asia. The traditional, continental armies of the Western democracies should not have been introduced there for both political and strategic reasons ("the wrong war in the wrong place at the wrong time"). Instead, the guerrilla and loosely organized irregular forces, the neoterrorists who for centuries have been despised by Western governments and identified with the ill-equipped, landless poor, now command attention, fear, or even admiration, not merely on political grounds, or even through any brilliance of combat, but rather because of their uncanny success at ambush and evasion of direct assault: they seek not to engage in *but rather to avoid infantry battle.* This failure to lure the North Vietnamese army into a Western-style shootout is what finally paralyzed the huge land army of the United States and forced it to abandon the entire theater:

> When the hideous Battle of Dak To ended at the top of Hill 875, we announced that 40,000 of them had been killed, it had been the purest slaughter, our losses were bad, but clearly it was another American victory. But when the top of the hill was reached the number of NVA found was four. Four. Of course, more died, hundreds died, but the corpses kicked, counted and photographed and buried numbered four. Where, Colonel? And how, and why? Spooky. Everything up there was spooky, and it would have been that way even if there had been no war. You were there in a place where you didn't belong, where things were glimpses for which you would have to pay, a place where they didn't play with mystery but killed you straight off for trespassing. (*Herr 95*)

And so Mao Tse-tung, Ho Chi Minh, and Fidel Castro became

media favorites to many, figures whom even the most diehard
traditionalists might grudgingly admire. Their military success
brought along with it political credibility, as the freedom fighter
who lies confidently in wait for the Westerners' clumsy, unaware
phalanx, a dinosaur-like, noisy body of men that lumbers forth
too late, in vain bringing enormous firepower to bear against an
enemy who is no longer there. Our nineteenth-century heroes
Wellington, Grant, and Sherman have now faded somewhat, and
perhaps, too, we have lost our admiration for that gallant, murderous charge of Cortes and his small band, men who, like
Xenophon's Ten Thousand before them, through disciplined formation and superior body armor and armament sliced a way
through a sea of swarming Aztecs and thereby earned their heroic
salvation:

> The number of the enemy was double that of the Christians, and it
> seemed as if it were a contest which must be decided by numbers and
> brute force, rather than by superior science. But it was not so. The in-
> vulnerable armor of the Spaniard, his sword of matchless temper, and
> his skill in the use of it, gave him advantages which far outweighed the
> odds of physical strength and numbers. After doing all that the courage
> of despair could enable men to do, resistance grew fainter. (*Prescott* 2.
> 65–66)

We still need to study the origins of Western battle if for no
other reason than the flicker of curiosity we feel, our morbid fascination with the frightful collision of men who, attacking in
massed formation, like their Greek hoplite predecessors, do not
wish to harass their enemy but prefer instead to seek victory in
the rawest, if not, as Mardonios said, the silliest sense: battle
where they face their enemy at arm's reach to kill and be killed.
Tyrtaios, the seventh-century elegiac poet who wrote for the Spartans in the second Messenian War, could simply say of the Greek
battlefield, "no man ever proves himself a good man in war unless he endures to face the blood and slaughter." (12.10–11) He
was referring to men who were clearly not cowards, yet not ex-
tremists but, rather, courageous amateurs who had somehow
found a way to face the enemy without flinching. Whatever the

future of infantry battle in the nuclear age, this inner craving for a clear decision, despite the carnage, will not fade; it cannot since, as the Greeks discovered, it resides in the dark hearts of us all. Yet it is essential to remember its moral imperative is to end the fighting quickly and efficiently, not simply to exhibit brave resolve.

This Western mode of attack has been so successful that we have essentially eliminated the very chance that it will take place again in our lifetime. We have put ourselves out of business, so to speak; for any potential adversary has now discovered the futility of an open, deliberate struggle on a Western-style battlefield against the firepower and discipline of Western infantry. Yet, ominously, the legacy of the Greeks' battle style lingers on, a narcotic that we cannot put away.

The cagey Spartan general Brasidas in the fifth century B.C., during a forced march through the hostile frontier of Macedonia, for the first time in European history defended this preference for direct battle and the accompanying disdain for the tactics of evasion. In a rousing speech to his troops, Thucydides tells us, he reminded his men:

> To the unexperienced these opponents present an image of fear: they are formidable in their numbers and nearly unendurable with all that shouting. The empty brandishing of their weapons offers a display of their taunts and threats. Yet, these men are not quite the same when it is a question of charging those who stay their ground. Since they do not have any formation, once under duress they have no shame at all in abandoning their position. To run away and to stand firm, these are all the same in their eyes, and so their courage can never really be tested. Battle is an individual affair to them and consequently everyone has a ready excuse to save his own skin. They think it is safer to bully you without any risk to themselves rather than meet you in pitched battle. Otherwise, instead of all this, they would join battle. Therefore, you realize clearly that the fear which they instill, in reality, is quite small, although granted it is annoying to the eye and ear. (4.126.4–6)

There is in all of us a repugnance, is there not, for hit-and-run tactics, for skirmishing and ambush? Does there not hide a feeling, however illogical and poorly thought out, that direct assault between men who, in Brasidas' words, "stay their ground" is somehow more "fair" and certainly more "noble" an opportunity to show a man's true character and test it before his peers? Hope of a Greek-style battle was for this very reason always in the mind of the Crusader, a figure who more than any other in European history was enamored with classical armament and a desire to kill at close range. At the battle of Arsouf (A.D. 1191),

> The Turks did not endure for a moment the onset of the dreaded knights of the West. The sudden change of the crusading army from a passive defense to a vigorous offensive came so unexpectedly upon them, that they broke and fled with disgraceful promptness . . . a dreadful slaughter of the Infidel took place. The rush of the Crusaders dashed horse and foot together into a solid mass, which could not easily escape, and the knights were there to take a bloody revenge for the long trial of endurance to which they had been exposed since daybreak. Before the Moslems could scatter and disperse to the rear, they had been mowed down by the thousands. (*Oman 2. 315*)

And how else can we explain the carnage caused by those who adopted this absurd manner of battle at the Somme, or Verdun, or Omaha Beach? To the Greeks who long ago formulated these ideas about battle, anything less than a "fair" fight—that is, a daylight clash of two massed phalanxes—was no fight at all, however decisive. "The policy which you are suggesting is one of bandits and thieves," snapped Alexander the Great when he was urged to attack the Persians by night, "the only purpose of which is deception. I cannot allow my glory always to be diminished by Darius' absence, or by narrow terrain, or by tricks of night. I am resolved to attack openly and by daylight. I choose to regret my good fortune rather than be *ashamed* of my victory." (Curtius *Alexander* 4.13) The Greeks of the past, wrote the Hellenistic Greek historian Polybius, had no interest in victory through tricks and deceit since it was only "hand-to-hand battle at close range that brought clear results." (13.3.2–3) Therefore, it was "madness" that the Hellenistic ruler of Macedon Philip V avoided pitched battle, "left war untouched," in Polybius' words, opting instead to attack the cities of Thessaly. Up to that time all others "had done everything they could to beat each other on the field of battle, but had spared cities." (18.3.7) Part of the romanticism and glory that we see here lies too in the struggle against vastly superior numbers. From the Three Hundred at the pass at Thermopylai, to Xenophon's Ten Thousand in Asia Minor, to the frontier Roman garrison, the Crusaders, and European colonial troops, outnumbered Western commanders have never been dismayed by the opportunity to achieve an incredible victory through the use of superior weapons, tactics, and cohesion among men.

This deliberate dependence on face-to-face killing at close range explains another universal object of disdain in Greek literature: those who fight from afar, the lightly equipped skirmisher or peltast, the javelin thrower, the slinger, and above all, the archer. (Eur. *HF* 157–63; Aesch. *Pers.* 226–80, 725, 813, 1601–3) These were all men who could kill "good" infantry with a frightening randomness and little risk to themselves. Worse yet, in the eyes of the Greeks, they were often men from the lower orders of society who could not afford their own body armor, or semi-Hellenized recruits from outlands like Crete or Thrace who had no stomach for the clash of spears, no desire "to play by the rules." When the Spartan infantry survivors at Pylos were asked how and why they inexplicably surrendered during that disastrous battle of the Peloponnesian War, and so handed themselves over alive to the despised light-armed and missile-equipped troops of the Athenian general Demosthenes, one prisoner dryly replied in his defense that arrows would be worth a great deal if they could pick out the brave men from the cowards. (Thuc. 4.40.2) Clearly, the indiscriminate and unexpected manner of death from distant warriors did not go down well; it dated from the very dawn of the hoplite age as we see in Homer's *Iliad:* "If you were to make trial of me in strong combat with weapons," challenged Diomedes to Paris, "your bow would do you no good at all nor your close-showered arrows." (11.385–87) No doubt we can believe the first-century A.D. geographer Strabo when he claims that he saw an ancient inscribed pillar of great antiquity which forbade the use of missiles altogether in the war on the Lelantine Plain during the eighth century B.C. (10.448) Plutarch, too, in an anecdote of uncertain date, reminds us that for a Spartan dying from a fatal arrow wound "death was of no concern, except that it was caused by a cowardly bow." (*Mor.* 234 E 46; cf. Hdt. 9.72.2) There is a note of pathos in the usually somber Thucydides when he describes the fate of a phalanx of five hundred of the best Athenian infantry who during the early years of the Peloponnesian War stumbled clumsily into the mountainous wilds of Aitolia only to be bled white by the javelins and arrows of lightly armed native irregulars. Nowhere was there an enemy phalanx visible to test the Athenians' spears and unbroken ranks. "They were," Thucydides sadly concludes, "many and all in the prime of life, the *best* men that the city of Athens lost in the war." (3.98.4) Another fifth-century Athenian, Aeschylus, wrote of Greek infantry who die far off in Eastern battle: "in the place of men, urns and ashes return to the house of each." (*Ag.* 434–36)

Like so much of their art and literature, the Greek manner of battle was a paradox of the highest order, a deliberate attempt to harness, to modulate, and hence to amplify if not sanctify the wild human desire for violence through the stark order and discipline of the phalanx. To the Persians, who reversed these concepts—their disordered, moblike frightening hordes had no fondness for methodical killing—the approach of a Greek column was especially unsettling. At Marathon they thought a "destructive madness" had infected the Greek ranks as they saw them approach on the run in their heavy armor. Surely, as those outnumbered Greek hoplites crashed into their lines, the Persians must have at last understood that these men worshiped not only the god Apollo but the wild, irrational Dionysus as well.

This Western desire for an awesome clash of arms was first expressed in Greece at the beginning of the seventh century B.C. There, for the first time in European history, heavily armed and slow-moving infantry, massed together in formation, by mutual agreement sought battle to find in a few short hours a decisive victory or utter defeat, where men's "knees settled in the dust and the spears shattered at the very outset." (Aesch. *Ag.* 64–65) This explains what went on in the mind of the fourth-century B.C. Spartan general Agesilaos when he purposely allowed his various enemies to combine so that he might fight them all together, in a single pitched battle, whatever their numbers: "he thought it the wisest course of action to allow the two enemy forces to combine, and, in case they wished to fight, to engage them in battle in the traditional manner and out in the open." (Xen. *Hell.* 6.5.16; *Ages.* 2.6) No wonder that after Antiochos returned from Persia he concluded that although he had seen vast numbers of Persians of various sorts he "was not able to find any who could stand up to Greeks in battle." (Xen. *Hell.* 7.1.38) Contrarily, nearly two centuries later, to Philip V's everlasting discredit among the Greeks, he chose to fight in rough terrain and thereby avoid pitched battle. (Polyb. 18.3.3)

The stark simplicity of Greek combat, bereft of heroics and romanticism, has not been appreciated by us, their Western heirs: for too long we have failed to include this austere legacy of Greek battle among the gifts—or burdens—of our classical heritage. This is a surprising omission when we consider that our general ideas about the conduct of battle even under the frightening conditions of contemporary warfare have not changed much in other respects from those practiced by our Greek ancestors. These men were the first we know of to relegate cavalry to a secondary role and thus to suppress for a thousand years to come the notion that the battlefield was the private domain of aristocratic horsemen. Nor did they have any liking for the landless poor, who were skilled only in missile attacks; they, too, were to be kept clear of the hard fighting. Instead, the hoplite class of the Greek classical age chose to ignore the bow or javelin in preference for the spear and massive bronze armor in a desire to eliminate entirely the critical "distance" that elsewhere traditionally separated men in battle. They alone introduced to us a novel type of frontal attack, where warriors of like class sought to eye each other at close range as they killed and died. Yet they displayed a minimum of heroics and gallantry in battle. The plumed general, the armchair tactician, and the bemedaled retiree were virtually unknown—left to the imagination of their Hellenistic and Roman successors. Battle was seen only as the domain of those men who actually experienced the carnage of spear and sword thrust, and these had no desire to make anything else out of it than the acknowledgment of unavoidable and necessary killing. No wonder theirs was a type of warfare which the poet Pindar called "a sweet thing to him who does not know it, but to him who has made trial of it, it is a thing of fear." (Fr. 120.5)

3   *Not Strategy, Not Tactics*

> I do not intend to say anything of logistics or strategy
> and very little of tactics in the formal sense . . . My pur-
> pose [is] to demonstrate, as exactly as possible, what the
> warfare, respectively, of hand, single-missile and multi-
> ple-missile weapons was (and is) like, and to suggest how
> and why the men who have had (and do have) to face
> these weapons control their fears, staunch their
> wounds, go to their deaths.
> —*John Keegan,* The Face of Battle

> Tactics are only a very small part of warfare.
> —*Xenophon,* Memorabilia

The origins of the Western infantry experience lie in classical
Greece, back past 2,500 years of military tradition to the battlefields of Marathon and Delion, or to that strange, terrible head-
on collision of Thebans and Spartans in 394 at Koroneia—"like
no other in our time," wrote the contemporary witness
Xenophon—where men in the West first drew themselves up in
dense formation, charged, killed, and then died. To the few students now who sometimes ask about war in ancient Greece, about
hoplites, phalanxes, Thermopylai and Leuktra, Agesilaos and
Epameinondas, I usually insist that they read first the ancient accounts of these battles, however brief, however inadequate by our
modern standards of accuracy and fairness. To those who return
and wish more, the advice to learn the classical languages, to
reread these passages in Latin or Greek is unwelcome. But this
is not perverse advice on my part to bolster enrollments in classics at our state university (I can think of only two students who
eventually pursued that interest and signed up for Introductory
Greek or Latin the next term). Nor is it because I think nothing
is to be learned from the research of the last two hundred years
of classical scholarship; *res militares,* after all, were among the fa-

vorite topics of inquiry of a most gifted group of nineteenth-
century Europeans. Rather, it derives from a quirk of my own personal experience, a belief that what little I have learned about
warfare has come out of an interest in battle and combat at the
expense of strategy and tactics. During my childhood, for example, I read every word of my father's popular paperback accounts of the "Air War over Japan," and memorized the specifications of the B-29 bomber in his strange collection of histories
of the aircraft. Yet now I remember very little of these books, and
of what I do recall, nearly all seems unimportant or detached
from any plausible frame of reference, so that I really have no
idea at all what went on in those last months of 1945 in the air
above Japan. But what I *do* remember are the stories of combat—
never of strategic bombing planning or an analysis of the damage inflicted—that my father told to my brothers and me, usually late at night after he had opened a bottle of good bourbon
or scotch. War to us, then, was never an antiseptic description of
strategy and tactics, but rather a lesson about what battle was,
about which men looked to maps, charts, and reports, and which
bombed, strafed, and were blown apart. To discuss anything other
than the latter class of soldiers called into question our very
morality. These sessions were "stories" only in the sense that they
were narratives about human conduct, but they were far more
than stories. Men, we were told, do unexpected things when they
are trying to kill each other, and so my father went on about those
who defecated in their flak suits, who wrapped their groins in armor only to suffer wounds to the head—if the loss of both the
face and jaw can be called a mere wound. And he told of the smell
of burned flesh from those set afire ten thousand feet below, of
doomed bombers that did not "crash" on lift-off or even crum-
ble to pieces, but rather simply vanished, overloaded as they were
with fuel and incendiaries.

    In his defense, it must be said that my father was only follow-
ing a family tradition, for his father had taught him about the nature of battle by describing his own wartime experience, lost in
the Ardennes in 1918: about the Lewis machine gun which finally

melted in his hands from the monotony of shooting German teenagers, about the gassed food that slowly ate away at his insides, transforming him not only bodily but also in outlook, so much so that on his return his forty acres no longer were a mere farm but had become a refuge from those around him. My own memory of my grandfather is of a man in his late seventies riding a donkey about his farm, quite an anomaly to his young neighbors, professional farmers riding the boom of the late 1960s who considered him, rather than themselves, so odd. Much of the same could be said of so many cousins, uncles, and friends, those lucky enough to come back from war, although damaged and unable to do more than prune a few vines in the winter— like my cousin Beldon, brain damaged from tropical fever, yet far luckier than his brother Holt, who died of a head wound on Omaha Beach.

From the haphazard descriptions told by these Americans (and despite what many Europeans may think, there is a tradition of battle in many families in this country), a coherent picture of war overseas was created in my mind at a very young age. After learning the classical languages, I looked for similar descriptions in the ancient authors who wrote about Greek warfare, such as Thucydides and Xenophon, veterans themselves of land battle, expecting the same detail, comparable stories of soldiers under fire.

Yet within their histories of war there is a scarcity of detail about most of the action on the field once the two sides joined in battle; the overall campaign, the city-states that formed the battle alliance, the number of respective combatants, the speech of the general before the battle—all these warrant their attention instead. Modern scholars have chosen likewise to concentrate either on tactics, provisioning, deployment, drill, or on the structure of command. Of course, ancient Greek writers composed their narrative for an audience of veterans, hoplites like themselves who knew all too well the slaughter that took place once men in armor met, but it is not entirely accurate to state that therefore they omitted in-depth accounts of the subsequent wounding and killing because this would bore their experienced readers: in fact, Herodotus, Thucydides, and Xenophon do tell us much about men in battle, if little detail about any *one* battle. Their many offhand remarks, such as the one by Xenophon concerning the Spartans drinking before the battle of Leuktra, or Thucydides' strange interest at the fight at Mantineia in the universal tendency of hoplites to drift toward the right side, have a cumulative effect. These anecdotes give us a good idea of what the fighting, killing, and dying were like. Equivalent information can be found throughout Greek literature (and on Greek vases). Battle, then, was known by the Greeks to be the essence of human conflict.

We must ask ourselves what the hoplites in the phalanx were faced with, for they are the key to our understanding ancient Greek warfare. Because of the peculiar nature of classical Greek society "battle" rather than "war" may be the only apt description of conflict between city-states. Classical scholars, with their long university training in philology and limited exposure to, or affinity with, veterans of infantry combat, have neglected this view and have misinterpreted the spirit and, most importantly, the lesson of classical Greek military history—the nature of which we have always felt we have understood so well.

From the research of the past two centuries we have learned a great deal about how the classical Greek hoplite was armed, drilled, and deployed and the strategic limitations which confronted his general. For example, the nineteenth-century Germans Köchly and Rüstow (1852), Droysen (1888), Delbrück (1920), and, later and most importantly, Kromayer and Veith (1928), drawing on their practical experience in the German army—their *Kriegskunst*—as well as their knowledge of the classics, conceived the modern study of ancient military theory and practice as the natural complement to a wider, contemporary interest in the diplomatic and political history of the Greek city-state. Yet, their *Handbücher*, exemplars of nineteenth-century scholarship at both its best and its worst, view conflict strategically, topographically, logistically, tactically—in the end, nonsensically and amorally. There is a marked *distance* in their viewpoint, as if they were suspended above the killing on the battlefield in an observation balloon looking downward, detached from if not uninterested in the desperate individuals below.

Hans Delbrück, for example, felt it necessary to begin his massive work on the history of the art of war with the problem of the relative number of men present at each battle:

> Whatever the sources permit, a military-historical study does best to start with the army strengths. They are of decisive importance, not simply because of the relative strengths, whereby the greater mass wins or is counter-balanced by bravery or leadership on the part of the weaker force, but also on an absolute basis.

Delbrück was not merely wrong, but also misleading: wrong, because in the world of the classical phalanx, the army was without any reserves, coordination of specialized troops, or integration of cavalry, and at the mercy of rumor, superstition, misinformation, and panic to a degree unknown on the modern battlefield, so that the relative strengths were *not* so important, and the historical accounts of Greek battle make this clear. He was wrong again because the numbers of combatants usually cannot be known to the level of accuracy which his argument requires; given the nature of our source material, they can only be guessed at, often through faulty modern analogy and comparison. Finally, that Delbrück presents this issue within the first paragraph of his massive encyclopedia is misleading because it suggests that the actual behavior of Greek hoplites and the unique atmosphere in the phalanx are of secondary importance. In fact, he never discussed them. "To these late nineteenth-century specialists who had experienced the limited confrontations of their own day and who remembered the 'piecemeal' wars of the last century," Yvon Garlan has written, "war was insubstantial and unreal, as gratuitous as a game of chance, an outlet for the energy of a social group which it did not affect deeply, or else a luxury activity." (19)

Later English scholars—for example, Tarn (1930), Griffith

(1935), or Greenhalgh (1973)—sought to understand Greek warfare either topically or chronologically, to trace the origins and evolution of battle through one specific type or era of warfare. Yet they too did not wholly abandon the previous obsession with deployment, drill, weapons, and tactics. But a shift in focus was dramatically accomplished by the three volumes of Kendrick Pritchett's *The Greek State at War* (1971–79), where for the first time Greek warfare was really seen in its proper function as a social institution, as commonplace and integral an activity to the Greeks as agriculture or religion: in Garlan's words, "ancient war has a reality, a manner of being, a practice and a mode of behavior that are as wide as society itself." (21) While Pritchett made no claim to comprehensiveness in the presentation of his material, the range of interests is nevertheless quite remarkable.

In all these recent studies of ancient Greek warfare, however, there was no substantial change in the manner of inquiry, what John Keegan has termed our "angle of vision." Battle between hoplites was seen from the vantage point either of the general, or of the state, or, more fashionably now, of the community as a whole. With the publication of Keegan's *The Face of Battle* (1976), however, combat as experienced on the battlefield became a legitimate subject of study by classical historians. Usually works in medieval or modern European history have little influence on current research in the ancient world; classical scholarship, after all, can pride itself on its near isolation from "trends" in the historiography of other disciplines. That a popular account of medieval and modern battles such as Keegan's would turn attention toward the neglected figure of the ancient Greek infantryman and his experience within his phalanx attests to the singular originality of Keegan's approach—an approach which, ironically, perhaps might have been even better suited for studying the Greeks' unique concentration on their one decisive clash, on the "battle" rather than episodes of "war." As some scholars sought to apply Keegan's approach and principles to ancient Greek military affairs, what had been for more than a century a laborious and often dry examination of Greek warfare finally became a more exciting exercise, to learn what battle was actually like for the men who did the fighting and dying. In the last ten years a number of articles and books have ignored strategy and even tactical considerations in an effort to learn the very nature of the individual's experience in battle, as if this was at last understood as the very key to unlocking the strange enigma of war and society in Greece.

Not surprisingly, it was Pritchett again who first collected the evidence, in a fourth volume on *The Greek State at War* (*The Pitched Battle*, 1985). There, he presented an in-depth account, based on close attention to the vocabulary of early Greek poets and historical writers, of the action when hoplites finally crashed together. Given the existence of this excellent, scholarly treatment, I make no attempt here to follow in similar fashion all the action on the Greek battlefield from the initial impact of the phalanxes to the final collapse and subsequent rout. Instead, I try to suggest what the *environment* of ancient Greek battle was, the atmosphere in which the individual struggled to kill and to avoid death, the sequence of events seen from within the phalanx. I ask the question, What was it like? at any given stage of the fighting.

If there is a theme to this brief essay, it is, I confess, the *misery* of hoplite battle. Few types of infantry battle in the West have required quite the same degree of courage, of nerve in the face of mental and physical anguish, as this, its original form, in which armed and armored hoplites advanced in massed formation with no chance of escape. The Greek battlefield was the scene of abject terror and utter carnage, but it was a *brief* nightmare that the hoplite might face only once a summer, unlike the unending monotony of warfare in the trenches of the First World War or in the jungles of Vietnam. A man could focus all his courage upon one pure burst of frenzied activity; for an hour or two he overcame the limits of physical and psychological endurance.

We must always remember that the Greeks' desire for this brutal confrontation was designed to *limit* war and martial gallantry, not to romanticize the warriors' inherent nobility. Yet, finally, is it enough for us to understand the noise, the dust, the wounds, the manner of death, the confusion and panic of ancient battle, if we cannot understand *why* these men marched forward? I do not believe that the Greeks in the hoplite age fought under coercion or fear of punishment. Their willingness to go into battle is not to be found in either their superior drill or their equipment. Nor were they drunk to the point of senselessness, or bent on plunder and booty, or in awe of God and country. Rather, they went into battle for the man on the left and right, front and back, brother, cousin, father, and son: out of respect for, or in fear before, men of like circumstance, they forged some code of honor and salvaged a certain dignity (if not pleasure) from the killing. When once a man had taken his place in the phalanx of his city, Socrates, the old veteran of hoplite battle, reminded his audience in the last speech of his life, "he must stay put there and face the danger without any regard for death or anything else rather than disgrace." (Pl. *Ap.* 28 D)

4   *The Hoplite and His Phalanx: War in an Agricultural Society*

Indeed, for a long time peace was understood in negative fashion, simply as the absence of war.

—*Yvon Garlan*

Sometime in the late eighth or early seventh century B.C. infantrymen in Greece gradually began to arm themselves with body armor, round shield, and thrusting spear, and so chose to get close and jab the opponent head-on rather than fling javelins from afar, advancing and retreating like the ebb and flow of native warriors whom Europeans encountered in nineteenth-century Africa and South America. The era of mounted fighters of the Greek Dark Ages (1200–800) who dismounted to throw the spear was also now over, for warfare no longer was the private duels of wealthy knights. On the left arm of this new warrior rested a round wooden shield some three feet in diameter, the *hoplon,* so radically different in concept from its cowhide predecessor that it was from this piece of equipment that the infantryman eventually derived his name, "hoplite." By the aid of an interior forearm strap and an accompanying handgrip, the hoplite could manage the unusually great weight of this strange shield, warding off spear blows solely with the left arm, or at times resting its upper lip on his left shoulder to save strength. In this way he could both protect his own left flank and, if formation was well maintained, offer some aid to the unprotected right side of the man to his left in the ranks. Yet, despite the shield's great weight and size, well over half a man's height, its round shape offered poor protection for the entire body, unlike the rectangular model of the later Roman legionary or the body shield of the earlier Dark Age warrior; there was little chance that a hoplite could save himself from most of the traditional sources of attack on the front and rear. The hoplite's shield offered no material advantage over earlier models in isolated skirmishes or individual duels. Even more importantly, the shield could not be easily slung over the back, as previous shields had been, to protect those who turned and ran—although this was a small drawback, since these fighting men now had no other intention but to stand firm together and push constantly forward.

We do not really know whether the use of this new equipment spawned a radical change in battle tactics, or vice versa. Yet it is at least clear that better success at warding off blows and striking home with the spear was accomplished by having the men mass in column, usually eight ranks in depth. There they could find mutual protection from an accumulation of their shields to the front, rear, and side—if care was taken to moderate and account for the natural tendency to drift rightward as each man sought cover for his own exposed, unshielded right flank in the shield of his neighbor. Although there was an accompanying loss of firepower overall, as every rank to the rear of the first three primary rows was effectively out of the initial action (the spears of these men in the middle and rear not immediately reaching the enemy), the added weight and density of the formation were believed to offer a crucial stabilizing force, in both physical and psychological terms, for the few men who first met the terrible onslaught of the enemy.

What followed this initial collision was the push, or *othismos,* as ranks to the rear put their bodies into the hollows of their shields and forced those ahead constantly onward. Some recent scholars have branded this image of a mass thrusting contest as ridiculous and absurd. Yet careful compilation of ancient descriptions of Greek warfare makes it certain beyond a doubt that this was precisely what happened in hoplite battle; it soon degenerated into an enormous contest of pressure, as men used their shields, hands, and bodies in a desperate, frantic effort to force a path

forward. Xenophon, an eyewitness of the last age of purely hoplite battle, remarked that any troops who were suspect belonged
in the middle of the phalanx, so that they would be surrounded
by good fighters at the front and rear "in order that they might
be led by the former and *pushed* by the latter." (Xen. *Mem.* 3.1.9)
The key, as the successful Spartan general Brasidas reminded his
men, was to maintain formation always, to stay in rank, and to
preserve the cohesive protection offered by the accumulation of
shields. Likewise, Thucydides notes that during the awful retreat
after the Peloponnesian catastrophe at Olpai in 426, only the
Mantineians survived, never once breaking rank, but rather
tightening up their formation to prevent any inroad between
their shields. (Thuc. 5.9; 3.108.3; Diod. 15.85.6)

The actual social and political sequence of events at the end
of the Greek Dark Ages that led to this movement toward the armament and subsequent tactics of hoplite battle cannot and will
not be known, given the nature of our sources. But surely by the
early seventh century B.C. the so-called hoplite reform—if we
may use such a dramatic term—must have attracted a growing
number of farmers, who now became restless at the idea that
anyone might traverse their own small parcels of land. (Hoplite
farmers usually owned properties outside the city walls of between five and ten acres.) It makes sense that the solidarity and,
more importantly, the success of their wartime experience in the
phalanx—a formation which, like Napoleon's columns, encouraged ties of camaraderie, if not revolutionary fervor—reflected
a growing confidence in their new, emerging function in the government of the Greek city-state as owners and producers of food.
By the late seventh century B.C. the security of most of Greek society depended on the arms and armor that each such landholder
possessed, hung up above his fireplace, and the courage which
he brought into battle when confronted with an army of invasion encamped on his or his neighbors' farms.

As long as these unlikely fighters, heavily armed men in
bronze armor, held their assigned places in the ranks of the phalanx, they were virtually impregnable from attack by any lighter-

armed, mobile infantry or by charges of heavy cavalry—provided that the ground was flat and free of obstruction. Because the great plain of Boiotia met these criteria, the legendary fourth-century Theban general Epameinondas once called it "the dancing floor of War." (Plut. *Mor.* 193 E 18) The phalanx (which Polybius reminds us must break its ranks when crossing rough ground [Polyb. 18.31.11]) then must first find such a battlefield, and only thereafter seek out its enemy. Polybius was correct in his famous comparison between the Roman legion and the Macedonian phalanx, when he remarked of the advantages of the Greeks that "nothing can stand in the way of the advance of a phalanx, as long as it maintains its customary cohesion and power." (18.30.11) Success, especially when depth increased and width diminished accordingly, required that the vulnerable flanks be protected by cavalry, skirmishers, and above all, rough terrain. Even well-trained enemy archers and slingers were seldom a threat if the hoplites stayed on level ground and could be brought to close quarters quickly. When infantrymen lumbered across the last 150 yards of no-man's-land and came into the range of the ancient arrows and other hand-propelled missiles, which could wound their arms, legs, faces, and necks, and at closer ranges penetrate their body armor, the "window of vulnerability" lasted not more than a minute. These airborne attacks, far from turning aside the onset of heavily armored men, most likely served to incite their anger and to guarantee a furious collision of leveled spears. In short, for nearly three hundred years (650–350) no foreign army, despite any numerical superiority, withstood the charge of a Greek phalanx. The battles at Marathon (490) and Plataia (479) demonstrate this clearly: relatively small numbers of well-led, heavily armed Greeks had little difficulty in breaking right through the hordes of their more lightly equipped and less cohesively ranked adversaries from the East.

The extraordinary integration of civilian and military service within the city-state also explains much of the Greek success. In most cases, men were arranged within the phalanx right next to lifelong friends or family members, and fought not only for the safety of their community and farmland but also for the respect of the men at their front, rear, and side. Small landholders and craftsmen with their own armor on their backs were liable to be called up from the city's muster rolls for military service any summer after their eighteenth birthday until they turned sixty. In the fifth and fourth centuries, battle broke out in the Greek world nearly two out of every three years, so the chances were good that a man would have to leave his farm, take up his arms, fight in repeated engagements, and fall wounded or die one summer's day in battle. Military service rarely was confined to peacetime patrols or to drill, and consequently hardly any figure in fifth-century Greek literature refers to his past tenure as a hoplite but rather only to the specific battles at which he fought. A service organization other than the Veterans of Foreign Wars (such as the American Legion) would be incomprehensible to the classical Greek mind.

In this world of perennial battle, fighting in the ranks of the phalanx required utmost courage, excellent physical condition, and endurance, but little specialized training or skill with weapons. The spear and shield, even when used in unison with other men in the crowded conditions of the column, were still much simpler to handle than either the bow or the sling or even the javelin. Besides, "there was little chance," Xenophon remarked quite rightly, "of missing a blow" through any lack of skill in massed combat. (*Cyr.* 2.1.16; 2.3.9–11) About the same time, Plato agreed that specialized weapon training was of little value except during retreat and pursuit, where for the first and only moment men had room to maneuver and to use their prowess in arms in duels or individual skirmishing. (*Lach.* 181E–83D) Pericles, in his famous funeral oration after the second year of the Peloponnesian War, castigated the Spartan system for its excessive (and unnecessary) attention to hoplite drill (Thuc. 2.39.1), and Aristotle likewise seems to imply that the Spartans were just about the only soldiers in Greece who felt it necessary to train at all for battle. (*Pol.* 8.1338 b27) In the utopia of the *Republic* Plato must have been reacting to this general Panhellenic amateurism when he complained that a man who grabbed up a shield could hardly become a skilled warrior on that very day. (2.374B–D) Yet, in a sense, that was very nearly the truth. All this would explain why on occasion we read of extreme cases in Greek history where men fought in the phalanx with virtually no training. These soldiers were not exactly "hoplites"; nevertheless, they were provided with heavy armor and ordered to fight as infantrymen with no experience or idea of hoplite combat. (E.g., Thuc. 6.72.4; Xen. *Hell.* 4.4.10; Diod. 12.68.5; 15.13.2; 14.43.2–3; Polyaen. *Strat* 3.8) For example, during the Athenians' invasion of the Ionian city of Miletos in 413, they brought along five hundred light-armed irregulars from Argos who were given armor and expected to fight as hoplites. (Thuc. 8.25.6) And the hoplite class of independent small farmers, as they have for centuries since, had little free time or desire for constant drilling. Yet they came to battle with an abundance of courage, if not controlled recklessness, and possessed a spirit of camaraderie with those of the same class and background: "I do not think," wrote the fourth century A.D. tactician Vegetius, "that there has ever been any question that the rural peasantry are the best equipped for military service." (1.3) These men were natural hoplites, in short, awesome soldiers turned loose to battle on their own turf, the farmlands of Greece, men to whom Pericles in his famous funeral oration was no doubt referring when he said they "would rather perish in resistance than find salvation through submission." (Thuc. 2.42.4)

Throughout the seventh, sixth, and on into the fifth century in Greece, a hoplite army of invasion quickly offered a challenge to pitched battle once it had made its way into the flatland of the enemy; indeed, its very occupation of precious farmland was an invitation to battle. Attacks against the walls of an enemy community were rarely successful, perhaps because siegecraft was both expensive and its techniques—the battering ram, artillery, and movable armor—were either unknown or not well understood. Only late in the fifth century and, more frequently, in Hellenistic times does one find the occasional successful siege. Nor were night engagements an option. At times the sheer daring of an attack after darkness could bring results, but more commonly it ended in chaos, misdirection, and disorder in the ranks. (Hom. *Il.* 2.387) The confusion of men trapped in tight formation without any visibility made such battle risky, as well as less honorable if successful, in the eyes of most hoplite generals. (Thuc. 7.43–44; 7.80.3) Instead, once an invading army had crossed the border, either the defenders usually marched out from their walled cities promptly to contest this occupation of their farmland, or they simply submitted to the terms dictated in order to clear the intruder from their property as quickly as possible.

Strangely, in the typically brief invasion and occupation, there was little discussion on the part of the invaded whether any enemy army actually posed a credible threat to their livelihood by causing *lasting* damage to their orchards, vineyards, and grainfields when they set to work with fire and ax. After all, the methodical destruction of trees and vines with hand tools is a time-consuming process, made more difficult by enemy sorties and the need to gather food. The trunks of olive trees can achieve enormous proportions of some ten to twenty feet or more. Because the wood is especially hard, systematic cutting of olive groves with hand tools then was nearly impossible. Uprooting olives was of course an absurd undertaking; it is a formidable task even for the modern bulldozer. Vines could fall to the ax, but under ancient methods of cultivation there might be upward of two thousand plants to the acre; the image of light-armed troops chopping away for hours on end in an alien vineyard belongs more to the world of stoop agricultural labor than to the battlefield.

Wheat and barley can be burned but only during a brief period right before harvest, which would require the ravagers to arrive in enemy territory at precisely the right time. And numerous difficulties limited that scenario: if they had delays in mustering troops, their arrival on the enemy flatland would be amid grain still green—cereals impossible to use as a supplement to their own rations and not at all combustible; while later invasions, in late June or July, might find fields harvested and a populace willing to ride out occupation, secure in the belief their produce was safe behind strong walls. The key, then, was to invade right at the beginning of harvest, to burn the barley and wheat, to deny the enemy the dividends of an entire year's work and investment, to use the produce to feed the very agents of its destruction. Yet, there remains one final irony; the invading hoplite army of small farmers had their own responsibilities back home; and the time they spent torching the grain of the enemy might mean that their own fields were left without adequate help just when harvest labor was most precious. In short, agricultural devastation was far from a simple process; even when accomplished it usually had few long-term effects.

The psychological turmoil among the influential, landed class of hoplites within the city walls, peering out at an enemy running among their ancestral fields, was generally felt to be enough either to draw the citizen body out to fight or, better yet, to make them simply give up. In this strange ritual of agricultural poker, a few cities, usually closely tied to the sea, occasionally persuaded their citizens to "ride out" an enemy invasion and not hazard battle, but only when they had men of vision and daring—men like Pericles of Athens who could at least convince all but the hoplite class to stomach foreigners on Attic soil. When this was the case, they suffered little agricultural damage of any lasting consequence from enemy ravagers and kept their city free and their infantry—though perhaps not their pride—unhurt. Oddly, few of the city-states understood, or rather wished to understand, the advantages that this unaccustomed inactivity within the walls could achieve. Such self-control was very rare during the age of the classical hoplite, as most Greeks felt that revenge in the old form of pitched combat was the most honorable and expedient way of resolving an insult to their sovereignty. Their tradition, their duty, indeed their desire, was for a ritualistic collision, head-on, with the spears of their enemy to end the whole business quickly and efficiently.

This paradox of Greek warfare—the threat of such a relatively ineffective tactic as crop destruction being successful in drawing men out to fight—helps to explain the frequency of pitched battle between mutually consenting hoplites throughout the Greek world. Yet, if battle was so incessant among the small city-states of classical Greece, how did the social fabric endure the frequent death and destruction year after year and such a vast amount of collective time and labor seemingly wasted on defense? The answer must lie again in the sheer simplicity of phalanx tactics and strategy, a mode of battle that did not require extensive peacetime drill and training or public expenditure on arms and provisioning. More importantly, until the late fifth century, there was no need for the expense of extended campaigns, with men marching for months on end, fighting in battle after battle. The enemy was usually nearby, on the other side of a range of mountains, no farther than a few hundred miles at most. Once the invader arrived in the spring, the entire "war," if that is the proper word, usually consisted of an hour's worth of hard fighting between consenting, courageous hoplite amateurs, rather than repeated clashes of hired or trained killers. The harvest demands of the triad of Greek agriculture—the olive, the vine, and grain—left only a brief month or two in which these small farmers could find time to fight.

Nor was combat fatal to most combatants; annihilation of entire armies was rare in the classical age, as the nearly uniform adoption of the panoply—the Greeks' bronze breastplate, shield, helmet, greaves, spear, and sword—ensured protection from repeated attacks. (It was left to the Hellenistic Greeks to record staggering deaths in battles between huge phalanxes of poorly protected infantry.) After the clash between the front ranks of armored infantry determined the direction of momentum and one side made an inroad into the ranks of the other, battle degenerated into a massive, pushing contest as rank after rank struggled to solidify and increase local advantages until the entire enemy's formation was destroyed. Yet, if the defeated could somehow maintain enough cohesion, a fighting withdrawal of sorts was possible. A great number died only when there was a sudden collapse, a collective loss of nerve, when the abrupt disruption of the phalanx sent men trampling each other in mad panic to the rear, either in small groups or, worse, individually to save themselves from spear thrusts in the back. Even when one side was swept suddenly off the battlefield, casualties in such a disaster remained low by modern standards, well below 20 percent of the original force—a "tolerable" percentage as long as such a decisive engagement entailed both the beginning and end of the "war." However, several such repeated clashes, such as the missions which caused the notorious casualty ratios among American bomber crews in the Second World War over Europe, would have bled a small city-state white in short order.

Long-drawn-out pursuit was also rare; unlike Napoleon, the victors were not aiming for the complete destruction of an enemy army. Indeed, pursuit of fleeing hoplites was not even crucial: most victorious Greek armies saw no reason why they could not repeat their simple formula for success and gain further victory should the enemy regroup in a few days and mistakenly press their luck again. Besides, it was always good propaganda for a Greek general to profess no taste for slaughtering fellow Hellenes from the rear after the issue of battle had already been decided face-to-face. (E.g., Polyaen. *Strat.* 1.16.3; 1.45.5; 2.3.5; Thuc. 5.73.3.; Plut. *Mor.* 228 F 30) When told of the slaughter of Corinthians by his Spartans, the legendary old battle veteran and king of fourth-century Sparta, Agesilaos, was supposed to have remarked, "Woe to you, Greece, those who now have died were enough to have beaten all the barbarians in battle had they lived." (Xen. *Ages.* 7.6) Both sides were usually content to exchange their dead under truce. The victors, after erecting a battlefield trophy or simple monument to their success, marched home triumphantly, eager for the praise of their families and friends on their return.

For more than three hundred years Greece thrived under such a structured system of conflict between amateurs, where the waste of defense expenditure in lives and lost work and agricultural produce was kept within "limits." Unfortunately, nearly all of the conflicts of the seventh and sixth centuries remain unrecorded. At this time hoplite battle remained a "pure," static, unchanging match between men in the heaviest of armor, void of support from auxiliary cavalry, missile throwers, or archers, and they were proud of their close bonds to their farms. In the later fifth century, when we learn a great deal more from our sources about hoplites, two events occurred that upset this fragile equilibrium inherent in Greek battles between city-states; these led not merely to fundamental changes in the manner of fighting, but also to uncharacteristically catastrophic losses throughout the Greek city-states, as their most logical and in one sense unheroic system of resolving disputes was transformed into an unending nightmare.

First, the two great Persian invasions of the early fifth century pitted Greek hoplites not against each other in the accustomed ritual of battle, but rather against a huge army of Eastern troops with unfamiliar equipment and tactics, specialized contingents, and, most importantly, different aims and responsibilities. Battles such as Marathon and, especially, Plataia were longer, involved greater numbers of combatants, and were certainly more violent than the domestic clashes of the prior two centuries. The outcome of infantry battle was now more decisive. The issue that induced pitched battle no longer concerned the temporary swing of influence over a nearby rival, the occupation of a few acres of disputed borderlands, or the threat to chop down a few trees, but, rather, the final status of the Greek-speaking world. Battle was now with an enemy that had at his disposal cavalry brigades, missile troops, and an array of variously armed infantry: the Persian Wars became the training ground for the murderous years of the Peloponnesian War, as—reversing the contexts—the Spanish Civil War was for the Second World War. The Greeks were to learn that battle could be more than a simple pushing contest between armored men, and that war was more than a single collision of phalanxes.

Sparta and Athens, the two great Hellenic powers that emerged dominant from the Persian conflict (only to divide the Greek world fifty years later into two armed camps), were—unfortunately, perhaps—unrepresentative of what might be termed "normal" Greek city-states, and thus immune from those accompanying "normal" restrictions that had traditionally prevented Greek battle from evolving into a deadly struggle of annihilation. Supported by an entire class of rural, disenfranchised servants known as *helots* who worked their farms, Spartan hoplites were free to drill and campaign without any obligation to work their farms or to return from battle to harvest their crops. "Not by caring for the fields," the Spartans could brag, "but rather by caring for ourselves did we acquire those fields." (Plut. *Mor.* 217 A 3) In other words, Sparta's closed, militaristic society produced an army of professionals, immune from pressing economic or other peacetime obligations; they were free to threaten the farms of others, to fight year round if need be, secure in the knowledge that in their nightmarish system of apartheid, servants were busy with their own harvests. In answer to the complaints of his allies that they had contributed too many men for too long, the Spartan king and general Agesilaos asked the assembled army of the alliance to stand up by profession— potters, smiths, carpenters, builders, and others. At last only the small minority of Spartiates remained seated, the few who had no jobs other than war. "You see, men," Agesilaos laughed, "how many soldiers more we send out to fight than you do." (Plut. *Mor.* 214 A 72)

Yet, neither were their Athenian adversaries obliged to go home to their countryside to resume work on their farms, nor was their government overly worried about a rapid depletion of capital from the constant drain of wartime expenditure. Already by the fifth century Athens had a majority of craftsmen, traders, and small businessmen who felt it was not in their own interest to march out and risk their lives in the old way to defend the cropland of the minority of small farmers who tilled the surrounding countryside. Whatever their shrill appeals to the glorious tradition of pitched battle, these "Marathon men" of Aristophanes' comedies may have had as much influence in the foreign policy of their government as their rural American counterparts do today. So it was from the sea that Athens found her "*helots*," for it was from the maritime empire in the Aegean that the men came who provided the lifeblood of imported goods, foods, and tribute which kept Athens strong. Massive long walls running down to the port of Piraieus ensured that Spartan infantry were kept out, while vital maritime trade could reach Athens uninterrupted, protected as it was from the Peloponnesian fleet by Athenian naval superiority. By the late fifth century, the Athenians, in hopes of spreading their untraditional ideas about the avoidance of hoplite battle on the plains, sent out corps of "long-wall builders" to other cities, such as Argos or Patras, to advocate the construction of similar systems of defense. (Plut. *Alc.* 15.2–3) Consequently, there was less chance now that a single, simple clash of Spartan and Athenian infantry would be the decisive factor in determining the outcome of a war between the two states; throughout Greece the old way of massing in formation to decide a conflict on a battlefield was nearly forgotten. War was now to drag on for countless years in a variety of land and sea encounters over a vast theater of operations, involving soldier and civilian alike, until both sides were finally exhausted, having suffered the steady misery of battle so well known to modern civilization.

5   *Sources of Inquiry*

> Moreover, a truly definitive history of Greek warfare
> would require a knowledge of many aspects of Greek life.
> The would-be investigator would have to be familiar with
> terrain in the case of any given battle, have an acquaint-
> ance with the archaeological artifacts of various types,
> close familiarity with the written sources, and most impor-
> tant, an understanding of the general economic picture.
> He would also need some insight into ancient religion
> and acquaintance with military and naval procedures and
> strategy.
>
> —*W. K. Pritchett, introduction to*
> The Greek State at War

From Greek literature we learn most about how the infantrymen
of the city-state fought and died, and Greek literature begins with
the two great epic poems the *Iliad* and the *Odyssey*, which have
come down to us under the name of Homer. Of the two, the *Iliad* is the more important for our purposes here, inasmuch as its
15,000 hexameter lines sing of battles rather than war—a series
of grisly, violent struggles between Greeks and Trojans in the
tenth year of the Greeks' siege of Troy. From Homer we can learn
a great deal about the early Greek attitude toward war and death
in battle. More importantly, because the poet saw combat as essentially a struggle between individuals, he alone in Greek literature describes in explicit detail the blows and wounds which armored men inflict and receive, regardless of the formation in
which they fight:

> The son of Telamon, sweeping in through the mass
>   of the fighters,
> struck him at close quarters through the brazen cheeks
>   of his helmet
> and the helm crested with horse-hair was riven about the
>   spearhead

to the impact of the huge spear and the weight of
    the hand behind it
and the brain ran from the wound along the spear by
    the eye-hole, . . .

(Il. *17.293–98*)

Yet there are questions of a historical nature which cloud the use of the Homeric poems as unambiguous sources for aspects of Greek hoplite battle. One, of course, is the matter of chronology. The author of the *Iliad* may have composed his epic as early as the latter half of the eighth century—a time when archaeological evidence suggests that hoplite armor (but not necessarily the associated tactics of massed attack in the phalanx) was just appearing for the first time in mainland Greece. Many therefore argue that we can obtain no sure knowledge of the arms and armor that the hoplite infantrymen wore from the descriptions of Homeric heroes. Secondly, the manner in which his epic warriors typically fight does not closely resemble the later custom and practice of phalanx infantrymen. In Homer, we find some traces of the Mycenaean world of the Linear B tablets some five centuries earlier, mixed together with more frequent references to the material culture of the Dark Ages and Homer's own eighth-century Greece. The resulting picture is an amalgam-mosaic spanning five hundred years, the exact nature of which is still uncertain; it may not reflect an actual historical society at all. Remember, too, that the *Iliad* and *Odyssey* are epics, heroic poems that were not intended to be a precise historical reflection of contemporary life. Many of their battle descriptions, even when they do not employ the formulaic conventions of oral poetry, must, like all epics, entertain, romanticize, and so sing of a strange, far-off world no longer present:

    But Tydeus' son in his hand caught up
a stone, a huge thing which no two men could carry
such as men are now, but by himself he lightly
hefted it.

(Il. *5.302–4*)

Nevertheless, throughout the *Iliad* a surprising number of passages show men fighting in unison, in massed formation of some sort; they cannot have fought and died much differently than their successors several generations later, even if they were not armed and deployed exactly like hoplite warriors.

More can be learned from the remaining fragments of Greek Lyric poetry, the new genre of literature of the Greek Archaic Age of the seventh and sixth centuries B.C., which followed the epic poems of Homer and Hesiod. Their usefulness as historical sources for information on Greek battle is less problematic, inasmuch as the authors were usually living when hoplite armament was first introduced and the tactics of the phalanx within the Greek city-state were developed; they are near witnesses of the so-called hoplite reform. For example, the poems of Archilochos, Tyrtaios, Kallinos, Mimnermos, and Alkaios all mention most of the components of the classical hoplite panoply, and suggest at times the voice of a man who has fought in the massed ranks of the phalanx. Because this focuses for the first and nearly the only time in Greek literature on the personality of the speaker and the particular circumstances of its delivery, we receive an unusually vivid, fresh view of battle, unlike that found earlier in the Homeric poems or even later within the prose narratives of the classical historians:

> No, no, let him take a wide stance and stand up strongly
>   against them,
> digging both heels in the ground, biting his lip with his
>   teeth,
> covering thighs and legs beneath, his chest and his
>   shoulders under the hollowed-out protection of his
>   broad shield,
> while in his right hand he brandishes the powerful war-spear
>   and shakes terribly the crest high above his helm.
>   (*Tyrtaios 11.21 ff*)

The camaraderie of combat in close order, the fear of the collision of armed men, the agony of wounds to the unprotected neck and groin, and, above all, the need to stay together without flinching in the face of the enemy are described in a first-person realism found nowhere else in Greek literature:

> For once a man reverses and runs in the terror of battle,
> he offers his back, a tempting mark to spear from behind,
> and it is a shameful sight when a dead man lies in the dust there,
> driven through from behind by the stroke of an enemy spear.
>
> *(Tyrtaios 11.17–20)*

Battle in these poems is fresh and vivid, reflecting the poet's fascination with a new type of combat, a new type of warrior who seeks ultimate victory not by himself but rather in concerted effort with men of his own class and circumstance. Much of the power of these poems is attributable to the rapidly changing environment in which the poets wrote, for many were among the first generation of hoplite fighters in the Greek-speaking world. One ought also to remember that proportionately few of these poems have survived intact from antiquity; most have been pieced together through quotations in extant prose authors or have been found fragmented on scraps of papyrus. Because of this lack of textual continuity and also because most of the poets lived well before the fifth century, we know few facts about the circumstances of the authors' lives. All too often the fragments are detached from any reference points—an exact date, a known war, an incident in a poet's career. Naturally these shortcomings have impaired the use of Lyric poets such as Tyrtaios as sources for the study of early Greek strategy and tactics or even Greek history in general. Yet in simply trying to catch a glimpse of battle, to learn how individual infantrymen fought and died in the great age of the hoplite, their value is unmatched.

Unfortunately, we have no contemporary prose accounts of the latter seventh and sixth centuries B.C., during the high point of the hoplite; our knowledge of that period must rest with less adequate archaeological finds—representation on vases and stone sculpture, and those precious few lines from the Lyric poets. Yet we must concentrate precisely on this very age of "pure" hoplite battle, where there was little variation from generation to generation in armament or in the manner of personal combat, if we are to learn about ancient Greek battle. For it was from this era of hoplite battle that the soldiers of the fifth century, so prominent in the accounts of Herodotus and Thucydides, learned to fight. However, we have no real accounts of these battles, and so the struggle on the Lelantine Plain, the battles at Hysiai (669), Tegea (560), Sepeia (494), and Dipaia (471), and even the later encounters in the first Peloponnesian War at Koroneia (447), Oinophyta and Tanagra (457) must all remain little more than mere names from a distant age.

Consequently, when the first prose writers of European history appear, in the latter fifth century B.C., and describe the warfare of the classical Greek city-state and thus the contemporary battles between hoplites in phalanxes, the great age of soldiers covered from helmet to toe in plate armor (700–500 B.C.) was already waning. Infantrymen like those of Xenophon's Ten Thousand had gradually begun to reequip themselves with lighter body armor, often of nonmetallic construction. The use of additional contingents of lighter-armed infantry, occasional javelin-throwers, professional skirmishers, and the independent deployment of cavalry all modified warfare; and yet, through such adaptation, paradoxically, this ensured that phalanx battle would be preserved for another hundred years, even if the heavy infantry was no longer now the only force on the battlefield.

From the three great historians of the fifth and early fourth centuries, Herodotus, Thucydides, and Xenophon, we receive the first clear account from beginning to end of a Greek hoplite battle where two massed armies square off to collide on level ground, such as occurred at Delion (424) or Mantineia (418). And while each author saw war and battle as the theme of their histories, they also took for granted an understanding of battle practice on the part of their audience, mostly male and veterans themselves. Occasionally, it is true, there is a brilliant exception—such as the fascinating description of the battle at Mantineia where Thucydides goes to great lengths to ensure that we understand the confusion and disorder that confronted the Spartan commanders in the field. There he describes the tendency, universal among hoplites in the phalanx, to drift slightly to the right, each man in search of protection for his own unshielded right side. But in general the historians placed much more emphasis on political history, and so they considered detailed accounts of the campaigns or theaters of operations (as part of some larger plan), more than graphic descriptions of the actual fighting between individual hoplites, to be the more effective technique in chronicling the change in fortune among Greek city-states. Consequently, when it comes to the clash of armed men, there is a sparsity of detail, an economy of style on the part of these writers—something Thucydides himself labeled "an absence of storytelling" (1.22.4)—which limits their battle pieces in most cases to a brief notice of a charge, "heavy fighting," the inevitable rout, and the final exchange of the dead.

Yet there is a wealth of information found in nearly all other literature of the fifth century—drama, comedy, oratory, and philosophy. Most Greek writers knew of battle firsthand; like the generation of American writers who went through the Second World War—Jones, Heller, Manchester, and Mailer—these veterans returned to their experience in combat to clarify or broaden their thoughts on whatever subject they were discussing. In the same way as the experience on board B-17s over Europe or jungle fighting in the Pacific became known to readers through postwar novels, so too in Aristophanes or Plato we hear often of the bothersome clumsiness of hoplite armor or the need to stay in rank during the fighting—in the course of a speech or dialogue otherwise unconcerned with war. From Aristophanes we learn that men might defecate before the onslaught of battle, in a scene where he intends no exaggeration in his ridicule of the fancy, though now *soiled*, cloak of a pompous commander. (*Pax* 1175–76) Plato, likewise, returns to battle imagery in his *Laches*, when he says that the brave men are those who hold their rank in the formation and do not run from the approach of the enemy. (190 E) We should not be surprised with the epitaph that Aeschylus was purported to have left behind for himself on his death in

Sicily. It makes no mention of his some seventy great tragedies presented in the Athenian theater but, rather, refers only to his service at the battle of Marathon as an ordinary hoplite in the ranks:

> Under this monument lies Aeschylus the Athenian
> Euphorion's son, who died in the wheatlands of Gela.
> The grove of Marathon, with its glories, can speak of his
>   valor in battle
> The long-haired Persian remembers and can speak
>   of it too.
>
> *(Aesch.* Vita *[Lattimore translation])*

Hoplite battle was second nature to nearly all these writers, and mention of the use of the spear and shield, the shame of flight, the art of weapon handling, the terror of a sudden collapse in the ranks, all appear at unlikely moments in allegory, metaphor, or simple storytelling. These allusions to battle, which can appear anywhere in Greek literature, cannot easily be located through the use of indices and concordances; yet, it is from these sources that much of the most helpful detail concerning combat between hoplites can be found.

Many classical scholars are hesitant to consult the later Greek writers of the Roman period, such as Diodorus, Pausanias, and Plutarch, who may be more than five hundred years distant from their subjects of inquiry. Yet most of the Lyric poets' accounts of battle in the great age of the hoplite are lost, while the ensuing fifth-century historians witnessed an altered and thus less representative type of phalanx warfare, which scholars are willing to accept as valuable evidence. Also, in defense of these less gifted inquirers of the Hellenistic and Roman periods, it should be noted that they sometimes drew on good (and often lost) contemporary sources about Greek hoplite battle of all epochs and, more importantly, their biographical approach and interest in an individual's role in history often preserved personal detail that otherwise would have been left unrecorded. If they are less valuable for the traditional study of tactics and military strategy due to their anecdotal, idiosyncratic, and unsystematic approach to historical writing—their bothersome omissions of crucial battles or treaties, and confusion over or misunderstanding of chronology and important changes in government—they nevertheless may be of even more interest to us by the sheer perversity of information which they do choose to include. For example, while we rarely hear of individuals fighting in hoplite battles in the more traditional (and reliable) histories of Thucydides and Xenophon, and so are not told much about wounds from sword and spear, there is an abundance of gore in both Diodorus and Plutarch— striking descriptions of battle injuries that can bring us much closer to the carnage of the battlefield: the image of the Greek general Philopoemen limping along "held as if by a fetter" when a javelin pierced both thighs simultaneously (Plut. *Phil.* 6.4–7), the dying Epameinondas at Mantineia with a broken spear protruding from his chest (Diod. 15.87.1–6), the nameless Spartan who hobbled from the battlefield on all fours suffering from multiple wounds to the legs and feet (Plut. *Mor.* 241 F 15), or Dionysius struck in the genitals at Rhegion (Diod. 14.108.6).

A final genre of literary evidence is the military manual or handbook, formal treatises on tactics from the late Hellenistic and Roman age, as well as the accompanying *strategemata,* which are essentially collections of old battle adages and clichés. These works of Aelian, Arrian, Asklepiodotos, Onasander, Polyaenus, and Frontinus (all in Greek but the last) are usually dismissed by military and classical historians alike as dry exercises in pedantry: "There is a collection of stratagems," wrote F. E. Adcock in his Sather Lectures on Greek and Macedonian warfare, "hastily compiled by Polyaenus to illustrate the dim mind of Lucius Verus on his Parthian campaign. It is uncritical, as is its Roman counterpart, the work of Frontinus, but it is, at the worst, the sediment left behind by the tides of war." (102) However, on occasion their uncritical approach allows them to include almost inadvertently interesting detail about how infantrymen reacted under specific conditions. While they do not intend to tell us anything about the men in the ranks, they often do, nonetheless; the

first-century A.D. Platonic philosopher Onasander advised his
general:

> When the enemy commander is distant, yell out, "The hostile general
> has fallen," or the king or whoever it may be. And it is crucial to call
> this out in such a way that the enemy also hears, since his own men,
> on hearing that their side is winning, are encouraged and even more
> eager to continue fighting, while the enemy, when they learn the de-
> pressing news, suddenly becomes discouraged, so much so that on oc-
> casion they run away immediately. *(23.1)*

We should note here the surviving chapter entitled "On the
Defense of Fortified Positions" (part of a much larger, lost work
on military operations) by one Aeneas Tacticus, and seven "minor" works of his better-known fourth-century contemporary,
Xenophon. These treatises, written in the chaotic world of the
early and mid fourth century, view military practice from an especially idiosyncratic viewpoint in a variety of different genres:
the political pamphlet, the biography, the didactic handbook, the
single-subject essay or monograph. From such wide-ranging discussions on horsemanship, hunting, municipal security, mining,
fortification, and cavalry sorties a good deal of information can
be gleaned concerning individual problems of armament and
weapons handling during combat.

Archaeological finds—excavations, topographical studies,
and examination of sculpture and vase painting—are the second kind of source material from which we learn about the
Greek infantryman in battle. The Greek practice in the Archaic
Age of dedicating captured arms and armor as votive or thank-
offerings at Panhellenic sanctuaries—a custom contemporane-
ous with the rise of the hoplite—has ensured that we know quite
a lot about how even the earliest Greek hoplites were armed and
protected, and more importantly, how difficult such equipment
was to wear into battle. The collections of shields, breastplates, helmets, greaves, ankle and thigh guards, swords and spear points,
and butts uncovered at Olympia and elsewhere (Delphi, Argos,
southern Italy, and Athens) not only provide information about
weight and size, but also illustrate regional specialties and even

individual modifications in arms. There is evidence too of a gradual trend over some 250 years toward lighter and less cumbersome armament, showing the hoplite's increasing desire for greater mobility and maneuver. Some idea of the rich flavor that archaeological evidence adds to the study of Greek battle is illustrated nicely in a small, obscure footnote in G. B. Grundy's classic *Thucydides and the History of His Age*. In his masterly chapter on Greek warfare—an account based almost exclusively on literary sources, written as it was before most archaeological and epigraphical evidence was known, much less organized and published—he remarks on the discomfort of hoplite armor:

> I have tried on a Greek helmet found at Delphi, and I have also tried on various helmets of genuine armour dating from various periods in the Middle Ages. The iron [*sic*] of the Greek helmet was extraordinarily thick, and its weight was, I should say, nearly double that of the heaviest helmet of the medieval period, even than those used by the Spanish common soldiers of the sixteenth century, which were naturally made of comparatively inexpensive metal. *(244)*

Finally, the excavation at Greek battlefields can add some knowledge about combat. But the resulting topographical studies are more valuable for tactical and strategic reconstructions of battle when literary descriptions are fragmentary or in need of supplementary detail. Not only can the size of ancient armies be envisioned (they must fit into the confines of the battle plain), but traces of the dead sometimes have been recovered. For example, at the Kolonos hill of Thermopylai, arrowheads of an Eastern type were found not far from the place that corresponds to the last stand of King Leonidas and his Spartans against the Persians in 480 as described in Herodotus and Diodorus. Spartan dead, buried at the end of the Peloponnesian War, were unearthed in the Athenian municipal cemetery with spear and arrowheads lodged in their skeletons, intact after 2,400 years and confirming an incident known previously only from Xenophon's brief remark that "Chairon and Thibrachos, both *polemarchs*, were killed there, and Lakrates, the Olympic victor, and the other Lakedaimonians who lie buried beneath the gates of

Athens in the Kerameikos." (Xen. *Hell.* 2.4.33; cf. Van Hook)
Likewise, under the lion monument at Chaironeia, 254 skeletons were unearthed, which may suggest the spot where we are
told the Theban Sacred Band of Three Hundred finally perished
in battle against Philip of Macedon in 338.

Men in battle, or on their way to war, were also a favorite topic
of red- and black-figure vase-painting and sculpted relief on public and private monuments on stone. While scenes were often
heroic in nature—the fight over the body of Patroklos, or the
farewell of Hektor to Andromache—the artist quite naturally portrayed his figures in the battle dress of his own time, although
occasionally reverting to easily identifiable "heroic" nudity. There
are frequent pictures of swordplay, spear thrusting, hoplites arming, or infantrymen stumbling in an attempt to ward off a blow.
Again, these representations are not so helpful for learning about
ancient tactics: the "group" effort in the phalanx is a difficult one
to portray successfully in iconography, and therefore never really appears. Yet, for the discovery of the sequence of events in
combat between individuals or small groups, these paintings are
quite useful and provide a glimpse of individual life-and-death
encounters after the two phalanxes collided and became one
mixed mass of humanity. Unlike the narrative accounts of Herodotus or Thucydides, they naturally concentrate on the individual, not the state's or the community's, experience with war; therefore they capture even the minutest detail: the bleeding thigh
wound of an injured soldier, the last movements of a trampled,
smashed hoplite, the final seconds before a fatal spear thrust. In
a sense, this interest in the individual in battle is not unlike the
personal voice of the Lyric poets, and so it comes as no surprise
that our best knowledge of Greek battle may derive from these
two sources.

Finally, epigraphy provides the third source of our knowledge
of Greek military history; examination in recent decades of hundreds of public documents on stone concerning the financial
structure of fifth-century Athens is a good example of a revolutionary change in the scholarly study of the city's imperial admin-

istration. Records of leases, public sales, honorific decrees, inventories, contracts, and civil and criminal legislation unearthed from the American excavations in the Athenian Agora have provided material for a social and economical history of Athens unknown from the literary evidence. Understandably, however, most of this epigraphic material is of a public nature, more important in learning about the army's enlistment, command structure, and casualty figures than about specific detail concerning the fighting and killing in the phalanx. There are occasional exceptions. For example, public casualty lists usually recorded the dead by tribal affiliation; this may suggest that the men in phalanx were more than a mere collection of citizens, but rather were drawn up and arranged by familial and kin relationships in order that those stronger ties might extend to the close-in fighting of the battlefield.

II

The Ordeal of the Hoplite

6   *The Burden of Hoplite Arms and Armor*

> We shall never know quite how Marathon was won, but
> we can be fairly certain that valour alone would not have
> won it, nor even perhaps the combination of courage
> with the somewhat rudimentary tactical skills which the
> style of Greek warfare at that time gave scope. The su-
> periority of Greek equipment must have been an im-
> portant factor here and elsewhere, and at times perhaps
> a decisive one.
>
> *—Anthony Snodgrass*

Classical scholars who have cataloged the archaeological finds
of Greek arms and armor, collated the references in Greek literature, and surveyed the painted ceramic evidence are struck
by the magnificence of the Greek achievement: their unrivaled
skill in metalworking, the attention to beauty in form and finish,
the matchless protection offered by the bronze panoply, which
gave its wearer a confidence in his superiority over all other contemporary soldiers. To the ancients, the excellence and outward
beauty of their own military equipment were matters of natural
pride. "The great hall is aglare with bronze armament and the
whole inside made fit for war," wrote the Lyric poet Alkaios in
obvious admiration, "with helms glittering and hung high,
crested over with white horsemanes that nod and wave and make
splendid the heads of men who wear them." After paying homage
to the various articles of the panoply—the greaves, breastplate,
shield, and sword—Alkaios simply finishes, "These shall not lie
neglected, now we stand to our task and have this work to do."
(54) Aeschylus, a veteran of the battle of Marathon, saw the infantry success at Plataia as a victory of the "Dorian spear" (*Pers.*
817)—a battle in which Herodotus likewise felt that the weapons

and the armor of the Greeks had been the key to success: "in war-like spirit and strength the Persians were not inferior, but they were unprotected by armor." (9.62.4) Apparently, in his view any-thing less than Greek plate was hardly worthy of consideration as real protection. (Cf. 9.63.2, 3.94.4) In a speech to the assem-bled Athenians he makes his Aristagoras (an Ionian Greek who should have been familiar with the enemy equipment in nearby Persian territory) remind the audience that the Asians used "nei-ther spear nor shield and so could be easily conquered." (5.97.1; cf. 7.211.2; Diod. 11.7.3) Like the German soldier of 1940–41, the Greek hoplite of the classical period drew an almost smug assurance from the natural superiority of his own weapons over any other in the Mediterranean world.

In their appreciating this unusual Greek contribution and in being dazzled by its unique durability and beauty, both ancient and modern authors have been reluctant to discuss the disadvantages of hoplite arms and armor, but they were many. Heavy, uncom-fortable, unbearably hot, the panoply was especially poorly suited for the Mediterranean summer; it restricted even simple move-ment, and in general must have made life miserable for the men who were expected to wear it. Most modern estimates of the weight of hoplite equipment range from fifty to seventy pounds for the panoply of greaves, shield, breastplate, helmet, spear, and sword—an incredible burden to endure for the ancient infantryman, who himself probably weighed no more than some 150 pounds. (Cf. Donlan and Thompson 1976: 341) Whatever the advantages this equipment offered in face-to-face battle, the Greek hoplite knew well that he was not really envied by his lighter-clad adversary. My own students at California State University, Fresno, who have cre-ated metal and wood replicas of ancient Greek and Roman armor and weapons, find it difficult to keep the weight of their shield, greaves, sword, spear, breastplate, helmet, and tunic under seventy pounds. After about thirty minutes of dueling in mock battles un-der the sun of the San Joaquin Valley they are utterly exhausted.

Before we examine the problems of the panoply in detail, four general trends must be kept in mind that illustrate quite clearly the discomfort which armed hoplites faced:

1. a gradual but steady tendency over some 250 years to alter, modify, and then discard entirely some elements of body armor;

2. the understandable habit of delaying arming until literally the very last seconds before the collision of spears;

3. the regular use of personal servants to transport hoplite equipment;

4. the natural urge to cast aside at a moment's notice expensive hoplite armor which usually was purchased by the individual and not supplied by the state.

There was a definite trend over some 250 years not to augment defensive armor in an effort to enclose the entire body like some medieval knight, but, rather, to lighten or omit some pieces altogether. Ankle guards and protective cover for the thighs and upper arms, which seem better adapted anyway for dueling than for battle in a phalanx, were the first to go; they seem to have faded already by the sixth century B.C. The introduction of a so-called race in armor at the Olympic Games (520) and the final Greek charge at Marathon (490) may reflect a newfound mobility arising from a reduced panoply. Such activity would have been quite impossible for the original hoplites of the seventh century, whose limbs were virtually encased in bronze. In any case, it is clear that the hoplites of the fifth century never had such auxiliary protection for the arms, thighs, and ankles. Their helmets, body armor, and greaves all became sleeker, lighter, and at times disappeared altogether, again suggesting continual displeasure with the weight of the old equipment of their forefathers. To judge from vase paintings of the mid-fifth century B.C. and the descriptions in Thucydides' history, some infantrymen of the phalanx must have gone into battle without greaves, the Corinthian helmet, or the bell corselet. Instead, they often wore the Athenian *pilos*—a mere conical cap, possibly of bronze but more likely of felt—and either lighter bronze body armor which fitted more closely to a man's torso, or linen corselets which contained little, if any, metal protection. By the early fourth century B.C. we even hear on occasion of something called the "half-corselet" which apparently protected the chest alone. (Plut. *Mor.* 596 D) Perhaps, by the end of the Peloponnesian War, soldiers might have seemed as ill-equipped to their hoplite ancestors of 250 years earlier as their lighter-clad adversaries from outside Greece; no doubt the staggering number of battle casualties in the Hellenistic period reflects this trend toward abandonment of body armor by the men of the phalanx.

Nor did all hoplites necessarily wear identical equipment—which is not surprising, considering that men brought along their own equipment and were never really provided with "general issue." Most would have their own individual preferences for certain designs that provided greater comfort (and at less cost) and therefore might also modify (that is, lighten) their arms to their own individual tastes. Outside the parade ground, it is unlikely that the soldiers who fought in the phalanx were as uniform-looking as modern representations might suggest. While the degree of variety may not have been as rich as one saw among American ground troops in Vietnam, it is clear, from vase paintings, that hoplites on both the same and opposing sides often wore different helmets, body armor, and weapons; this suggests again that the difficulty of the panoply may have encouraged modification by individual soldiers who learned of the advantages of certain changes, or who thought that both money and weight could be saved by reducing the amount of bronze protection. (E.g., Anderson pl. 7; Ducrey pl. 48; Snodgrass 1964: pl. 15b) The breastplate was often discarded entirely by poorer hoplite infantry who probably had neither the money nor the desire to wear it; later, during the fourth century in the Syracusan army under the tyrant Dionysius, only officers and cavalry were likely to have worn body protection. (Diod. 14.43.2–3) Thrasyboulos' "people's army," which overthrew the Thirty Tyrants at Athens right after the Peloponnesian War, carried both wood and wicker shields. (Xen. *Hell.* 2.4.25 and cf. too Thuc. 4.9.1) Xenophon, as a young man in Asia, was supposed to have been especially distinguished because of his unique arms (*An.* 3.2.7), though perhaps not to the same degree as the millionaire Nicias, who was said to have carried a purple and golden shield. (Plut. *Nic.* 28; cf., e.g., Ael. *VH* 3.24; Xen. *Mem.* 3.10.9–14; Plut. *Dion* 28.3) In contrast, it was to Agesilaos' credit that on his return from Asia during the early fourth century he still wore his regular Spartan issue, which suggests that a few of his men on duty there had incorporated some Persian tastes. (Plut. *Ages.* 19.5) A few years later, on Epameinondas' entry into the Peloponnese, it was rumored that the Athenians' allies who followed him were wearing some "new" type of armament—the nature of which we are never told (Plut. *Mor.* 193 F 20); this may be further evidence of considerable variation in the panoply. Indeed, the story that after the fall of Pellene in 241 soldiers marked their allotted captive women by putting their own helmets on them makes no sense unless we understand that each hoplite's headgear was easily distinguishable to wearer and onlooker alike. (Plut. *Arat.* 31.3) While most evidence of individual modification in armament comes from the fourth century and later, we remember that even earlier, in Thucydides' famous description of the great preparations for Athens' ill-fated expedition to Sicily (415), he makes an incidental remark that there was rivalry of sorts among hoplites as they readied their individual equipment, again implying that, in addition to regular mending and polishing, these men were perhaps making small changes in their offensive and defensive arms. The rise of the hoplite and his phalanx, where men of like background massed in formation, did not mean that they were always armed identically or even that men looked alike in the column. The actual conditions of battle made demands on men quite different from those of drill and parade, as they have ever since. We should imagine, then, that the hoplites, despite their interlocking formation, were not all that different from their Homeric predecessors in adapting their arms to their own particular tastes or the conditions of battle:

> The kings in person marshalled these men, although
>   they were wounded
> Tydeus' son and Odysseus, and Atreus' son Agamemnon.
> They went among all, and made them exchange their
>   armour of battle,

and the good fighter put on the good armour, and each
    gave the worse gear
to the worse.

                          (Hom. Il. 14.379–83)

    There also seems to have been a special reluctance on the part
of the Greek infantryman to put on his body armor, strap on the
shield, and don his helmet until the last possible moment before
battle. This expresses his sensible aversion toward wearing arms
and armor until their life-saving potential was more significant
than the inherent discomfort. Hoplites in sculpture and on vase
painting, for example, usually have the Corinthian helmet
pushed far back on the head, visorlike, suggesting that it was
brought down over the face only when the hoplite began his
charge. At times, we hear of men who are caught surprised without their armor and weapons, although there is no doubt that
battle is only a few moments away. Like modern infantrymen, who
have a natural tendency to go bareheaded whenever possible, the
ancient hoplite gladly risked the chance of being surprised unprotected in order to be free as long as possible from the great
weight and discomfort of his arms, and to enjoy unobstructed vision and hearing. Right before his attack on the Athenian oli-
garchs (403), Thrasyboulos, Xenophon relates, ordered his men
to ground their shields while he made a last-minute address. (*Hell.*
2.4.12) Earlier, during the battle of Plataia, in the last moments
before the charge the Spartan general Pausanias had his men re-
lax their arms before they lumbered out. (Plut. *Arist.* 17.6) It
seems quite natural to put down the spear and shield whenever
possible, since both could be picked up in a matter of seconds.
Yet, at other times we even hear that soldiers removed not only
shield and spear but also their entire body armor. Perhaps they
never put it on in the first place until they were absolutely sure
they were about to charge. How else can we explain the strange
behavior of the Mantineian horsemen who unbuckled their
breastplates during a brief lull in the battle there? (Xen. *Hell.*
7.5.22) Plutarch expresses surprise that, after their victory at

Kynoskephalai in 364, the Thebans did not unfasten their corselets but rather, in their eagerness to reach their fallen general Pelopidas, "ran up still wearing their full armor." (*Pel.* 32.2–3) Although the Athenian army was drawn up for their first hoplite engagement since landing in Sicily, waiting in formation on the Syracusan plain, the Sicilians were somehow caught off guard and suddenly realized battle was imminent. Thucydides remarks that "they hastily picked up their arms and marched out," again implying perhaps that they lacked body armor as well as shields in these last moments before combat. (Thuc. 6.69.2) When the fourth-century officer Polydamas bragged that he always led his mercenaries in full armor, he apparently was convinced that for most other soldiers that was certainly not the case. (Xen. *Hell.* 6.1.6)

Even when men were finally drawn up for battle, awaiting the moment to begin their charge, and their personal weapons-carriers had exited the ranks, any slight delay in the action caused them instinctively to drop their shields. Chabrias' men, for example, in 378 were ordered to stand fast and receive the Peloponnesian invaders of Boiotia rather than charge forth; they took their shields off, rested them against their knees, and at the same time lodged their spears upright on the ground—something most hoplites must have done whenever they had the chance. (Diod. 15.32.5; cf. Plut. *Eum.* 14.4–5; Xen. *An.* 1.5.13) We often see that very scene on vase painting, where hoplites stand or even crouch down with their shields resting against their legs. (Anderson 1970: pls. 6–7; Ducrey pl. 84) The Thebans before the battle of Leuktra in 371 were heartened that the statue of Athena had "picked" up her shield—a shield which Xenophon tells us was usually resting at her knees. (*Hell.* 6.4.7)

Yet another indication that hoplite arms and armor were intended to be worn only during combat is the undeniable presence in nearly every Greek battle of personal servants for both regular soldiers and officers alike, their chief function being to carry the masters' weapons and hand them over only in the very last seconds before the charge. Besides the standard battle equipment (breastplate, greaves, spear, sword, helmet, and shield), there were also provisions and utensils to carry; it is likely, then, that more than one "batman" accompanied each soldier to battle. The evidence for this constant presence of orderlies and personal attendants—either slaves, indentured servants, or the extremely poor—is found in nearly every Greek author. (Pritchett 1.49–51) But these servants were more than generic helpers of sorts during the campaign, since there are good indications that they not only carried the hoplite's arms and armor but passed them over only *in the very last seconds before battle*. Anaxibios, in a desperate situation near Antandros in 389, for example, after his last address to his men was finally handed his shield by his servants and immediately perished along with those hoplites remaining with him. (Xen. *Hell.* 4.8.39) When the Theban general Pelopidas commanded his infantry to charge against the Thessalians at Kynoskephalai in 364, we are told by Plutarch that he too joined in "after picking up his shield"; this suggests again that most would entrust their weapons to the help until the actual combat commenced. (*Pel.* 32.4) That is exactly the picture we receive in Aristophanes' *Acharnians*, when Lamachos repeatedly bids his servant to pick up his shield. (1121–25; 1135–39) Xenophon himself in the heat of battle during the march of his Ten Thousand in 401 became separated from his weapons-carrier and so separated from his shield; he was nearly caught helpless until aid arrived. (*An.* 4.2.21–23; cf. Plut. *Tim.* 27.2) From a later drill manual we learn that the shield bearer held his master's weapons until literally the last moment before the charge, when he was finally ordered to exit the ranks of the phalanx as the infantrymen picked up their spears: "Prepare arms! Let the orderlies depart from the ranks! Silence and pay attention to command! Take up arms!" (Asklepiodotos 12.11)

That hoplites themselves were not always up to carrying the great weight of their panoplies until the final moments before the charge is also clear from the curious carrying cases we sometimes hear were used to transport weapons. Apparently, both the shield and spear were packed away in leather bags to facilitate handling when not in use; indeed, we even know of wooden tripods designed exclusively to prop up shields while they rested on the ground. (Ar. *Ach.* 574; 1120; 1128) This also illustrates nicely the hoplite's pride in his own weapons, for it is hard to imagine modern infantry taking such care of their government-issued arms. Like modern golfers who are supplied clubs from their caddies' bags only before each swing, so too ancient Greek infantrymen picked up their heavy, awkward tools of the craft only when combat was inevitable. The general weight of the equipment, rather than any Greek notion of "equality" among the troops, explains why all soldiers, regardless of rank, were served by personal servants.

Finally, throughout Greek literature we find constant references to the abandonment of hoplite arms on the field of battle: again, I suggest, this illustrates the universal tendency on the part of Greek heavy infantry to be rid of their great weight and the general discomfort at the first sign that it might be dangerous to keep them. Remember that this equipment was paid for by the hoplite out of his own purse, an item of family honor to be hung up over the hearth on his return—in short not an easy thing to throw away unless there were good reason. The charge of *rhipsaspia,* or "tossing away the shield," is associated with cowardice in combat. Those so accused were assumed to have been among the first to have abandoned their friends in an effort to save their own lives during a general collapse of the phalanx; that is, they had endangered the men who had kept their arms and were not able, or had no desire, to make good such an ignoble escape. The frequency of this charge in Greek literature is not limited to Athenian comedy or oratory, where we would not be surprised to find such slander in the plays of Aristophanes or the speeches of Lysias. Indeed, men like Demosthenes and the poets Archilochos and Alkaios were all said to have flung away their equipment in battle. That this shameful conduct was attributed to such well-known authors is not really an indication of the martial timidity of Greek literary artists, but rather an illustration of just how widespread this tendency was. "Some barbarian is waving my shield, since I was obliged to leave that perfectly good piece of equipment behind," bragged the Lyric poet Archilochos, "but I got away, so what does it matter?" (5) Much has been made of Archilochos' new antiheroic stance at the very dawn of the hoplite age. His very flippancy perhaps suggests a particular sensitivity or defensiveness about the loss of such a "perfectly good piece of equipment"; this is quite a different view of the panoply than Alkaios' undisguised pride in the beauty of his arms (expressed in his poem 54). We can be certain that the poet gave up its damnable weight only, as he says, when his very life was in danger. Herodotus reminds us that "in a battle which the Athenians won, Alkaios saved himself by fleeing, and so they gained possession of his arms and hung them up in the temple of Athena at Sigeion" (5.95.1); apparently he lost the love of his hoplite panoply once he left the banquet hall and walked the battlefield. Two hundred and fifty years later Aristophanes joked that Kleonymos threw his shield away whenever possible—on land, sea, and in the air (*Vesp.* 22); shields had become no lighter since Archilochos' time.

The shield was probably the first piece to be discarded since it could be detached and cast aside most easily, and of course it was also both the most awkward part of the panoply to carry and the cheapest to replace (being the only item made largely of wood). But the helmet, greaves, and even breastplate were also left behind on occasion. What accounts for the particular emphasis on the shield in literature is the natural Greek notion that its loss alone affected everyone in the formation who were similarly equipped and thus was, in a sense, a crime against every citizen within the phalanx: "men wear their helmets and breastplates for their own needs," wrote Plutarch, "but they carry shields for the men of the entire line." (*Mor.* 241 F. 16; cf. 220A; Polyaen. *Strat.* 3.9.4) After the Athenian debacle on the heights of Epipolai during the Sicilian expedition in 413, Thucydides wrote, "more arms were left behind than corpses"—a picture startlingly reminiscent of the modern battlefield. (7.45.2) Simply put, for most hoplites (unlike light-armed troops or archers) who decided that flight was preferable to a glorious end in battle, there was no chance of escape from the pursuit of victorious enemy infantry and cavalry if they were burdened with arms and armor on their backs. Thus there was always in Greece a desire to lighten hoplite equipment, always a reluctance to carry the panoply or even put it on until the last seconds before battle, always a tendency to throw it away when flight was imminent.

The Shield

The hoplite's most important piece of defensive armament was his shield, a rounded, concave piece of wood some three feet in diameter, the exact size somewhat depending on the length and strength of the individual wearer's arm. The thickness and type of hardwood used (and thus the real weight of the shield) are not really known, since most wood cores have long since perished, but it has been estimated at some sixteen pounds. (Donlan and Thompson 1976: 341) While this was a considerable burden for the armored hoplite to carry, the advantage over the earlier ox-hide models of the Dark Ages was the greater protection against standing spear and sword thrusts, allowing the warrior the chance to approach his enemy at much closer range. Originally, the shield may have been rimmed with a bronze strip around its outer edge to prevent rot and splintering at the edges, but by the fifth century B.C. literary references and archaeological examples suggest that much of the face, like the old Homeric shield of the Dark Ages, was covered by a thin sheet of bronze, often in the shape of a distinctive blazon. This added little to the shield's protective capability or even weight, but apparently imparted a sense of ferociousness to its wearer if it could be brought to a high polish and thus dazzle or even frighten the opponent.

Scholars make much of the shield's distinctive arm and hand-grips, the *porpax* and *antilabe*, which for the first time distributed the weight all along the left arm rather than concentrating it at the hand and wrist alone. These innovations made it possible to hold such an otherwise clumsy thing for the duration of battle. Yet it is usually forgotten that this grip also had severe drawbacks for the men in the field. Overall body movement was impaired as the left arm—for most men the more awkward and weaker one—had to be held rigidly, stuck out in front of the body waist high, elbow bent and the forearm straight and parallel to the ground, the hand tightly clenched to the grip. If the hoplite bent down or slipped, the lower rim of the shield would scrape the ground—a likely occurrence when its wearer was not much over five and a half feet in height. Balance was affected as well, and crouching or even bending over was difficult. Nor could the shield be easily handled once battle commenced. Because the entire arm was needed to maintain its great weight, the angle of deflection could be adjusted only with difficulty, and its shape suggests that it may have been really designed largely for pushing ahead. The shield could not be brought over at any angle to protect a man's right side, and we hear of entire phalanxes caught helpless by a flank attack upon the extreme right, where the last file of hoplites had no protection at all for their unshielded sides. (Xen. *Hell.* 4.2.22; 4.5.13)

It is worthwhile to examine some of the frequent references to the discomfort of the hoplite shield. "It is not right, Xenophon," complained Soteridas, a dissident member of his Ten Thousand, "that you sit on your horse while I struggle under the weight of my shield." (Xen. *An.* 3.4.47–48) Those first few brave Plataians who chose to break out from the Spartan siege in 429 during the Peloponnesian War went out only with offensive weapons, followed closely behind by others who brought along their shields. Apparently they knew that there was little chance of escape if one man had to carry both (Thuc. 3.22.3); there is no mention here of body armor, but even the weight of the spear and shield alone must have been considered excessive. We can understand why "Right Logic" in Aristophanes' comic play the *Clouds* (987–999) remarks that the youth of his day could only hold their shields thigh high; in other words, these soft young men were not up to the rigorous demands of the old hoplite standard, which expected men to maintain the more difficult chest-high position of battle. The often quoted aphorism (of unknown date) of the Spartan mother who admonished her son to return from battle with his shield, or on it, also reveals the shield's intrinsic immobility and awkwardness: there was always present a natural (though repressed) tendency to discard it, while its unusual size and bowl shape made it ideal to double as a bier for the corpse should the hoplite perish. (Plut. *Mor.* 241 F 16) No wonder, then, that the Spartans punished those soldiers found lax in their duty by making them stand and hold their shields in position (Xen. *Hell.* 3.1.9): merely wearing the panoply, without the rigors of battle, was considered penalty enough.

Indeed, so great was the effort needed just to hold their equipment that when hoplites became worn out or lost concentration they instinctively first dropped their shields. The famous shield of Aristomenes, which Pausanias claims to have seen hundreds of years later at Lebadeia, had supposedly been lost by the legendary hero during the Messenian Wars. (Paus. 4.16.7) Two centuries later the Spartan general Brasidas, upon landing on the shore at Pylos to challenge the Athenian garrison there, was overwhelmed by blows, and after "he fell into the bow of his ship his shield slid off into the sea." (Thuc. 4.12.1) Likewise, the Theban general Epameinondas lost his shield when he was wounded at Mantineia; brought out of the battle conscious, he asked if his servant had managed to bring it too out of the fray. (Diod. 15.86.5) The wind over the pass at Kreusis blew many of the shields right off the arms of the Spartan hoplites who were trying to make their way over the pass. (Xen. *Hell.* 5.4.18) This difficulty in retaining the shield must be what Epameinondas had in mind when he remarked that his Thebans could not maintain their power if they could not keep hold of their handgrips. (Plut. *Mor.* 193 E 18) Heroes such as Brasidas, Epameinondas, and Aristomenes, and Spartans on the march, unlike the poets, "lost" rather than "cast away" their shields; but whatever the truth, we know that their weight and difficult configuration ensured that shields were a constant bother.

Recently when scholars conducted tests to reproduce the physical requirements which faced the soldiers at Marathon, they discovered that their modern-day subjects in these experiments had the greatest difficulty in holding the shield chest high:

> It is significant to note that running the prescribed distance with the shield in chest high position required an average increase of 28% in energy expenditure for each subject . . . The experiment also showed that the weight and size of the shield were the critical factors. The hoplite shield, which appears to have weighed about sixteen pounds, could only be carried isometrically, and the considerable energy expenditure required sharply limits the distance over which troops could sustain great effort. (*Donlan and Thompson 1976: 341*)

Even with the handgrips and armgrips, the only way ancient infantry could hold onto this shield for more than a few minutes in battle was to rest it occasionally on the left shoulder—a point that is all too often forgotten. This was possible because of the extreme concavity of the shield, a shape that allowed the soldier "to put both the chest and shoulder into the belly of the hollow shield." (Tyrtaios 8.24 ff) The lip of the shield very nearly made a ninety-degree angle, creating a veritable bowl, rather than a plate shape. While it is true that such an unusual bowl shape helped to deflect blows and offered additional protection to the forearm, far more importantly, it allowed the shield's great weight *to fall upon the shoulder*. Other shield types of smaller size and less weight—the Macedonian, Roman, and Persian, for example—lacked this radical concavity, perhaps because there was not the need to relieve the arm.

Once the two armies collided, a pushing match usually ensued, and so we can imagine that the hoplite naturally rested the entire weight of the shield on his left shoulder as he leaned into the men ahead. Perhaps this concavity, so radical in conception, rather than the more heralded armgrips and handgrips, was the real revolution in armament: it allowed a disproportionately large piece of equipment to be carried by even a small man (of some 150 pounds) and enabled him to find the perfect surface for channeling his power into the backs of those ahead of him.

After Homer, as we would expect, the infantry shield was described for the first time as "hollow." (Tyrtaios 11.24; 19.7; Mimnermos 13a) Thucydides remarked that Athenian prisoners on Sicily were forced to "fill four inverted shields" with their money—an image difficult to conceive unless one remembers the distinctive shape of the hoplite shield. (7.82.3) In Euripides we read that the warrior chafes his beard with the rim of his shield, another suggestion that the lip was resting on his shoulder right under the side of the jaw. (*Troades* 1196–1200) Indeed, a nearly completely restored Argive hoplite shield in the Vatican Museum confirms that a man could hang the inside of the rim on his left shoulder. (Connolly 54) We see this posture often on vase paintings, where men appear to rest their shields on their shoulders both when stationary and when in battle; often, too, a crouching hoplite protects himself from a blow from above by holding his shield horizontally, the lip on his shoulder tucked under the chin. (Ducrey pls. 2, 62, 84, 85, 187; Chase 74) A better representation may be found on an Attic grave relief of the late fifth century. (Anderson pl. 12) There a hoplite, probably with his shield on his shoulder, has both hands occupied: he is shaking hands with his right, while gripping the spear with his left. This important function of the hoplite shield rim can also explain its later disappearance during the Hellenistic period of the late fourth, third, and second centuries when infantrymen suspended their smaller shields from the neck in order to grasp the much longer and heavier *sarissa,* or pike, with both hands. The neck strap and decreased weight required no support from the shoulder, and so it is not surprising that the later military analyst Asklepiodotos could call the Macedonian version "not very hollow." (5.1)

Another reason why the advantages of the shield's lip are often neglected by scholars is the usual emphasis in vase paintings on the front ranks—the place where the initial stabbing occurred and where the shield more often than not was thrust out from the chest to deflect a variety of incoming blows. It could not be rested then at any time. Besides, the inherent action within the front ranks drew the artist's interest and was much easier to portray than rank upon rank of nameless infantry pushing and leaning their shields against the men ahead.

Besides the weight and cumbersome shape, a final drawback of the shield was its relative *thinness,* being not much more than an inch to an inch and a half thick. As armor has been for more than twenty-five centuries since, the thickness was sacrificed for surface area; its three-foot diameter demanded that it be thinly constructed to keep overall weight within tolerable limits. Although they could not guarantee absolute protection from all incoming blows, the Greeks knew that these cores, unlike the shields of past centuries, were sufficient to withstand most attacks from spears and swords, provided these were stabs and thrusts at close range, where it was difficult to create momentum. The stories of weapons handed down from father to son (Plut. *Mor.* 241 F 17), arms hanging above the ancestral fireplace (Ar. *Ach.* 57, 278), shields seen hundreds of years later on display in sanctuaries (Paus. 9.16.3; 2.21.4; 1.15.4; Diod. 17.18; Arr. *Anab.* 1.11.7) are probably all plausible, since most hoplites were not posted on the front line and did not subject their equipment to that first awful crash, where spearhead collided head-on with shield, breastplate, helmet, and greave. On the other hand, for those few men who faced this enemy charge at the front of the phalanx, the shield as well as the spear was likely to crack or fall apart upon impact. We see broken shields in vase paintings and should remember, too, that this is a frequent occurrence in literature. Brasidas' untimely death at Amphipolis in 422 was supposedly due to the failure of his shield to fend off a spear thrust. Asked how he received his wound, Plutarch has him reply, "It was due to my shield which turned traitor on me." (Plut. *Mor.* 219 C; cf. Xen. *An.* 4.1.18) That same image is captured in Xenophon's eerie account of the aftermath of the battle of Koroneia in 394, where after the collision of Spartans and Thebans shields lay smashed to pieces around the bodies of the slain. (*Ages.* 2.14) And in Menander's *The Shield* we recall the slave of Kleostratos, Davos, who finds his master's crumpled shield beside his supposed corpse. (75f) Finally, there are instances of entire armies which were reequipped after battle, or eager to exchange their own armament for new issue, an indication, perhaps, that quite a few shields—the only member of the defensive panoply not made entirely of bronze—must have been shattered in the initial clash. (Xen. *Ages.* 1.26; Polyaen. *Strat.* 3.8; Diod. 17.39.2)

The Helmet

The favored type of headgear throughout Greece in the great age of hoplite warfare (700–500 B.C.) was the so-called Corinthian helmet. Unlike infantry helmets employed in Western armies of the twentieth century, a hoplite's bronze helmet covered both the head and most of the neck, extending in the back all the way down to the collarbone. In its last and most elegant form, the cheek pieces and nose guards swept forward to such a degree that they nearly met in the center of the face, thereby ensuring that the eyes, nose, and even mouth were virtually enclosed. In theory, the massive bronze provided needed protection from spear thrusts to the face and head, and shielded the jaw from both lateral and frontal blows. Yet it must have been a most uncomfortable and difficult thing to wear. The obvious difficulty was that it impeded sight and hearing—there were no orifices for the ears. It would not be surprising if the simple formation and tactics of phalanx warfare—the massing into formation, charge, collision, and final push—grew, at least in part, out of the lack of direct communication between soldiers and their commander; dueling, skirmishing, and hit-and-run attacks were out of the question with such headgear, and the isolation created by the helmet demanded that each individual seek close association with his peers.

Even though the helmeted hoplite could scarcely see or hear, there was hardly any problem in locating the enemy, or any danger in being blindsided—as long as the cohesive formation of the phalanx was kept intact. Consequently, what sounds we do hear in the phalanx are usually singing in accompaniment with the flute (Thuc. 5.70.1; Plut. *Lyc.* 21; Xen. *Cyr.* 7.1) or yelling (Xen. *An.* 1.8.18; 6.4.27; *Hell.* 2.4.31; Thuc. 7.44); orders to advance or retreat were given by blasts of the horn. (E.g., Thuc. 6.69.2; Xen. *An.* 4.4.22) The Theban general Epameinondas' purported command at the battle of Leuktra in 371 "to give me one step forward" (Polyaen. *Strat.* 2.3.4) in the heat of the fighting, if true, was probably not heard by many, unless he was wearing the so-called Boiotian helmet, which left the face entirely open.

If the Corinthian helmet curbed communication between soldiers and thereby mandated that commands and tactics be simple, the restriction in vision also necessitated battle by daylight. Night attacks were understandably rare and, if attempted, usually ended in confusion; the ordinary dust raised by thousands of marching or shuffling feet burdened by armor must have made daytime battle difficult enough. Also, much of the fear and panic that often swept the ranks of a phalanx before battle can be attributed to the frightful sense of isolation created by the Corinthian helmet as the wearer entered a world of his own, cut off from the men around him, his perception of the fighting deriving largely from the sense of touch, or rather, to be more exact, from the pressure of men to the rear, side, and front. If not through this pushing and shoving within his own immediate vicinity, how else might a man receive accurate knowledge of the fighting around him? Conditions of battle only added to the lack of perception. The headgear was never molded precisely to match the skull, so even deflected blows could knock the helmet askew, forcing it not merely to nod up and down, but also turning it sideways and thus at times eliminating vision altogether.

Besides the loss of perception, the helmet was uncomfortable because of its weight (five or more pounds) on the neck and because of the heat it generated around the eyes, mouth, nose, and ears. The campaigning season, we should remember, was almost exclusively confined to the summer months. During that time temperatures in Greece routinely exceed 90 degrees F; there

could not have been a more stifling type of headgear for a wearer—
who was bearded and wore his hair long. (E.g., Hdt. 1.82.7–8;
Plut. *Nic.* 19) Long hair, not the shaved head of our own time,
was the proper sign of militarism, as the custom in Sparta at all
times shows clearly. (Ar. *Av.* 1281; *Vesp.* 476; *Lys.* 1072; Plut. *Phoc.*
10.1; *Lyc.* 22.1) There was no ostensible reason for this preference, since the beard and hair provided a grip for any adversary
on the battlefield, and could only make the helmet more uncomfortable and stuffy. Perhaps this is why we sometimes see in
vase painting a hoplite smoothing his long hair carefully, pressing it down firmly to the skull before putting on the helmet, as
if that will somehow make the fit more tolerable. (Ducrey 222)

The third drawback, in addition to reduced perception and
general discomfort, was the lethal absence of interior netting or
any suspension system other than a man's hair that could absorb
the shock of direct blows to the head. Although punched holes
around the perimeter of extant helmets suggest that there was
some type of interior felt or leather padding attached to the
bronze surface, this cushioning provided no air space between
the metal sides and the cranium and could not absorb fully the
force of incoming blows. Most likely the material's prime objective was to protect the wearer's head and face from the roughness and heat of the bronze (Lazenby pl. 4); understandably,
then, often we hear of soldiers who perished from blows to the
head. Most ancient remains of Corinthian helmets are cracked,
dented, or patched (e.g., cf. Weiss 195ff), suggesting that the
wearer might often have suffered serious contusions even if the
bronze managed to prevent actual penetration. (Ar. *Ach.* 1180)
Strong blows could drive the metal hard against the padding
around the head, shattering the cranium and perhaps pushing
metal, leather, and bone deep into the brain.

Most helmets in the Archaic and early classical periods were
equipped with horsehair crests. Some were attached directly to
the helmet itself; others made use of a special bronze holder that
arose from the top of the helmet. Apparently, they added height
and frightfulness to the appearance of the small hoplite; at least

that is how Hektor's young son thought of it when he saw his father's nodding crest. (Hom. *Il.* 6.469) Even Dikaiopolis was disturbed by the same sight in Aristophanes' *Acharnians* (567, 586) and Tyrtaios' call to "shake terribly the crest high above the helm" (11.26) was intended to create that same impression.

In a more practical sense crests may have blunted blows aimed directly downward to the center of the helmet (e.g., Snodgrass 1967: pl. 23) or arrows that rained down amidst the phalanx. Lykon, for example, in the *Iliad* "struck the horn of the crested helmet, and his sword broke at the hilt." (16.339) Alexander the Great at the Granicus River in 334 was saved when his helmet crest blunted an attack by the Persian Spithridates. The Persian's battle-ax split the crest, sliced away the plume, and nearly cleft the helmet, yet Alexander suffered only a nick on the scalp. (Plut. *Alex.* 16) But to anyone who has worn any modern headgear similarly equipped with some type of extensive ornament—a ceremonial hat or Halloween mask—it is easy to understand how the crest only made the helmet more unwieldy, especially when putting it on or removing it. If the crest allowed the hoplite to appear taller and therefore fiercer to his foe (e.g., Polyb. 6.32.13), it was even more likely to obstruct his own sight of incoming arrows and missiles, or even a spear thrust between shields. Vase paintings sometimes show hoplites being grabbed by their crests, so it also offered the same liability as the beard or long hair. (Ahlberg pls. 6, 10, 11) Finally, it is hard to imagine that the crest could really stay intact during the general pushing and shoving; Lamachos' plume, for example (if we can believe Aristophanes), fell off when he tripped while leaping over a trench. (*Ach.* 1182) Can we be surprised, then, that crests are often absent on vase paintings and that extant helmets sometimes show no trace at all of them? Perhaps in many cases they were never worn in the first place.

The Corinthian crested helmet of the great age of the hoplite took a physical toll on its wearer. No wonder that in both sculpture and on vase paintings it is nearly always shown propped back on the head, suggesting that it was probably not pulled down over the face until the last seconds before the charge. (Snodgrass 1967: pl. 42) That it seems to have been superseded in the fifth century by a simple conical cap or other headgear that left the face open makes perfect sense. Finally, the Corinthian helmet, the shield, and, as we shall see, the breastplate, were too uncomfortable to be worn until the final assault; this is evidence, again, that a man's equipment, like the very tactics of Greek warfare, was designed for only a few hours of battle each summer.

Greaves

The lower legs could not be adequately protected by the downward movement of the shield, and so the vulnerable shins and calves were guarded either by an apron of sorts attached to the shield's lower rim or, more commonly, by greaves—thin sheets of bronze extending from the kneecap all the way down to the ankle. Unlike the short, rather stubby leg guards of the Mycenaean period, the classical hoplite's more elegant leg protection often lacked metal or leather laces. Instead, the two edges of the greave nearly met at the rear of the calf muscle. The punched holes we find on surviving examples may not be eyes for leather straps to hold the bronze steadfast, but rather, as in the case of the helmet, signs of the presence of interior felt or leather padding which was stitched to the bronze to protect the wearer's leg from both the heat and chafing of the metal and perhaps to provide some additional protection. Modern scholars believe that these metal eyes in the hoplite's greaves had nothing to do with a fastening system; greaves were "snapped on," remaining in place by the sheer elasticity of the bronze and thus the snugness of the fit. The advantages of greaves were that they apparently offered the infantryman some protection from missiles whose high trajectory might enable penetration into the interior of the phalanx, wounding a man's vulnerable tibia, which is without much flesh or muscular protection. Of course, too, they provided the men in the first few ranks some defense against low sword and spear thrusts. Also, unlike the other pieces of a hoplite's body armor, the thin greaves did not add unreasonable extra weight. Yet, ironically, of all his equipment, greaves may have been precisely the most bothersome: like the awkward leggings of the First World War infantrymen, the greave was likely to chafe when running or even simply walking. Worse yet, regardless of how precise their fit and malleability they could not ride snugly on the leg without the aid of straps; perhaps those holes in the bronze served for both interior padding *and* leather or metal ties. While on the march or in battle, the constant movement of the leg, and more importantly, the occasional distortions caused by spear and sword blows, could well have modified the original fit, and so caused the hoplite constantly to rebend his greave. That would be a difficult task, with some fifty pounds of metal riding on his head and chest. Understandably Polybius remarked that it was crucial that soldiers take care to ensure that their greaves "look and fit well." (11.9.4) In the Roman period their use by infantry nearly dies out completely; those examples which do appear are always equipped with ties—suggesting that the elastic models of the Greeks were not entirely successful.

The Breastplate

The standard breastplate for the initial two hundred years of hoplite battle was the simply designed bell corselet, which consisted of front and back sheets of bronze connected together at the shoulders. Above the hip socket, the armor curved outward to form a flange, thereby creating the characteristic bell shape and apparently aiding the movement of the hips during walking or trotting as well as offering some protection against downward thrusts to the lower stomach. The groin and neck, however, were both left unprotected, if the wearer was to retain at least some mobility. (Xen. *Eq.* 12.2ff) Strangely, although there was little fear of an attack from the rear, this type of plate, which covered both the entire torso and the back, did not drop out of use in

Greece until the early fifth century when lighter versions, of either bronze or even leather and fabric, finally appeared. Even then, infantrymen felt some type of body protection was necessary, and suggestions by some that hoplites in the latter fifth century wore no body armor at all are probably mistaken. (E.g., cf. Lazenby 32) Rather, what is surprising is that generation upon generation were willing to endure the plate corselet—a type of armor which through its great weight and inflexibility probably wore out its wearer within minutes.

Some idea of the discomfort of the breastplate can be found in frequent references throughout Greek literature to the importance of a good fit, the difficulty of movement, and the need for help in arming. Interestingly enough, such citations are mostly from the fifth and fourth centuries when the bell corselet was being replaced by lighter types; yet, even these improved, lighter versions were annoying enough to the wearer. The breastplate seller in Aristophanes' comic play the *Peace* makes an impossible promise in advance to Trygaios that his product will be a perfect fit, for he knew body armor had to be made to the exact specifications of the wearer to be of any value. (1225) "The breastplate," Xenophon remarked in his treatise on the art of horsemanship, "quite simply must be constructed to fit the body"; he added that a loose fit put an impossible weight on the shoulders, while body armor that was too tight was a "prison rather than a defense." (*Eq.* 12.2; cf. *Mem.* 3.10.9–15) He worried in any case about the lack of mobility caused by the plate corselet; "the shape," he said, "should not prevent either sitting or stooping." To throw a javelin with the right hand, he added, required that a portion of the plate be removed entirely. (12.3–7) Just to put on his body armor the hoplite was forced to ask for assistance. In literature and on vase painting, fellow soldiers or attendants must hold the helmet or buckle the straps on; greaves are usually already attached, suggesting, whatever Xenophon apparently believed, that once the breastplate was on, stooping might be a problem. (Anderson 1970: pl. 5; Hom *Il.* 3.330–38; 11.17–44; 16.131–44; 19.369–91)

Much of the difficulty in wearing the corselet was, of course, due to the weight of the bronze. Although the remains of bronze armor from Panhellenic sanctuaries in Greece and sites in Italy have usually been found corroded or damaged in the nearly 2,500 years since their fabrication, and so make exact calculations of their original weight impossible, estimates that the bell corselet of the seventh, sixth, and early fifth centuries weighed somewhere between thirty and forty pounds are reasonable. (E.g., Donlan and Thompson 1976: 341) Even during the Hellenistic period, when the weight of body armor was as a rule reduced, at times we hear of heavier models. Demetrios of Macedon, we are told by Plutarch (*Demetr.* 21), wore a breastplate of forty pounds; one of his infantry officers supposedly wore a panoply of well over one hundred pounds—twice the weight of most others in the army. Diodorus remarks that the breastplate of Agathokles, the infamous tyrant of Syracuse, was so heavy that no one else could handle it. (19.3.2) Indeed, many of the general references to the encumbrance of hoplite armor must refer to the breastplate specifically; after all, it accounted for at least half the total weight of the panoply. Medieval plate armor, for example, which bears a close resemblance to the hoplite's helmet and breastplate, weighed between sixty and seventy pounds even without offensive weapons. (Wise 48) Even in much later times, when we know that body armor was far lighter than the bulky bell corselet worn by the first generation of hoplites, we still hear of complaints and difficulty: once the Macedonians under Philip V lost the cohesion of their phalanx, they fell easy prey to the Romans under Flamininus since "in hand-to-hand fighting they struggled with armor which was both heavy and uncomfortable." (Plut. *Flam.* 8.3–4) Similarly, Lucullus reminded his Roman troops of the drawbacks of the enemy's heavy armor: "it will be easier to defeat them in battle," he said only half in jest, "than it will be to strip away their armor once they are dead." (Plut. *Mor.* 203 A 2) We are told that once when the Greek general Philopoemen dismounted and marched ahead on foot, the weight and awkwardness of his breastplate (which must have been heavier than normal issue in Hellenistic times and thus perhaps not unlike the notorious bell corselet some four hundred years earlier) slowed his progress and nearly got him killed. (Plut. *Phil.* 6.3–4) Xenophon himself had a similar experience centuries earlier during the retreat of the Ten Thousand when he dismounted to push Soteridas out of the ranks. Because of the very weight of his corselet of plate armor he could scarcely make his way forward. (*An.* 3.4.48) It was probably this widespread unpopularity of metal body armor among fifth-century Athenians that Aristophanes was playing on in his *Peace;* there Trygaios suggests that the plate corselet could just as well be used as a chamber pot. (1224)

As difficult as the weight of the breastplate was, a greater problem was the lack of ventilation, since the solid, continuous plate of metal upon the body gave little relief from either heat or cold. In the summer, perspiration must have soaked the hoplite's inner garment: the shiny bronze which could dazzle the enemy across the battlefield could just as well act as a solar collector of sorts that would make the entire surface hot to the touch. The leather, felt, or linen worn beneath helmet, greaves, and breastplate to cushion the shock of blows and give some relief from the temperature and roughness of the bronze upon the skin could also increase the general discomfort; the sweat from his chest and back must have bathed this underwear very quickly. We often hear, then, of hoplites who came near collapse from dehydration, or became delirious as a result of heat prostration— surely a likely phenomenon for armored men in a country where it is so hot in the spring and summer. Thucydides states, for example, that after a series of attacks on Pylos, both the Athenian attackers and Spartan defenders were worn out by "thirst and the sun." (4.35.4) It was probably the discomfort of fighting in full armor under the summer sun that prompted the famous retort of Dienekes the Spartan at Thermopylai in 480: when he was told that the multitude of the incoming Persian arrows would blot out the sun, he replied calmly, "Then we might have our battle with them in the shade." (Hdt. 7.226.1–2) That difficulty of wearing body armor in the summer months probably also explains why the last Athenian retreat from Syracuse in 413 quickly turned into a rout. Once the fully armed hoplites finally reached the river Assinaros, Thucydides relates, "the majority of them were fighting among themselves to have a drink of it." (7.85.1) The danger of heat prostration for men in armor is also clear from Thucydides' descriptions a little earlier of the fighting around Syracuse. At one point the Syracusan defenders grew lax on their guard against Athenian attacks upon their fortifications; once they had left their posts to seek relief in the shade, the Athenians sent out a sudden sortie against the unmanned wall. (6.100.1) Frontinus, too, recalls what must have been a favorite stratagem of ancient commanders: the Roman general Metellus Pius kept his own men in the shade while the enemy waited fully armed in the sun for his attack. Once they showed the effects of the rising temperature, he led his troops out to victory. (2.1.2,5)

In his *Republic,* Plato suggested that hoplites prepare themselves for the rigors of extreme temperatures by constant gymnastic training (3.404); he, too, surely knew the dangers that hoplites in full armor faced under a summer sun. Certainly, we can see why the so-called race in armor at Olympia and ritualistic hoplite dances in arms almost never required wearing the breastplate; so great was the weight and discomfort of the corselet that during even moderate activity it could never really be worn during such exercise in "full" armor. (E.g., Paus. 5.8.10) When hoplites were called out to fight in the spring, thunderstorms and showers could also make life miserable. The body temperature of any man caught in full armor would decrease rapidly as his wet undergarments became uncomfortably cold and sticky against the flesh. Agesilaos' Spartans, for example, found that their battle gear was poor protection from the cold once they had been exposed to a hailstorm. To save their lives, he ordered fires in pots to be brought so that his men might be rubbed down with warm oil. (Xen. *Hell.* 4.5.3)

Even more crucial was the condition of the soil once it began to rain. A drenched hoplite carrying fifty to seventy pounds of arms and armor could scarcely maneuver once the ground was soft and muddy. Modern efforts to duplicate the difficulties faced by men in such armor have shown that ground that is sandy or merely loosely packed—not to mention wet or muddy—requires a 20–25 percent increase in oxygen demands. (Donlan and Thompson 1979: 420) Naturally, then, the approach of rain or hail had a depressing effect on the Sicilian hoplites at the first battle against the Athenians in 415 before Syracuse. (Thuc. 6.70.1) Demosthenes in a speech during the fourth century similarly remarked later that lightning, thunder, and heavy winds were likely to cause depression among infantry. (50.23) But the best example in ancient literature of what adverse weather could do to an entire army equipped with heavy body armor was the great catastrophe again in Sicily at the river Krimesos in 341 where everything imaginable went wrong for the invading troops of Carthage once they marched into the face of the storm and encountered Timoleon's Greeks.

> Then the gloomy darkness above the hills and mountain heights descended onto the battlefield, bringing with it a mixture of rain, wind, and hail. It swept over the backs of the Greeks from the rear, but struck the faces of the Carthaginians and blinded their vision, since there was an absolute deluge and unending lightning pouring out of the clouds. Under the circumstances there was widespread difficulty, but to the inexperienced the clashes of thunder seemed to cause the greatest harm as well as the noise of their armor being struck by the sleet and hail, which prevented any commands of their leaders from being heard. In addition the Carthaginians were by no means lightly armed, but rather, as I have stated, fully equipped in heavy armor; therefore, both the mud and the folds of their undergarments as they filled with water impeded them. As a result they were both weighed down and ill-equipped to fight effectively, and so they were easily overturned by the Greeks. Once they slipped and fell they were completely unable to rise again from the mud with their weapons in their hand. (*Plut.* Tim. *28.1–3*)

Of course, the reason why men would endure such discomfort, such misery, beneath bronze breastplates so poorly suited for even simple movement was the unusual protection the metal offered against the blows of the spear and sword and against the rain of airborne missiles—the javelin, the arrow, and the slinger's stones and bullets. The linen corselets that Pausanias saw hanging up on display at Athens in the second century A.D. were poor substitutes, in his view, for bronze armor, which alone could often turn back the thrust of the spear. (1.21.7) We remember, too, that at Kunaxa in 401 the breastplate of Cyrus the Younger withstood a direct blow from a javelin and allowed him to continue into battle. (Plut. *Artax.* 9.3) Yet, the breastplate did not offer its wearer absolute protection from all incoming attack (unlike that strange corselet of golden scales which the Persian Masistios wore at Plataia in 479 and which kept out all the spear thrusts of the Greeks even when he was finally forced to the ground. [Hdt. 9.22.2; Plut. *Arist.* 14.5]) We often also find both in Greek literature and on vase paintings hoplites who perish from blows that make their way right into the flesh. (E.g., Diod. 19.109.2–3; Xen. *An.* 4.1.18–19) No wonder, then, that Aeschylus, in his *Seven Against Thebes* (278), could describe body armor as "spear-pierced." Usually in such cases the victims were subjected to the direct fire of slingers or archers at very close range; more often, the initial thrust of the spear was driven home through the momentum of a running hoplite:

> With a sudden rush he turns to flight the rugged
>   battalions of the enemy, and sustains the beating
>   waves of assault.
> And he who so falls among the champions and loses his
>   sweet life, so blessing with honor his city, his
>   father, and all his people,
> with wounds in his chest, where the spear that he was
>   facing has transfixed
> that massive guard of his shield, and gone through his
>   breastplate as well.
>
>   *(Tyrtaios 12.21–26)*

Those instances were rare, however, in comparison to the repeated blows from sword and spear by standing hoplites in the shoving melee of the phalanx. There, slaps and jabs at the breast could be turned, since the enemy had no chance to "tee off" and charge with his spear on the run. Consequently, there was a good chance that the bronze breastplate might turn back literally dozens of blows of all types, giving its wearer all-important time, a new lease on life on each occasion to strike down his foe. Often when we do hear of men who are finally overcome from wounds to their chest, the breastplate is stuck full of broken shafts, dented, or cracked from repeated assault, suggesting that the wounded hoplite became the focus of a frenzy of thrusts that finally—but only finally—overwhelmed his metal body armor. The Theban leader Pelopidas, for example, was eventually overcome at Kynoskephalai in 364 when the enemy backed away and targeted him with repeated jabs until his armor finally gave way. (Plut. *Pel.* 32.6–7) Likewise, the fourth-century Spartan king Agesilaos was severely wounded, although not mortally so, only after he was caught surrounded and subjected to a multitude of spear and sword blows: his men "were not able to keep him untouched since he had received repeated blows which pierced his armor all the way to the flesh." (Plut. *Ages.* 18.3–4) Even the outnumbered Spartans on Pylos in 425, who were trapped and outgunned by a host of Athenian light-armed troops, were not totally annihilated. Although their felt conical caps were a poor substitute for the bronze of the Corinthian helmet and thus allowed arrow wounds to the head, Thucydides nevertheless relates that many missiles "had broken off" in the armor of others, suggesting again that their breastplates had at least dulled the incoming hail of darts and so allowed them to continue their resistance. (4.34.3)

The Spear

To the Greeks, the use of the thrusting spear was proof of the desire to approach the enemy at close quarters and stab him face-to-face—the choice of men who had no taste for the bow or missile and contempt for soldiers who would or could not come in close to fight. For Aeschylus, veteran of Marathon, the contrast between the archers of Darius and the spearmen of Greece left a lifelong impression of the moral superiority of men who strove to kill at close range. (E.g., *Pers.* 85–86; 147–49; cf. 25–32; 52–57; 278; 728–29; 816–17) The Greek spear was a heavy weapon for the right hand to manage alone, some six to nine feet in length; it was made of cornel or even ash wood; but it was only about an inch in diameter, and thus only two to four pounds in weight. There were no allowances made for left-handers, but this caused few problems, since the chief requirement for a spearman was strength rather than dexterity: the idea was not to find the target but rather to penetrate it. As the hoplite approached the opposing phalanx he brought the spear off his shoulder into an *underhand* position, both to make his final run easier and to enable him to jab the spear in the groin or under the shield of an enemy hoplite as he crashed into the front rank. Once the two sides met, however, there was a better chance to find an opening with the spear held *overhand;* in fact, most vase paintings show hoplites jabbing downward at the neck, arms, and shoulders. Since the chance for a running thrust was now well past, this change of grip to an overhand position could put enough power behind the blow to kill or even severely wound the enemy and thus create a gap in the opposing line. (Cf. Anderson 1970: 88–89)

Besides the iron spearhead, most spears also had a bronze butt spike at the base which made the weapon an ingenious device with a lethal point at both ends. The advantages of the butt spike were not merely the counterbalance it provided to the weight of the lance head, or even the protection it gave the shaft end from rot or wear when propped on the ground. It also allowed the infantryman an added dimension of attack, whether he was stationed in the first line or well back to the middle and rear of the phalanx. As we shall see, there were really two markedly different worlds of simultaneous combat within the phalanx: the stabbing and jousting in the first three ranks, and the pushing, shoving, and stumbling in the five ranks behind. For those at the focal point of the collision of infantry, the butt spike proved useful once the fighting became an entangled mass of hoplites; it gave the spear a killing point at both ends, allowing its holder to thrust backward should an attacker come on around him from the side or rear. In some extreme cases it might save a man's life, as it gave him some defense, however awkward, from such blind attacks.

More importantly, however, these men in the initial three ranks were likely to have their spears shivered in the initial collision of bronze armor, wooden shields, metal swords, spearheads, and flesh. Apparently this tendency of the hoplite spear to shatter on impact was well recognized, and it is not so surprising, given the relatively small diameter of the shaft. Also, on vase paintings, sculpture, and in literature there are many examples of hoplites forced to beat or cut away enemy spears with their short swords. (Polyb. 2.33.5; Anderson 1970: pl. 10) Yet there must have been plenty of instances where the spear was not immediately abandoned once the lance head was snapped off or the shaft broken or cut off by a sword: the remaining shaft, with its butt spike, could be used for a time in close-in fighting. The Greek historian of Rome, Polybius, makes this clear: the problem with early Roman spears, he relates, is that "they were not equipped with butt spikes and so they were used only for the first blows with the spear hand; after that they broke off and were of no further use." (6.25.9) In his view, the Greek version was far superior because it allowed the fighter to continue his attack with the spike once his lance head was lost. In any case, the butt spike allowed the hoplite a few more thrusts until he was finally forced to go to his secondary, and much less adequate, short sword. Indeed, the Spartan mother's famous reply to her son's complaint about the drawbacks of his short sword, "Add a step to it," was really no reply at all, but rather an indication of just how vulnerable a hoplite had become once he was forced to adopt that posture. (Plut. *Mor.* 241 F 18)

Men in the middle and rear of the phalanx usually kept their spears upright, where they helped to deflect incoming missiles, and also kept the points clear of hoplites to the front and rear, preventing accidental wounding. (Polyb. 18.29–30) While held in this position, the only mode of attack was to slam downward with the shaft, driving the butt spike and its square, short shaft into an enemy lying at one's feet. This was not a rare occurrence, as the square holes driven into the remains of ancient armor unearthed at Olympia show clearly. (Snodgrass 1967: 56, 80) Once the front ranks created an initial momentum, those to the rear would be pushing with their shields at the backs of their friends, but also stumbling over the debris of battle: the abandoned arms, the wounded, and the corpses of those already fallen. Many of the enemy who were already down and were being passed over by an advancing phalanx were not yet dead, but were trapped near the ground as the rear ranks walked over and around them. The best way of dispatching these unfortunate troops was to keep the spear upright and then jab it downward, allowing such a powerful thrust to send the butt spike right through the enemy's bronze armor.

Although the butt spike increased the spear's versatility in attack, the hoplite spear nevertheless had two distinct disadvantages. The first, of course, was the difficulty of movement within a massed formation. A shaft of some eight feet mandated that a hoplite's range of movement and mobility be restricted by both the butt spike and the spearhead of his own men to the rear and front. For example, men in the second and third ranks of the column would have the sharp butts of those ahead (in the first and second rows) constantly before them. Likewise, soldiers in the first and second lines would have to contend with the spear points of those men to the rear which were jostling right at their own flanks. The use of the hoplite spear also meant that a man's range of movement was limited laterally by the weapons of his own comrades. Besides the need to keep in formation and thereby protect against enemy inroads, besides the constant attention to uniformity of advance, to maintain balance in the face of attack, to prevent falling and thus a horrible death by being trampled, the infantryman must also have been aware ironically of the dangerous bronze of his *comrades,* who were constantly moving at his side, changing angles right and left, and threatening a most ignoble death by accidental wounding. An extreme case was Pyrrhus' phalanx, which became trapped in the cramped streets of Argos during the battle there in 272. So tightly was the formation pressed together, Plutarch relates, that the men were unable to raise their leveled spears again. Consequently, "many died from the accidental blows which they inflicted among each other." (*Pyrrh.* 33)

Besides these restrictions in mobility, the spear of the hoplite, like the other wooden element of the panoply, the shield, had inherent structural weaknesses. (Xen. *Eq.* 12.12) Although usually constructed out of tough cornel wood or occasionally ash, the diameter of about an inch clearly was not sufficient to prevent the lance head from being snapped off (or the shaft itself from disintegrating in a sea of splinters) in the initial collision where the advancing hoplite slammed his spear into the bronze or wood protective cover of the enemy. At times, his thrust could be parried and his shaft broken by the sword blow of a downed hoplite. We often hear, in ancient descriptions of battle, of the widespread loss of the use of the spear relatively soon in the course of combat. Xenophon remarks that when Agesilaos encountered Tissaphernes' troops near Daskyleion in 396, his men all shattered their spears on the initial clash. (*Hell.* 3.4.14) At Mantineia, Diodorus recalled that the sheer closeness of the fighting resulted in the destruction of the spears—requiring that the battle was to be played out, at least among the front ranks, with sword thrusts. (15.86.2) He apparently had an image of the ceaseless pressure from the rear forcing the spears of each successive front rank against the immovable bodies, wood, and bronze of the enemy; yet one wonders how there was any room at all for swordplay, given the density and pushing of armored men. At Thermopylai, only when the spears of Leonidas' brave Spartans were all shattered were his troops overcome under a sea of missiles. (Hdt. 7.225; cf., too, Plut. *Alex.* 16.4; *Eum.* 7.3; Diod. 19.83; 17.100.7) When soldiers lost their spears, they were never allowed to filter inside the enemy ranks, which would have allowed hacking away with their shorter swords at cumbersome spearmen who were unable to bring their eight-foot weapons to bear against them. Instead, the wall of shields and spear tips of the men to the rear kept the intruders out and ensured that they would be smashed or impaled by the steady pressure.

If the spear thrust was sufficiently powerful to make its way intact through the bronze armor of an opponent, there was no guarantee that the hoplite could draw it back out in one piece. Epameinondas at his last battle at Mantineia in 362 perished from a spear thrust through his breastplate; the shaft had snapped on impact and left its spearhead embedded deep within his chest. (Diod. 15.87.1) On occasion, however, some desperate troops who had lost their weapons could dodge the initial enemy thrusts and then grab the shaft from the side, perhaps even snapping the lance head off with their bare hands before the hoplite could inflict any damage. For example, at Plataia in 479, Herodotus says, the Persians were at first successful in taking hold of the Greeks' spear shafts and then shearing them off. This could only be true if we understand that the enemy had at least one hand free and that the length and thinness of the hoplite spear made it vulnerable to easy breakage by grabbing with the hands or cutting with the sword. (9.62.2; Polyb. 16.33.2–4) The relatively short life of the hoplite spear among the front ranks explains why hoplite battle quickly became a confusing contest of pressure. In a way, the frequent destruction of this eight-foot-long weapon allowed the battle to draw both sides even closer together. The few feet of protruding shafts on each side of the battle line no longer kept the enemies apart, and men now could meet together, pressing their very flesh face-to-face and hand to hand in a manner unknown in later military history. Once a man lost his spear and sword, his very body, encased as it was in bronze, became his best weapon, as his friends to the rear attempted to push him on through the enemy ranks.

7   *The Old Men*

> Yet who would have thought the old man to have had
> so much blood in him?
>
>   —*Shakespeare*, Macbeth

In most city-states of ancient Greece, once a citizen reached eighteen years of age, he was liable to be called out to duty each spring, if necessary, to serve as a hoplite in his city's phalanx for the next forty or so years of his life until he reached sixty. (Xen. *Hell.* 6.4.17; Arist. *Ath. Pol.* 53.4) For the citizen of the fifth-century Greek city-state who saw battle of some type on an average of two out of every three years, the chances were good that he would not die a natural death: in one of those years of his long service he would likely become one of the dead or wounded. More importantly, this long tour of duty meant that in the phalanx as a whole a great number of hoplites were always men over thirty. Like their younger colleagues, they were expected to carry nearly half their body weight in arms and armor, without concession to their age. And when battle commenced they were obliged to match their younger colleagues step for step, thrust for thrust, all the while keeping their shields chest high; any who could not fulfill this obligation to the men at his side endangered the integrity of the phalanx and thus the lives of all stationed within it. In physical terms, then, the single collision of hoplite battle was ideally suited for armies composed of men of all ages: they needed only be effective in a single day's engagement, not throughout a long and demanding campaign. Thus, they were judged by their courage and strength, rather than their health and mere endurance. The fourth-century Thessalian mercenary Polydamas, for example, bragged that his own hired troops were all men in top physical condition—unlike the citizen-armies of most city-states "which are made up of both those who are well

past their prime and those not yet in full manhood." (Xen. *Hell.*
6.1.5) He seems to imply that the aged within the ranks of most
hoplite armies were a limiting factor on the mobility (but not
necessarily the courage) of the phalanx. That image of the still
brave though now slower warrior is captured well by Homer's old
Idomeneus:

> Idomeneus wrenched out the far-shadowing spear from his body
> but had no power to strip the rest of his splendid armour
> away from his shoulders, since he was beaten back by their
>   missiles,
> and no longer in an outrush could his limbs stay steady beneath
>   him
> either to dash in after his spear, or to get clear again.
> So in close-standing fight he beat off the pitiless death-day
> as his feet no longer quick to run took him out of the fighting.
>   (Il. *13.509–15*)

Elsewhere, we hear that the old are always represented among
the city's soldiers and, too, among the city's dead. Nor was the
orator Andocides exaggerating entirely when he complained
that the young waste their time in court while the old were
forced to fight (4.22); after all, thirty of forty-two age classes liable to military service were composed of men over thirty years
of age.

Strangely, in modern battle, where the use of firearms and
mechanized transport might seem to make the fighting less rigorous than phalanx warfare, those over thirty now tend to be
commissioned officers or higher-level NCOs stationed in the
rear—in the general belief that men of that age cannot face even
the modern, less physical requirements of combat and, through
years of service in a professional army, have "earned" the safety
of the command post. Indeed, frontline fighters in their late
twenties, even in a state of national emergency, are a rarity. "One
of my people, a twenty-eight-year-old Vermont high school principal," wrote William Manchester in his memoir of jungle fighting in the Pacific during the Second World War, "was known because of his advanced age as 'Pop.' " (121) That the presence

of men over thirty on the modern battlefield was not so frequent is well illustrated by the nickname Robert Graves earned in the trenches of the First World War: although then only twenty-one, he was, nevertheless, known as "Old Gravy." (262) In sharp contrast, as we learn from Alcibiades in Plato's *Symposium* (221), the philosopher Socrates stalked the battlefield of Delion in 424 when he was well into his forties. Indeed, he was one of the few to hold his ground and avoid the general panic besetting his younger colleagues who had run away from the Athenian disaster. Demosthenes, although he apparently lacked Socrates' fortitude, also was well past forty when he saw service against the Macedonians at Chaironeia in 338. (Davies 126ff) In Greek battle, then, no consideration was given to a man's age during active service; the only deference—and a wise one at that—was the practical decision to deploy the younger members in the formation as skirmishers, an acknowledgment of their greater chances of success in ranging out at the front of the phalanx to deal with harassment and hit-and-run attacks. At Sparta, for example, usually the first five, ten, or fifteen age groups—men of eighteen to twenty-two, twenty-three to twenty-seven, or twenty-eight to thirty-two years—were called on for such duties in the belief that these troops were the only ones quick enough to catch light-armed enemy ambushers. Similarly, the great Athenian statesman Solon thought that a man reached his peak by his early thirties, when "every man reaches his highest point of physical strength where men look for prowess achieved." (27.7–8) Not much earlier Tyrtaios had confirmed that those well past thirty were not confined to rearguard duty or camp guards, but rather often expected to serve right up in the front ranks, and on occasion, as the cutting edge of the collision:

> This indeed is a foul thing, that the older man falls
> among the forefront and lies before the younger
> His white head and his grey beard breathing out his
> strong soul in the dust,
> Holding in his dear hands his groin all bloody.
>
> *(10.21–25)*

Indeed, the image of the old man horribly wounded or left to die in the tumult of battle goes back to Homer:

> For a young man all is decorous
> when he is cut down in battle and torn with the sharp
> bronze, and lies there
> dead, and though dead still all that shows about him is
> beautiful;
> but when an old man is dead and down, and the dogs
> mutilate
> the grey head and the grey beard and the parts that are
> secret,
> this, for all sad mortality, is the sight most pitiful.
>
> (Il. 22.71–76)

It is remarkable that when we examine the social register of the wealthy in classical Athens we find so many who continued to fight and die in battle well into their forties and fifties, although most were well-established men of property and influence. No doubt the unsurpassed morale found within the phalanx derived in part from the implicit understanding that *all* citizens, whatever their personal or social circumstance or even age, were first of all lifelong hoplites of their city, liable to fight and die without exception during any summer of their lifetime. One Menexenos, for example, was killed at the battle of Olynthos in 429 when he was at least forty; Kephisophon in 341 was in his mid-forties while on duty at Oreos, Skiathos, and Byzantion; Glaukon was fifty when he was general at Samos and later on he served at Corcyra; Pyrilampes, who fell at Delion in 424, was fifty-six. Nor was it rare to find even older citizens, in their sixties and occasionally even in their seventies, among the hoplite ranks. The elder Andocides may have been sixty while on duty at Samos in 441. Likewise, Phaidros, the son of Kallias, was approaching seventy when he closed out his career in a campaign against Styra in 323. (Cf. Davies 29, 145, 292–93, 339, 525) Outside of Athens we hear of even older soldiers. Philopoemen was seventy on campaign in Messenia (Plut. *Phil.* 18.1), and Agesilaos was apparently still an effective fighter when he finished out his career in Egypt well over eighty. (Xen. *Ages.* 2.28) One wonders if he could still manage to wear the panoply.

The presence of so many older men within the ranks tended, along with the use of hoplite armor, to focus warfare into a brief, single collision of massed infantry in deference to their reduced physical endurance. Yet there were also important advantages in having so many men past thirty among the troops. The psychological power derived from having all segments of society take part in battle was enormous; even more important was the experience of prior battle which these men brought into combat. Frequently in Greek literature we hear of the steadying role these veterans had upon the troops. In the moments before the battle of Delion in 424, the Theban general Pagondas urged his army of Boiotian confederates to emulate their veteran comrades within the phalanx, the old men at their sides who already had routed the Athenians years ago at Koroneia in 447. Apparently, there must have been many in the ranks (including Pagondas himself) who had faced the Athenians successfully twenty-three years earlier and had been in service each summer since. (Thuc. 4.92.6–7) Pagondas reckoned they could comfort the uninitiated with their living proof of Boiotian invincibility; he assumed, too, that they might repeat those long-ago acts of youthful bravery.

King Archidamos also referred to the presence of senior troops in the Peloponnesian army in hopes of boosting morale when he reminded his men on the eve of his first entry into Attica in 431 that their own fathers and "the elder men in this army of ours" were experienced veterans of many campaigns, thereby making it clear that there were at least two generations of Spartan hoplites in the ranks who knew exactly what to expect once battle commenced. (Thuc. 2.11.1) Archidamos was appealing to one of the great advantages that has manifested itself throughout the long history of the regimental system—the unifying force of tradition. Generals like Pagondas and Archidamos knew that their young men from boyhood onward had heard from their fathers and grandfathers of the illustrious deeds of their city's phalanx. In view of this legacy they would not want to disappoint those old veterans beside them, living reminders of the many more who were now buried, fallen long ago in defense of their fatherland. Their attitude toward hoplite battle was always one of emulation, of a shared experience of killing with an older generation, rather than a wild initiation rite among youthful peers. This was akin to what, in the modern world, we remember as a nineteenth-century sense of a father's careful shared observation of his son's first encounter with shooting and killing in the hunt, so far removed from our present-day American nightmare of armed youth turned loose in rural areas to go it alone after any accessible target.

At times we hear of even more specific references to the value of older troops. The historian Diodorus relates that the crack infantry corps of Alexander the Great, the phalanx of "Silvershields," continued to serve as pikemen in the Macedonian phalanx long after their general's death. (19.41.2) At the close of their careers even the "youngest" of the Silvershields was at least seventy. (Plut. *Eum.* 16.4) All were prized veterans, distinguished for their skill with the Macedonian pike and their long experience in combat: in short, a fearsome regiment of grim professionals to worry any potential adversary. Alexander was said not to have wanted men who were merely "strong, not yet mature in their manhood," but rather "veterans who had already served their time." (Just. 11.6.4) Often we hear of older troops who took a more active, advisory role, rather than merely serving as models of courage in the face of battle. At the first battle of Mantineia in 418, Thucydides mentions an "old man" in the army who yelled to the Spartan king Agis not to commit the phalanx to such a disadvantageous position, thereby saving the Spartans from a prebattle blunder (5.65.2); apparently, he had seen enough of hoplite battle to know when the situation boded ill. And during battle between the Arcadians and Spartans in 365 when hostilities were about to resume, one of the "older men" in the ranks shouted out to the surrounding soldiers, "Why, men, is it necessary that we are fighting each other?" (Xen. *Hell.* 7.4.25) Although he was probably not so polite or formal in his speech as

Xenophon reports, on hearing his words both sides immediately ceased further, needless slaughter. Perhaps, then, those older men in the ranks are further evidence that the Greeks of the classical age saw the pitched battle as a means to limit warfare, not as a youthful exercise to display bravery in facing down the enemy. They took the romanticism out of the fighting and taught soldiers and civilians alike why the whole business should be gotten over as quickly as possible.

The presence of so many men of rather advanced age affected hoplite battle in two other contrasting ways. The physical difficulty of wearing the bronze panoply may have helped to determine originally the very nature of combat, creating the common desire for one decisive clash each summer, rather than long campaigning and repeated skirmishing, a type of battle where all members of society, whatever their age or infirmities, could be expected to be included. Yet, in a type of combat where the greatest danger to success was panic which might scatter the entire phalanx in an instant, those past thirty who had often undergone the charge into the enemy were especially valuable. Their presence gave to the untried (and mostly younger) the assurance that there were men among them who had in the past not flinched from advancing into the spears of the enemy, and were hardly likely to do so now. In hoplite battle, there was no great need for the speed or agility of youth. The most important quality was a dogged determination not to falter, thereby leaving a lethal gap in the line. The crippled Spartan Androkleidas illustrated well the attributes needed in the phalanx: when questioned about his battle worthiness, he supposedly replied in his defense, "But there is no need of running away, but rather to stay put where I am to fight against those who are arrayed against me." (Plut. *Mor.* 217 C)

8   *The Dread of Massed Attack*

> Do not fear the multitude of their men, nor run away
>> from them.
> Each man should bear his shield straight at the
>> foremost ranks
> and make his heart a thing full of hate, and hold back
>> the flying
> · spirits of death as dear as he holds the flash of the sun.
> <div align="right">— <i>Tyrtaios</i></div>

> I do not believe that any man fears to be dead, but only
> the stroke of death.
> <div align="right">—<i>Francis Bacon</i></div>

Besides the peculiar discomfort of their armor, the poor protection offered from the heat and cold, and the constant service until advanced age, hoplites faced a further difficulty, unlike any other, that put demands on their strength and stamina: the unique terror that accompanied the onset of Greek battle. The idea of prebattle jitters is as old as Homer:

> the skin of the coward changes colour one way and another,
> and the heart inside him has no control to make him sit steady,
> but he shifts his weight from one foot to another, then settles
>> firmly
> on both feet, and the heart inside his chest pounds violent
> as he thinks of the death spirits, and his teeth chatter
>> together
> <div align="right">(Il. <i>13.279–83</i>)</div>

The nature of classical phalanx battle intensified this feeling, common to all warriors, in a way like none other. Crammed into the tight mass of the column, few outside the first rank could see or hear the enemy or even the voices of their own officers. What knowledge they had of the upcoming collision came only from the pressure of those around them who likewise were captives to rumor, the shuffling, and the widespread murmuring throughout the lines. Accidental shoving or even tremors of perceived pressure might suggest to the hoplites in the center and rear that battle had begun, or worse, was about to be lost. We can understand Thucydides' remark on the inherent confusion inside the phalanx, as he tried to put the disastrous Athenian night attack on Epipolai into perspective: "Even in daytime those men do not perceive anything, indeed nobody knows anything more than what is going on right around himself." (7.44.1) Later, during the last retreat of the doomed Athenians on Sicily, he added, "and upon them fell the very thing which happens to all armies and especially the largest: panic and fear." (7.80.3)

This initial "panic and fear," which could spread throughout the phalanx in the moments before the battle, most likely made its way *backward* from the front ranks where men first gazed upon the opposing enemy mass. Yet, once those in the rear felt that there were problems ahead, they were likely to run, and if this happened, they collapsed the entire formation. The tension could only have been heightened by the peculiarly formalized nature of Greek warfare: battle was "by agreement," and it required that both sides be drawn up face-to-face, eyeing each other anywhere from a few minutes to hours on end. Ambushes, surprise attacks, and entrenchment were not popular options. Instead, the no-man's-land between the two armies was purposely bare, ensuring unimpeded advance by both sides and, consequently, unobstructed clear views of the enemy. This made it quite plain that there could be no alternative but to march right on at the spears leveled a few yards away.

We often hear of the dread which the visual spectacle of an opposing phalanx could instill. To the Roman general Aemilius Paullus, as Plutarch tells us, the nightmarish sight of the Greeks opposing him at the battle of Pydna in 168 and the realization that those men with their long pikes would soon be at his face, left him with a lifelong image of terror: "he considered the formidable appearance of their front, bristling with arms, and was taken with both fear and alarm; nothing he ever had seen before was its equal. Much later he often used to recall that sight and his own reaction to it." (*Aem.* 19.3) Did Aemilius suffer that syndrome—so well known to the modern warrior—the unforgettable dread of dying, the terrible prebattle anticipation that haunts him for the rest of his life? Plutarch also records the fearful picture of the approach of a Greek phalanx at the battle of Plataia in 479: "suddenly there came over the entire phalanx the look of some ferocious beast as it wheels at bay and stiffens its bristles." (*Arist.* 18.2) Onasander commented on the same peculiarly frightening sight of an opposing phalanx in language quite unlike his usually dry narrative: "more dangerous the advancing formations appear through the splendor of their equipment, and that terrible sight frightens the very souls of the enemy." (28.1) For some warriors the reflection of the bronze weapons in the sun held a particular terror as they gazed on the enemy across the plain, and saw men like Mimnermos' image of the warrior, who had faced down the ranks of the Lydians: "no man ever in the strong encounters of battle was braver than he, when he went still in the gleaming light of the sun." (14.10–11) No wonder that the second-century Achaean Philopoemen told his men that the sheer brightness of their arms and armor would create shock in the enemy (Plut. *Phil.* 9.3–8), or that commanders often ordered their troops to polish their shields so as to dazzle the foe. (Xen. *Lac. Pol.* 13.8–9; Diod. 14.23.3) But it was not only bright shields that caused courage to falter: the first-century tactician Asklepiodotos remarked that rows upon rows of leveled spears created terror in the eyes of the enemy (4.5.2); other times it was due simply to the disciplined order of the Greek advance. (Polyaen. *Strat.* 2.2.3)

Soldiers were always aware of the nature and caliber of the troops posted opposite them; the sight of the scarlet cloaks and long hair of the men of a Spartan phalanx especially brought fear into the hearts of most opponents. (Xen. *Lac. Pol.* 10.3.8) And poor Kleon, commanding the Athenians in their defeat at Amphipolis in 422, we are told, took off at a run as soon as he saw the Lambdas on the Spartan shields shining across the plain. (Eup. F 359) The Spartan phalanx—with reason—was carefully groomed by Agesilaos so that his troops might look like "one mass of bronze and scarlet." (Xen. *Ages.* 2.7) Once the Persians made their way around the pass at Thermopylai they had to be assured that the Greek pickets there were not really Spartan hoplites— so great had the fear of those soldiers become to them. (Hdt. 7.218.1–2) Just as frightening was the infamous sound of the Spartan pipes, which signaled to the front ranks of the enemy across the battlefield the onset of their slow, dreadful advance. (Xen. *Cyr.* 3.3.58; Aesch. *Sept.* 270; *Pers.* 389; Thuc. 5.70) "It was a sight at once awesome and terrifying," Plutarch remarked, "as the Spartans marched in step to the pipe, leaving no gap in their line of battle and with no confusion in their hearts, but calmly and cheerfully advancing into danger." (*Lyc.* 22.2–3) Lysias' Mantitheos, in a speech after the Athenian defeat at Corinth in 394, summed up the general feeling: "It is a terrible thing to fight the Spartans." (16.17) The Athenians must have agreed when they first landed on Pylos in 425 since we are told that "they were overwhelmed by the notion that they had to face the Spartans." (Thuc. 4.34.7) Ironically, perhaps because they were assured that they would never have to face men quite like themselves, the Spartans alone of the Greeks were able to act somewhat immune to the fear rampant in the prebattle face-off: at Thermopylai, for example, a Persian scout reported that in the moments before the final assault he had seen those doomed men exercising and calmly combing their hair: "He carefully observed the men who were stationed outside the wall. At that very moment they happened to be Spartans; some were stripped, ready for exercise, while others were combing their hair. The Persian spy watched them in astonishment." (Hdt. 7.208.3)

What were the reactions of the men in the front ranks, once the fearful specter of the enemy phalanx appeared and they realized that in a few short moments they would be advancing into its solid wall of long spears? For a few the symptoms were simply silence, an eerie quiet that came over the army, as if the men had all suddenly been stunned, struck dumb at the very sight. (E.g., Xen. *Cyr.* 7.1.25) At the ghastly battle at Koroneia, Xenophon makes it a point to state that as the two armies squared off "there was deep silence on both sides." (*Hell.* 4.3.17; *Ages.* 2.9) Indeed, it may have been in order to dispel that hypnotic trance-like state that armies institutionalized the *paian,* or war cry, which in the playwright and infantry veteran Aeschylus' view gave "courage to comrades as it rids them of the fear of the enemy." (*Sept.* 270) The fear-induced lack of communication among troops could have had a damaging effect on the ranks as they made ready to advance and as each man withdrew into his own shell of fear. The situation would not have been much different from modern warfare; the modern combat analyst S. L. A. Marshall, for example, in his review of battle performance in the Second World War, emphasized the crucial need for modern foot-soldiers to talk: "When you prepare to fight, you must prepare to talk. You must learn that speech will help you save your situation. You must be alert at all times to let others know what is happening to you." (137)

At other times, we hear not so much of the silence within the ranks, but rather of an accompanying shuddering, a literal *shaking* among the men in the phalanx, as if the entire mass of soldiers was somehow quivering in fear. There may have been some truth in Iphikrates' exaggerated complaint that he could not hear the usual clanging of his men's armor as they readied themselves for battle since the "chattering of teeth" was too loud (Polyaen. *Strat.* 3.4.8), for Brasidas detected this same phenomenon in the apparent confusion of the Athenians at Amphipolis when he remarked that "those people will never stand up to us; that is clear enough from all the jostling about of spears and heads. When soldiers get into that state they can hardly ever face an enemy attack." (Thuc. 5.10.8) Apparently, those poor Athenians also resembled the adversaries of Epameinondas before the battle of Mantineia, whom Xenophon described simply as "men about to suffer." (*Hell.* 7.5.22–23) Presumably to encourage those in the front ranks to get a grip on themselves, the old war poet Tyrtaios urged them "to dig their heels in the ground and bite their lips with their teeth." (11.22)

Modern military thinkers have considered this fear of battle as one of the greatest perils to new recruits. So, for example, army draftees in the Second World War were told: "You'll be scared, sure you'll be scared. Before you go into battle you'll be frightened at the uncertainty of the thought of being killed. Will it hurt? Will you know what to do? After you've become used to the picture and the sensations of the battlefield you'll change." (Stouffer 196) Postwar studies in combat psychology found that more than 90 percent of the respondents acknowledged prebattle fear of combat, ranging from a common "violent pounding of the heart" to a "sinking feeling of the heart" to the occasional "losing control of the bowels" and "urinating in the pants." (Stouffer 201) Although it may not be recorded in such explicit, dry detail in our sources, the ancient hoplite must have often experienced to an even greater degree these same sensations. Indeed, Greek warfare gave no opportunities for gradual induction into combat by smaller preliminary actions. To a much greater extent than modern warfare, every phalanx battle was *the* decisive action—a sudden one-shot do-or-die experience that each man in the ranks had to confront without psychic preparation.

In addition to silence and trembling, the men in ranks, like their modern infantry counterparts, were prone to occasional involuntary urination—or worse yet, defecation—in fear of the upcoming collision. In Xenophon's *Hiero* we receive perhaps some idea of the universal discomfort and queasiness which must have affected a man right before battle. To illustrate the constant tension that the tyrant must endure, Hiero turns to the example of the similar sensation of prebattle stress: "If, Simonides, you, too, have had experience with war, and you have ever had to draw up facing the line of the enemy's phalanx, just try to remember what type of food you ate at that time, and what type of sleep you slept. Those very pains which you suffered then are exactly the same, and even more so, as the ones the tyrant also experiences." (6.3.7) An even more graphic example of the effects of prebattle fear upon the gastrointestinal system is found in Plutarch's life of Aratos, where an old accusation against the general is again repeated—namely, that at the outset of battle he habitually came down with loose bowels and associated symptoms so much so that he had to exit the battlefield altogether: "right before battle he came down with cramps in his bowels while both paralysis and dizziness would come over him just as the trumpeter gave the signal to make ready." (29.5) In Aristophanes' play *Peace* we receive the most explicit picture in ancient literature of what must have been a not uncommon phenomenon among hoplites before battle. There the poet chides the overbearing, overdressed infantry captain who prides himself on his fine equipment and scarlet cloak. Yet, Aristophanes then adds, once it's time to begin fighting, that same "commander" begins to run away and his cloak is turned a different color—a direct reference to involuntary defecation soiling his garments. (1176ff) Earlier in the same play, Aristophanes had simply called war, "the terrible one, the tough one, the one upon the legs." (241) The ancient commentator to this passage adds, as if there were any ambiguity about the meaning, that this referred to sudden, fear-induced defecation by hoplites. Throughout his plays, this tendency to lose bowel and bladder control is a constant object of Aristophanes' ridicule, apparently easily recognized as such by his audience of male combat veterans. (E.g., *Ach.* 349–51; *Eq.* 1056; *Lys.* 216) Incontinence was an especially uncomfortable, if not embarrassing, experience among men who were heavily armored, and stationed packed together in close ranks under a summer sun. That Aristophanes could personify war, even in comic allusion, as the experience of excrement "upon the legs" must suggest that it was a known phenomenon among all fighters in the phalanx.

The ultimate expression of the fear of hoplite battle was not stupor, not dumb silence, or trembling, not incontinence, but rather simply the decision to turn around and run. In Hellenic warfare, sudden panic before the clash of armies was not routine, but we do hear of five or six instances in the history of battle between Greeks where troops could not endure the sight of the enemy across the battlefield and thus fled before the two sides even met. (Thuc. 5.10.8; Xen. *Hell.* 4.3.17; 4.8.38 and, especially, 7.1.31) At Sparta, men who could not face the terror of massed attack were scornfully known as the *tresantes,* often translated as the "runaways"—apparently a graphic label for those who had shown the visible shaking signs of fright and were literally unable to march out to battle at the sounds of the pipes. (E.g., Hdt. 7.231; Plut. *Ages.* 30.2–4; Xen. *Lac. Pol.* 9.4–5) This tendency for troops in mass formation suddenly to disintegrate entirely was so well known that the Greeks at times attributed this behavior to the entrance of the god Phobos ("Fear"), and later in the fourth century, to Pan (cf. the English "panic"), as if the appearance of some deity was required to account for occasional mass flight among men who usually mastered their fears. Euripides said that the god Dionysus "struck fear into troops armed and in formation *before* they reached the enemy." (*Bacch.* 303–4)

The Greeks knew well that normal phalanx battle put great stress upon the men in the ranks, and that only a fine line separated control of fear from the collapse of nerve. And so Greek authors miss no opportunity to contrast their way of doing battle with the less organized—and to their mind less courageous— barbarian manner of skirmishing. In Polybius' view there were few peoples who could endure the terror of formal, phalanx battle. The Cretans, he observed, were unexcelled in ambushes, skirmishes, surprise attacks, night engagements, but these were all minor fighting, where trickery was an integral, necessary part of war. When it came to face-to-face battle, head-on deliberate phalanx fighting, they were "utter cowards and completely fainthearted." (4.8.10–12) Brasidas had said the same thing years earlier about barbarians, who made "a lot of noise and look threatening in their posture, but turned out to be not so brave when it came time to face men who held their ground." (Thuc.

4.126.5) In the Greek view, few others could endure their manner of fighting; indeed even among themselves there was a constant recognition of the struggle to master the paralysis, trembling, incontinence, and sheer panic that Greek battle fostered. No wonder Greek writers of tactics called for the best men to be placed not only at the front but also at the rear so that "any cowards in between might be more frightened of them than the enemy." (Xen. *Mem.* 3.4; *Cyr.* 6.3.25; *Hipp.* 2.4–6)

III

The Triumph of Will

In war the chief incalculable is
the human will.
        —*B. H. Liddell Hart*

9   *A Soldier's General*

In Vietnam the record is absolutely clear . . . : the officer corps simply did not die in sufficient numbers or in the presence of their men often enough to provide the kind of "martyrs" that all primary sociological units, especially those under stress, require if cohesion is to be maintained.

— *Gabriel and Savage,* Crisis in Command: Mismanagement in the Army

If we look for the reasons why men of the Greek phalanx fought, answers do not lie in religion, although there was a prebattle sacrifice to the gods in the minutes before the charge; nor are they to be found in patriotism, although by the fifth century most hoplites had the insignia of their city-state riveted to the faces of their shields; nor finally did their daring arise from a desire for booty or fear of punishment, although many searched the bodies of the dead in the aftermath of an engagement and might be severely treated for breaking rank during the fighting. Along with regimental esprit, an even better incentive for hoplites to stand firm was the sight of their own commanding officer, the *strategos*, fighting alongside them in the very front ranks of the army. The simple sequence of Greek infantry battle in the sixth and fifth centuries—advance, clash, and retreat—eliminated the need for elaborate prebattle planning and deployment of both specialized troops and reserve contingents once battle had commenced. Consequently, the commanding officer of the entire phalanx had very few tactical options once the two sides met. Instead, all believed that their supreme commander could best further his army's cause by leadership through example, by fighting in the ranks on the right wing of the phalanx where his hoplites might be buoyed by his personal display of courage: many of those nearby, in the first three ranks, could see his prowess in arms, and soldiers to the rear could be assured by word of mouth that he was alive and still fighting the enemy at the forefront.

But his entry into hand-to-hand fighting was not determined solely by the sheer simplicity of the battle and the lack of tactical options once it commenced, as if he had nothing better to do, nowhere else to go. Our sources indicate that there was a genuine desire on the part of the general to fight and risk death alongside his men, like the Spartan king Leonidas at Thermopylai, rather than watch the killing safely from afar. At least in the sixth and fifth centuries, this was an important function of generalship. At Sparta, of course, the tradition never seems to have gone out of favor. In the early fourth century, for example, the Spartan commander Anaxibios chose death once it was clear he had led his troops into disaster; in words not much different from Tyrtaios' three hundred years earlier, he simply announced, "Men, it is a fine thing for me to die right here." (Xen. *Hell.* 4.7.38; cf. 6.4.13)

For the most part, this novel Greek idea—that the battlefield commander, along with his small staff of subordinates, should at least be near the hard fighting, if not an active participant in the killing—survived in the West until the onset of the twentieth century. Yet, by the First World War, at least, it had eroded entirely, as the general receded to the rear, to a point completely detached from the fighting, and a position undreamed of by the men of antiquity. It was said of Joffre, the great hero of the Marne, for instance, that "every day of the long retreat, while the dusty sweating columns fell back along the baking roads of northern France towards the capital, he stopped work exactly at noon, took his seat at a table laid with gleaming cloth, silver and glass outside his headquarters and, in full view of passers-by, spent the next two hours fortifying the inner man." (Keegan and Holmes 200) Justification for the general's absence from the field of fire has been found in his ostensible need to pay close attention to the myriad problems of planning and communication that modern battle requires. Yet the absence of the commander from contemporary combat has often had a demoralizing effect upon the troops. A poor argument for this modern practice is the idea that the present-day commander's survivability is of utmost importance: his enormous staff has, after all, invariably planned for the very possibility of his demise, and his survival—even if he be a Rommel or a Patton—may ironically be even less important to his men's immediate success on the battlefield than that of his ancient Greek counterpart, who had no replacement officers of comparable rank or status.

Once he plunged into the fray, a Greek commander's sudden absence on occasion could set off panic among the men at his side who watched him go down. On the contrary, the loss of a modern general might go unnoticed by his infantry in the field for hours if not days, suggesting that the bureaucracy of command has made sufficient allowance for everything but that one key ingredient for success in combat: the magnetic presence of a leader who fights and dies alongside his men in battle. The few twentieth-century exceptions demonstrate this clearly. Kellet, for example, remarks of the British officer corps in general, "Perhaps the most signal reason for the ability of the officers to carry their men with them, even in the most dangerous activities, was their own acceptance of risk and sacrifice." (156) An officer summed up the feelings of American ground troops of the Second World War: "In combat, you have to be out in front leading them, not directing them from the rear. The men say, 'If the officer's going to stay back a hundred yards, then I'm going to stay back with him.' You can't direct them—you have to lead them." (Stouffer 124) S. L. A. Marshall saw this years ago, right after that same war when he raised a solitary voice of criticism during the general euphoria following the American victory: "out of sedentary generalship arises the evil of troops which, while obeying mechanically, have no organic, thinking response to the command will." (103) William Shirer recognized the anomaly of twentieth-century battle practice among the young German officer corps in 1940 during their heyday in France:

> The German generals were younger—few not yet forty—most of them in their forties, a few at the very top in their early fifties. But that gave them the qualities of youth: dash, daring, imagination, flexibility, initiative, and physical prowess. General von Reichenau was first in

his army to cross the Vistula River in the Polish campaign. He swam it. Guderian, Rommel, and the other commanders of the Panzer divisions led many of their attacks in person. They did not remain, as the French were inclined to do, in the safety of the division command posts to the rear. (*547–48*)

The natural affinity in the classical Greek world between the general and his men derived from the shared knowledge that the commander was essentially little more than a hoplite who was stationed nearby on the right wing, the first to encounter the charge of the enemy, and a citizen who should surely serve as an ordinary soldier again once his tenure had expired. No wonder, then, that we rarely if ever hear of any attack on an officer by the hoplites he commanded; there is no mention, for example, of the fragging that appeared at such an alarming rate among Americans during the latter years in Vietnam. Indeed, when we do hear of such random attacks it is usually among troops for hire during the latter fifth and fourth centuries: for example, the hoplite dissident of the mercenary Ten Thousand who threw a hatchet at his commander Klearchos. (Xen. *An.* 1.5.12) Instead, in Greek literature we see very clearly criticism of any leader who was not one with his men, who by the nature of his dress or conduct sought to elevate himself above the rank and file within the phalanx, and so foster the impression that he did not share the same dangers or interests. Thus, the seventh-century poet Archilochos remarked of an unknown commander: "I don't like the towering captain with the spraddly length of leg, one who swaggers in his lovelocks and clean shaves beneath his chin. Give me a man short and squarely set upon his legs, a man full of heart, not to be shaken from the place he plants his feet." (114) Likewise, the point of Aristophanes' barbs against Lamachos in his *Acharnians* (1071–1234) and the unnamed captain in his *Peace* ("triple-crested, scarlet-vested, scarlet bright as bright can be," 1171) is the ridiculous figure of ostentation these commanders cut, so foreign to the men they lead and so suggestive that they might not be eager to charge with their soldiers into the faces of the enemy. On the other hand, the ideal Greek general, as the

Lyric poet Archilochos pointed out at the dawn of the hoplite age, must have had a definite presence on the battlefield, like the "short" Agesilaos who toiled alongside his men in simple dress and thereby gained not only "their obedience but also their affection" (Xen. *Ages.* 6.4–7), or perhaps that solemn, nameless leader sculpted in frozen relief on the Nereid monument, who appears to take his place as an ordinary soldier on the line to urge his men forward (Anderson 1970: pls. 13, 14); he reminds us of Plutarch's description of the great Athenian statesman Pericles at the battle of Tanagra (457) when "he more than anyone exposed himself to danger." (*Per.* 10.1ff) Asked why the Spartans faced battle so bravely, Polydoros was supposed to have replied, "because they have learned to respect rather than fear their leaders." (Plut. *Mor.* 231 F 4)

Later, in the fourth century, military theorists developed a more abstract interest in an idealized structure of battle; like modern military thinkers, they began to worry about the inherent dangers to the army as a whole in committing the supreme commander to hand-to-hand battle. Their ideal, though fanciful, image of the battle general was one who demanded close attention to set plans and new contingents of light-armed troops, cavalry, and reserves. Xenophon, for example, in reaction to the role of the hoplite commander in the heyday of hoplite battle, advised that a general be less rash, that he keep his head and thereby retain a full understanding of the ongoing action on the battlefield (*Mem.* 3.1)—in other words, that he stay away from the dangerous fighting entirely. Ostensibly, the increasing complexity of battle and its ever lengthening duration suggested to some that a type of overall command of the battlefield was necessary, while battle itself could be conducted by a staff of junior officers leading the men in the field. But the very fact that such a suggestion is made in dry tactical manuals suggests that these armchair tacticians were in a distinct minority, and that the traditional role of entering the fray was still of utmost importance to most generals. Indeed, even the battle commanders of mercenary armies of the fourth century—men like Iphikrates and Chabrias, who led forces that were quite different in nature from the purely citizen militias of the prior two centuries—continued to fight right beside their troops once battle commenced. Onasander, the military theorist and Platonic philosopher of the first century A.D., must have been reacting against that old code of the warrior-general when he complained: "Let the general fight with caution rather than daring, or even let him keep away entirely from hand-to-hand battle." (33.1) The apparent reason why writers worried about the role of the general was their fear of the effect on the ranks should their leader suddenly go down in the fighting: "For whatever you may accomplish by spilling your own blood," remarked Philo, "could not compare with the harm you could do to your interests as a whole if anything happened." (5.4.28; cf. Onasander 23) But was this professed concern for the morale of the hoplites in the phalanx the real cause for the advice that the commander abandon the battlefield and assume the role of what has sometimes been called "château" generalship? Perhaps, rather, a natural fear of the danger that old-style, active command entailed frightened these would-be generals.

Most likely, the Hellenistic and Roman conviction that military commanders should not endanger their own lives was a natural reaction against the slaughter in the classical hoplite engagements, where the losing side invariably lost its leader. Most later writers did not appreciate what the sacrifice of hoplite generals was, nor did they realize that such casualties were not always responsible for an army's collapse but, rather, symptomatic of a leader's close ties with his men once the battle had for other reasons already been lost. The Theban confusion at Mantineia upon the death of Epameinondas, and perhaps the Spartan fright at Leuktra when Kleombrotos went down, are the exceptions that prove the rule. The unusual morale and willingness to fight among hoplite armies of the sixth and fifth centuries is in part attributable to the astonishing, high mortality rate among battlefield commanders: the troops were assured that their own general would be among the first to face the spears of the enemy, not perched on a throne like Xerxes at Thermopylai.

When we survey briefly the major Greek land battles of the fifth and even fourth centuries, three general trends emerge. First, the battlefield commander of any defeated army inevitably perished along with most of those stationed in the first rank that met the charge of the enemy. This was true in every Greek city-state regardless of its own individual preferences in battle. So, for example, Kallias the Athenian perished at Poteidaia (Thuc. 1.63.3); Leonidas, the king and leader of the Three Hundred, at Thermopylai (Hdt. 7.224); the Corinthian Lykophron at Solygeia (Thuc. 4.44.1); the Athenian Hippokrates at his city's disaster at Delion and the demagogue Kleon at Amphipolis (Thuc. 4.101.2; 5.10.9); the Spartans' Pasimachos at Corinth, Teleutias at Olynthos, and Klearchos at Kunaxa. (Xen. *Hell.* 4.4.10; 5.3.6; *An.* 1.8.4–5)

In a number of instances both generals of a joint command, or perhaps the entire group that surrounded the general, were all annihilated in the defeat—this was a frequent occurrence during several well-known Spartan and Athenian catastrophes. For example, at Olpai both the Spartan generals Eurylochos and Makarios died with their men (Thuc. 3.109.1); likewise, Epitadas fell at Pylos and his successor Hippagretas was left for dead among the pile of corpses. (Thuc. 4.38.1) During the series of defeats on Sicily, Lamachos, Nicias, and Demosthenes, who all at various times shared command, perished on the island. Earlier, at the first battle at Mantineia (418), Thucydides tells us that both Athenian generals, Laches and Nikostratos, were killed beside their troops. (5.74.3) And at the less well-known Athenian misadventure at Spartolos all three generals—Xenophon, Hestiodoros, and Phanomachos—were killed. (Thuc. 2.79.7) Xenophon relates that at Leuktra in 371 the officers Deinon, Sphodrias, and Kleonymos all went down alongside their king Kleombrotos. (*Hell.* 6.4.14)

So predictable was this mortality rate among generals that at Sparta there seems not to have been a single instance in some six hundred years of warfare of any Spartan king's surviving the defeat of his men on the field of battle—that is, until the king Kleomenes III in the twilight of the Spartan state deserted his overwhelmed troops at Sellasia in 222. (Polyb. 2.65ff; Plut. *Kleom.* 28.5) The Athenians, to their credit, followed that same tradition well into the fourth century. In the aftermath of Chaironeia (338), they condemned the surviving general of their defeated troops, Lysikles, to death. Lykurgos brought the charges: "Lysikles, you were general when a thousand of our citizens have perished, two thousand have fallen captive, a trophy stands over our defeat, and all of Greece has become enslaved. All this occurred when you were both leader and general. Now you dare live and look at the light of the sun; you even go into the market; you, a living reminder of our city's shame and dishonor." (Diod. 16.88.2)

Secondly, in a surprising number of major battles, the *victorious* general is killed despite the success of his troops—again, perhaps a suggestion that his presence in the front ranks, rather than his safety from injury, was important if his men were to fight well: so much for the idea that the battlefield general's survival was always vital for military success. It is often forgotten, for example, that in the great Athenian victory at Marathon, Kallimachos, the colleague of Miltiades, lost his life. Brasidas, likewise, fell as his Spartans routed the Athenians at Amphipolis in 422, a battle where the generals on both sides perished. (Thuc. 5.10)

Lastly, we should remember that of those battlefield generals who held repeated commands, very few lived out their lives in quiet retirement; assumption of leadership to these men often meant death while on duty rather than a comfortable pension. In Agesilaos' way of thinking, "It was unworthy that he live out an idle life in town, and sit down as he waited for death." (Plut. *Ages.* 36.3) A great many generals perished in the line of duty, a most likely occurrence when a man stationed himself at the center of danger again and again. Although they had established their reputations years earlier and were near celebrities among the citizens back home, men like Cimon, Pelopidas, Epameinondas, Brasidas, and Lysander, to name just a few, continued to lead men into battle, and thus eventually were killed on the battle-

field. Even if these men of advanced age (normally men below
thirty years of age were not eligible for the generalship) somehow managed to survive this repeated exposure to the first clash
of spears, the yearly stress finally caught up to them, and many
succumbed to disease or utter exhaustion. The Athenian Miltiades, for example, suffered a thigh injury during his expedition
to Paros and eventually died of gangrene. (Hdt. 6.136) Nicias,
an Athenian general, was plagued by kidney stones the entire time
he spent as one of the commanders of the expedition in Sicily;
Agesipolis, the fourth-century Spartan king, contracted a sudden
fever during his attack against Olynthos and died on the spot.
(Thuc. 7.15; Xen. *Hell.* 5.3.19) Antigonos, according to Plutarch,
perished from consumption soon after his victory at Sellasia.
(*Kleom.* 30.2) Yet, few men, if any, could match the remarkable
career of the Spartan king Agesilaos, who survived countless battles, severe wounds, and a near-fatal bout with phlebitis, only to
die years later while on his return from a campaign in Egypt in
360—eighty-four years old and "his entire body disfigured by
wounds." (Plut. *Ages.* 36.1)

The only comparable example of this close—yet fatal—relationship between a battlefield commander and his troops in the
modern period occurred during the American Civil War. The
Confederate Army, steeped in the chivalric tradition of the Old
South, presumed like the classical Greeks that it was the duty of
their leaders to fight alongside their men on the battlefield. The
record of these generals in combat is one of shocking fatalities
among the officer corps. There must have been a realization on
their part that, to match the overwhelming numerical superiority and firepower of the Union forces, their troops had to maintain an unmatched morale. To accomplish that goal the general
in the field, like his hoplite predecessor, was obliged not only to
fight, but more importantly, to die beside his men. A. P. Hill was
shot through the head at Petersburg. Stonewall Jackson expired
after a severe arm wound at Chancellorsville. Elisha Paxton did
not survive that same battle, nor did Turner Ashby the fight at
Port Republic. Jeb Stuart suffered a fatal stomach wound at

Winchester. Others—Robert Rhodes, Dodson Ramseur, Dick Anderson, Wade Hampton, John Bell Hood, and Joe Johnston—
either were killed in action or suffered near-fatal wounds and
were consequently disfigured or disabled. It was said that after
Chancellorsville 30 officers were found dead, 148 wounded, and
59 missing—all from a single corps. (Freeman 2.650)

Leadership could help to overcome the enormous physical and
psychological pressures of battle. It was evident only when each
man in the phalanx realized that a comrade of like circumstance,
dressed and equipped like himself (like Grant, who preferred the
uniform of a Union private), had led him into battle and would
stand fast where the fighting was most dangerous. If a general
showed himself determined to advance forward or simply perish where he stood, rather than forsake his men to the rear, most
were encouraged to do the same.

10   *Unit Spirit and Morale: The Origins of the Regimental System*

> Set your men in order by tribes, by clans,
>   Agamemnon,
> and let clan go in support of clan, let tribe
>   support tribe.
> If you do it this way, and the Achaians obey you,
> you will see which of your leaders is bad, and
>   which of your people,
> and which also is brave, since they will fight
>   in divisions,
> and might learn also whether by magic you fail
>   to take this
> city, or by men's cowardice and ignorance of
>   warfare.
>
> *—Homer,* Iliad

> We must be very careful what we do with British infantry.
> Their fighting spirit is based largely on morale and regimental *esprit de corps*. On no account must anyone tamper with this.
>
> *—General Bernard Montgomery*

The unique cohesiveness that existed among individuals within a phalanx accounts for much of the success achieved by Greek hoplites, especially in contrast to foreign troops. Although fragmented by city-state rivalries, badly outnumbered, hastily assembled, and plagued by outright betrayal, the Greek defenders during the Persian Wars routed the Eastern invaders in nearly every land battle in which they met. Besides the presence of Greek generals on the battlefield, the key must have been the camaraderie in the Greek ranks, the confidence which grew out of the bonds among hoplites in the phalanx which could allow Leonidas, on the eve of his certain destruction, when told by Xerxes to send over his arms, to reply on behalf of his men simply, "Come and take them." (Plut. *Mor.* 225 D 11)

Confidence in their commander and weapons, even love of country and past experience in battle, can all explain why an army once engaged operates successfully on the battlefield, but does it explain entirely why individuals will endure the sight of combat and in those last seconds advance into the spearheads of the enemy? True, many of the Greek hoplites may have become inebriated, but the use of drink was not necessary so much to convince a hoplite to charge out as to make that prospect easier to stomach. The soldiers of the city-state met the charge of the enemy, I suggest, because of their general and because of the men at their side, the wish to protect them from the thrusts of the enemy, the shame of playing the coward before their eyes. The ideal of the brave man in their view was the hero of old Kallinos' poem: "while he lives, he is treated as almost divine. Their eyes gaze on him as if he stood like a bastion before them. His actions are like an army's, though he is only one man." (1.17–19)

After exhaustive interviews with American combat soldiers, researchers concluded after the Second World War that the reason "why men fight" was due to "a matter-of-fact adjustment to combat, with a minimum of idealism or heroics, in which the elements which come closest to the conventional stereotype of soldier heroism enter through the close solidarity of the immediate combat group." (Stouffer 112) In plain English, men say they fight to protect their comrades at their side. Under these circumstances, we should not be surprised, for example, that the innovative Athenian general Alcibiades was unable to forge two separate phalanxes into one army at Lampsakos in 409. Men who did not have any shared blood ties and who had no common experience under fire were hardly willing to form up together into the dense ranks of the phalanx: "The older soldiers had no wish," Xenophon says, "to be deployed with the troops of Thrasyllos, for they had always been unconquered while the others had just arrived from defeat." (*Hell.* 1.2.15) William Manchester, in his narrative of his wartime fighting in the Pacific, wrote:

> Those men on the line were my family, my home. They were closer to me than I can say, closer than any friends had been or would ever be. They had never let me down; and I couldn't do it to them. I had to be with them rather than let them die and let me live with the knowledge that I might have saved them. Men, I know now, do not fight for flag, country, for the Marine Corps, or glory or any other abstraction. They fight for one another. *(391)*

There were two factors, unique to classical Greek battle, that tended to create exceptional ties among soldiers, so much so that it is no exaggeration to say that such bonds among hoplites in the phalanx were stronger than any other among infantrymen in the long history of Western land warfare. First, the armament and tactics of the ancient phalanx were ideally suited to ideas of loyalty and friendship; fighting together in column, rather than spread along a line, drew all in close physical proximity with each other: a man's moment of bravery or lapse into cowardice was manifest to all who fought in rows and files to his rear, front, and side:

> Those who, standing their ground and closing ranks together,
>   endure the onset at close quarters and fight in the front,
> they lose fewer men. They also protect the army behind them.
> Once they flinch, the spirit of the whole army falls apart.
> And no man could count over and tell all the number of evils,
>   all that can come to a man, once he gives way to disgrace.
> *(Tyrtaios 11.11–16)*

Similarly, as Thucydides remarked, the nature of hoplite equipment—especially the shield—dictated that each became dependent on the man to his right for the protection of his own right side. Soldiers not only were drawn up in dense ranks before battle, but were also expected to stay put there in close formation once battle commenced. Indeed, there must often have been actual touching, bumping, tripping, and pushing among men as each sought protective cover throughout the battle, as each hoplite sought not to see or hear his friends as much as to "feel" those at his side. Plutarch reminds us that hoplites carried their helmets and corselets for themselves, but "they carry the shield for the men of the entire line." (*Mor.* 241 F 16) Any who failed to hold his assigned place and so offer cover to the man on his left was quickly found out and exposed as a coward.

Important, too, was the lack of any combat specialization among heavy infantry. All were armed alike with spear and shield, and thus there was no possibility of resentment toward the more talented or favored who were given specialized tasks or weapons, as happens in modern battle, often with more prestige and less exposure to combat. In Greek battle there were no machine gunners, spotters, point men, radio operators, riflemen, flamethrowers, or any of the myriad other classifications of modern foot soldiers. Instead, the knowledge that all men of the hoplite class were uniformly armed eliminated rivalry and resentment, giving all a wondrous sense of superiority as a group over those outside the phalanx, the clearly inferior and often landless light-armed skirmishers who lacked heavy armor.

The peculiar nature of space and time on the Greek battlefield ensured that the men on the line would not, could not, leave each other once they met the enemy. Unlike battles of later times, where combat could continue on through miles of separate engagements and skirmishes, where reserves could rush in, ignorant of the prior fighting of comrades (themselves strangers) that took place hours or even days earlier, and where men could break into small groups to find greater safety in both advance and retreat, the hoplites always met the enemy as a group, at the same time, and at roughly the same place. While this resulted in a brutal concentration of killing within a confined space, there was nevertheless always the realization that victory or defeat was due only to the men at one's side, and only within the clash at hand—a factor encouraging exceptional unity among all who made up the phalanx. Indeed, Kellet, as he looked back on nineteenth- and twentieth-century battle in his study of combat motivation, remarked that close-order formations such as the line and square contained powerful coercive properties, both social and physical; men trusted each other to stand firm because, if they did not, the consequences could be terrible. (137)

And there has perhaps never been any formation quite so "close-ordered" as the Greek phalanx. We can understand why Themistocles' purported last words to his men before the battle at Salamis with the Persians became so popular with later Athenians. He reportedly had seen some gamecocks fighting and, in an effort to incite his men forward, drew inspiration from that scene: "These animals," he said to the troops, "do not suffer such misery because of their fatherland nor their native gods nor out of respect for their ancestral heroes; nor is it because of glory or freedom or even their children. Rather, they do it simply because of the desire that each one might not become inferior to, or give way, before another." (Ael. *VH* 2.28)

The second and more important consideration is the peculiar nature of the ties among the men of the phalanx: unlike most modern armies, the bonds between hoplites on the line did not originate within military service or in weeks of shared drill in boot camp; they were natural extensions of already long-standing peacetime friendships and kinships. So far as we know, hoplites in nearly all city-states were deployed in their phalanxes by tribe, and most likely were of course well acquainted with those of their own town or deme. Men who knew each other through political, religious, and ceremonial associations and who may have been related strengthened these existing bonds as they fought side by side in the phalanx. Each subdivision of the phalanx fought to protect men who had known each other from boyhood and so were less likely to throw away their shields and thereby endanger friends and relatives.

There are numerous unambiguous references throughout Greek literature to show that individual contingents of the phalanx were drawn up on the basis of tribal affiliation, and that men were also well aware of those soldiers in the ranks who came from their own community. (E.g., Lys. 16.15; 13.79; Thuc. 6.98.4; 6.101.5; Arist. *Ath. Pol.* 42.1) We won't be mistaken, then, to suppose that each time the phalanx marched out, men knew exactly their own assigned place within the formation as well as the relatives and friends who served in front, behind, and at their side. Cimon, for example, on his return from exile, joined his Athenian comrades moments before the battle of Tanagra; immediately he took up his place among the men of his tribe, men who were apparently waiting for him with arms and armor in hand. (Plut. *Cim.* 17; Frontin. *Str.* 4.1) Even after a prolonged absence, he knew exactly where to line up in the phalanx. Oman writes of the similar organization of the medieval Swiss phalanx: "There was no need to waste days in the weary work of organization, when every man stood among his kinsmen and neighbors under the pennant of his own town, valley, or guild." (2.256)

According to Plutarch (*Arist.* 5), Aristides and Themistocles fought close to each other in the hard-pressed center of the Athenian battle line which bore the brunt of the Persian attack at Marathon. This proximity in a great battle occurred, he tells us, because they belonged to the tribes Leontis and Antiochis, respectively—the two contingents that composed the middle of the Athenian phalanx. Men of rank fought as ordinary hoplites alongside men they had known for years. And the same seems to be true outside of Athens. When the Athenians captured the muster rolls of the Syracusans in Sicily in 415, they were thereby able to learn the number and nature of the enemy force, since these lists of their hoplite soldiers were arranged by the tribal affiliations. (Thuc. 6.66) The importance of these tribal associations in most Greek city-states is also evident from extant casualty lists on stone and scattered references in literature to the battle dead. For example, Epameinondas was said to have been reluctant to re-form his phalanx of Thebans after a costly battle for fear that his men would lose heart when they noticed the sizable gaps in the ranks. (Polyaen. *Strat.* 2.3.11) Apparently, it was customary that decimated columns were not immediately reconstituted, but instead men simply moved over a spot to take the place of the deceased—most likely friends or family whose loss was noted by all around. Since armies in the classical period were not large by modern standards, it was likely that each man knew the members of his tribal contingent, if not the members of the entire phalanx. Individual deaths thus affected the group as a whole. Xenophon relates the sad story of the Spartans who had suffered a reverse at the hands of their Arcadian adversaries; the defeated became even more despondent after the battle "because they had heard the names of the dead who were brave and nearly all their most distinguished men." (*Hell.* 7.4.25) Apparently most Spartans within the phalanx knew all the men who had fallen. Elsewhere, we hear of particularly severe losses of an individual tribe (e.g., Lys. 16.15), which suggests that its members must have been at a point in the battle line which suffered a localized collapse or was simply overwhelmed by a concentration of superior numbers. Casualty notices, routinely drawn up by tribe, indicate that after the battle it was the responsibility of each tribe to collect their own dead and turn in an accounting to the city. From Athens and other Greek city-states—Mantineia, Corinth, and Argos—we have inscriptions on stone where the deceased are cataloged by tribal affiliation. (E.g., *IG* I² 929, 931, 943; Paus. 1.32.3; and cf. Pritchett 4.138–243) It seems likely that men who were recorded for posterity according to their tribal associations also fought in those contingents within the phalanx.

Evidence of the camaraderie among tribesmen and even those of the same deme can be found in a few passages from the Attic orators. A speech attributed to the great Athenian orator Lysias suggests that men of the same deme testified to the number of battles a man of their locale had actually fought (20.23); each of these men must have shared a rather intrusive mutual interest. In another speech Lysias says quite clearly that those of the same deme gathered together before marching out on campaign. (16.14) Isaeus, too—another of the Attic orators (and teacher of Demosthenes)—seems to confirm this very picture that those in the phalanx knew not only their tribesmen who fought next to them during the actual battle, but also their neighbors throughout the ranks; his speaker reminds the audience that he "had seen service in both his tribe and deme during the campaigns of that period." (2.42) From Theophrastus comes the well-known story of the coward who calls out to his tribesmen and demesmen to see how he had brought back a casualty to camp (25.3); apparently he knew these men intimately and valued their praise highly. At Sparta those who shared the common mess were probably also stationed alongside each other in the phalanx so that those close peacetime ties might also carry over into battle. (Plut. *Lyc.* 12.3; Polyaen. *Strat.* 2.3.11; Xen. *Cyr.* 2.1.28) And at Leuktra both Sphodrias and his young son fell together in the general massacre on the right wing around King Kleombrotos—yet another indication that close relatives fought side by side. (Xen. *Hell.* 6.4.14) Centuries later, the first-century A.D. Roman military writer Onasander looked back at the history of Greek warfare and concluded that men fought best when "brother is in rank beside brother, friend beside friend, lover beside lover." (24)

These uncommonly strong bonds among hoplites were merely the normal relationships of nearly all fighters in the phalanxes of most Greek city-states; they do not presuppose any unusual specialized training or concerted effort to form an elite corps. Occasionally we hear of select contingents at Syracuse, Thebes, and various states in the Peloponnese, and we can only assume that the morale and ties among those men were even more extraordinary. (E.g., cf. Pritchett 2.221–24) Throughout Greece there is also evidence that homosexual friendships were a contributing factor to unit morale. At Sparta, for example, the separation of the sexes at an early age, together with attitudes peculiar to other Greeks on the role of women, resulted in overtly homosexual relationships centering on life in the barracks. No doubt such strong ties extended to the battlefield and must help explain Spartan heroism, most notably in dramatic defeats from Thermopylai (480) to Leuktra (371), where men chose annihilation rather than the shame of flight. Yet, the most extreme example was not among the Dorians but rather in Thebes. There the Sacred Band, composed of 150 homosexual couples (something unknown even at Sparta), for some fifty years fought heroically in the city's most desperate battles and were wiped out to a man at Chaironeia (338); Philip was struck by the appearance of the huddled masses of their paired corpses. (Plut. *Pel.* 18–19; *Mor.* 761a–d; Xen. *Symp.* 8.32)

The peer pressure among friends and family within the Greek phalanx grew out of a pride that all men shared in facing danger together. Battle in this manner essentially eliminated rear-unit troops who never enter into actual fighting, those "fighters" who are often looked down upon by modern soldiers and the source of constant dissension throughout the army as a whole: "The code of being a man is here explicit. The rear-echelon soldier is resented and despised because of his misuse of army authority and his failure to share a community and sentiment." (Stouffer 135) That bond forged through shared combat is evident even today: years after the end of the Second World War, American veterans of the armored divisions of the Third Army could still recall with undisguised pride, "I rolled with Patton." Their spirit is hauntingly similar to the old Athenian hoplite veterans of the running (novel) charge at Marathon. Much later, to remind a younger audience of that legendary shared battle experience, they needed to say simply, "We ran." (Ar. *Ach.* 700)

11 *Drink*

Had it not been for the rum ration I do not think that
we should have won the war.
—A medical officer of a Black Watch battalion

And Dionysus also has a certain share of Ares' domain.
—Euripides, Bacchae

The use, or rather perhaps the abuse, of alcohol before battle
was another, though less significant, incentive for hoplites to face
the demands of phalanx warfare and so meet the first charge of
the enemy. There is little evidence in Greek literature to indicate
that commanders always issued hoplites a ration of strong drink
as a matter of policy before they marched forward, but it is nevertheless clear that there was routine drinking and drunkenness
in almost every Greek army. Even the customary silence about
the formal issuance of drink does not prove that most hoplites
did not fight under the influence of alcohol. Writers may have
considered such a detail insignificant in their overall description
of the battle, and they may also have been reluctant to make a
point of the drinking. The mention of alcohol raises the possibility of abuse and disorder, which could bring rebuke upon a
general if his troops fared poorly on the battlefield, or even di-
minish the glory of a victorious army if the enemy in their defeat
alleged drunken disorder. In any case, the idea of drunken soldiers seems inconsistent with our notions of the rigidity, discipline, and order required within a Greek phalanx.

What are the advantages that alcohol would have offered to
most hoplite armies? The formal nature of Greek battle created
mounting, relentless tension as troops were deployed in sight of
each other and yet at the same time provided a lull before this
storm, when soldiers might well have tried to steel their jittery
nerves in any possible manner. Since Homer, the Greeks had recognized that alcohol had some analgesic value against wound

trauma. (*Il.* 11.639; 14.5) Many soldiers may have been drinking simply to dull the sensations in expectation of a painful penetration wound to come. Keegan, in his study of Western battle practice, has noted the traditional use of some such drug among infantry:

> Yet the prospect of battle, excepting perhaps the first battle of a war or a green unit's first blooding, seems always to alarm men's anxieties, however young and vigorous they be, rather than excite their anticipation. Hence the drinking which seems an inseparable part both of preparation for battle and combat itself. Alcohol, as we know, depresses the self-protective reflexes, and so induces the appearance and feeling of courage. Other drugs reproduce this effect, notably marijuana; the American army's widespread addiction to it in Vietnam, deeply troubling though it was to the conscience of the nation, may therefore be seen if not as a natural, certainly a time-honoured response to the uncertainties with which battle racks the soldiers. (*326*)

Wine, as is generally known, was the daily drink of choice throughout the ancient Mediterranean world, not only essential in the average citizen's diet, but also a standard ration of the hoplite's meal, an inseparable fact of military life on any campaign. This close association between soldiers and wine is assumed throughout the history of Greek literature. In the midst of the fighting before Troy, for example, Homer's Nestor remarks to Machaon before he goes forth into battle:

> Now Nestor failed not to hear their outcry, though he was drinking
> his wine, but spoke in winged words to the son of Asklepios:
> "Take thought how these things shall be done, brilliant Machaon.
> Beside the ships the cry of the strong young men grows greater.
> Now, do you sit here and go on drinking the bright wine,
> until Hekamede the lovely-haired makes ready a lovely bath
> for you, warming it, and washes away the filth of the bloodstains,
> while I go out and make my way till I find some watchpoint."
>
> (Il. *14. 1–8*)

A few years later Archilochos sang:

> By spear is kneaded the bread I eat, by spear my Ismaric
> wine is won, which I drink, leaning upon my spear.
>
> (*2*)

The ubiquity of wine in camp life is also reflected by various references to the standard rations of the hoplite soldier while on the march: figs, cheese, and wine. (E.g., Xen. *An.* 6.2.3–4; 6.1.15; Ar. *Av.* 544–54; *Pax* 1129; Thuc. 3.49.3; Plut. *Lyc.* 12) For example, in the negotiations concerning the trapped Spartans on Pylos, the Athenians allowed them two quarts of water and a pint of wine per day. (Thuc. 4.16.1) In Xenophon's *Cyropaedia,* Cyrus prepared his troops for a march across the isolated desert by gradually weaning them from wine to water, suggesting that the immediate withdrawal from the normal wine ration would be too great a shock for most soldiers who considered it a daily necessity. (6.2.28–29) A variety of sources show that most hoplites traveled with either a wine cup or a flask as part of their pack and thus were always prepared at a moment's notice for a quick draught. (Archil. 4; Ar. *Ach.* 549; Plut. *Lyc.* 9.4)

More importantly, some evidence suggests that troops frequently drank to excess. Hoplites could become disorderly and rebellious when inebriated, making themselves both a danger to their commander and, through their laxness, vulnerable to enemy attack. Xenophon remarks that during the invasion of Corcyra in 374 the Spartan-led mercenaries foraged liberally throughout the island, consuming only the best of the local wines. It seems that very soon after their arrival they had turned to drinking, ruining their morale and making them vulnerable to counterattack. When they were finally expelled by the natives, they left behind stockpiles of wine and grain. (*Hell.* 6.2.5ff) The same sequence of events is told in Menander's *Aspis* (53ff) when Davos explains how his detachment was sliced to pieces by an enemy incursion: they had all retired to their tents in drunken stupor. (Cf., too, Polyb. 5.48.1–5) The Macedonian general Antigonos was said to have drummed out some of his men whom he caught drunk—apparently playing ball while still in their breastplates. (Plut. *Mor.* 182 A 2) And in his fourth-century speech against Konon, Demosthenes reminded his Athenian audience that while on garrison duty at the Attic border fort of Panakton, the sons of Konon were drunk and abusive toward his company; they were saved from physical violence, he adds, only by the timely arrival of their officers. (54.4) In Xenophon's *Constitution of the Lacedaemonians* (5.7) there is mention of the Spartan practice of group messes where hoplites were required to walk home from compulsory mess meals without aid of a torch—apparently an official effort to discourage drunkenness among the men.

The evidence, then, from Greek literature makes it clear that infantry drank daily as part of their allotted rations and frequently were liable to become intoxicated either before or right after battle with disastrous results for the safety of the entire army. But an important distinction must be made here. Does this activity also indicate that hoplites deliberately drank right before combat to calm their nerves before the clash, and that such use of alcohol was officially condoned, an acknowledgment of the lift it might give the men?

First of all, many of the accounts of Greek hoplite battles make references to the midmorning breakfast where both sides took their last meal before the afternoon's battle. It was this traditional last meal that Leonidas referred to in his famous farewell to his three hundred Spartans before the final encounter at Thermopylai; after bidding his troops to lunch well, he added, "Tonight we will dine in Hades." (Diod. 11.9.4; Plut. *Mor.* 225 D 13) Polybius points out that the Carthaginians at the Trebia River during the second Punic War were caught unaware without a chance to have their accustomed breakfast and so suffered from hunger during the ensuing battle. (3.72.5–7) We know that all hoplites expected alcohol to be part of their daily ration, and were prone to drink wine to excess in times of celebration after the battle or in general camp relaxation. It may be likely that many were, in fact, drinking wine as part of their traditional brunch right before the battle. Xenophon relates how in 378 each day Agesilaos' army of invasion could wait confidently in expectation of meeting the Theban defenders at the same place near their fortifications, since "it was always after the midmorning meal that the enemy appeared." (*Hell.* 5.4.40–44) At one point the usually superior Theban cavalry inexplicably was

beaten back by the inferior Spartan horsemen and their accompanying younger, mobile hoplites. The reason, as Xenophon
relates it, was that they had thrown their spears senselessly well
before the enemy troops were even within range; accordingly,
he remarks that these Thebans acted like men "who had drunk
a little at noontime." Is he implying here that they had consumed
too much wine during their customary prebattle brunch, or
merely recognizing that reckless soldiers resemble those who
commonly overindulged at their meal of bread, cheese, and
wine?

Elsewhere, we occasionally hear of a more deliberate attempt
to raise the spirits of troops about to go on the offensive. Plutarch,
in his life of *Dion*, declares quite clearly that Dionysius issued his
men a strong liquor ration before they charged out: "In early
morning he filled his mercenary troops with unmixed wine and
sent them on at a run against the siege-wall of the Syracusans."
(30.3–4)

A better example in Greek literature is found in Xenophon's
description of the Spartan catastrophe at Leuktra. There he reminds us that part of the initial Spartan confusion in the battle,
which began an entire succession of fatal blunders, was caused
by the wine the troops had drunk right before the battle:

> However, in this battle everything turned out disadvantageously for the
> Lacedaemonians, while for the other side all was favorable even by
> chance. For it was after the mid-morning meal that the final plan of
> battle was held by Kleombrotos. And they say that the wine stirred them
> up as they were drinking a little at noontime. (Hell. *6.4.8–9*)

Perhaps that explains why Kleombrotos led out the charge against
the Thebans before the men under him "even perceived that
he was advancing." (6.4.13) In both accounts of the Theban
recklessness against Agesilaos and the Spartan disorder at Leuktra, Xenophon acknowledges that the prebattle ration of wine
might have aroused the troops a little too much. Instead of steeling their nerves for the upcoming encounter, drink could just
as well endanger their chances of success due to alcohol-induced

recklessness. Perhaps in most cases hoplites wisely drank only enough to calm, rather than excite their nerves. It seems possible, too, that most authors assumed this customary practice to be quite commonplace, so that again we hear more of the exception rather than the rule—the incidents where troops became drunk rather than the less exciting but more commonplace customary last drink or two before the charge.

Did ancient Greek soldiers march into battle drunk? The most likely answer is "almost." It may be naive to assume that the Greek hoplite, who drank daily both at home and while on the march, would not realize that an extra cup or two of wine at his customary last supper might stanch his fear, dull his sensitivity to physical injury and mental anguish, and make the awful task of facing an enemy phalanx that much easier.

IV

Battle!

De l'audace, encore de
l'audace, toujours de l'audace.
— *Danton*

12 *The Charge*

> The Athenians made ready to move and advanced at a
> run against the Barbarians, who were not less than a
> mile away. The Persians, as they gazed on them ap-
> proaching on the run, prepared to meet them. They
> attributed a suicidal madness to the Athenians who
> would risk such an attack without either cavalry or
> archers. In any case, that was what the Barbarians
> thought. Yet, the Athenians, nonetheless, all down the
> line closed with the enemy and fought worthy of record.
> Indeed, these were the first Greeks, as far as we know,
> who charged at a run, and the first too who endured to
> face Persian dress and the men who wore it. Up until
> that time, the mere name of the Persians brought on
> fear among the Greeks.
>
> —*Herodotus, on the charge at Marathon*

> C'est magnifique, mais ce n'est pas la guerre.
>
> —*Marshal Bosquet, on the charge of the Light Brigade*

The Need to Move Forward

After the men had drawn up in their formation, after they had
heard the final battle harangue of their general, when there was
now no apparent choice but to meet the enemy, there was left
only the problem of moving the men across the plain. Yet, must
we assume that a clear-cut, simple collision of opposing phalanxes
on the run always occurred in the near center of no-man's-land?
Sometimes we hear of some final transference of troops along
the battle line in an apparent effort to isolate one allied contingent who might be particularly well-matched against an enemy
across the plain. (Hdt. 9.26–27) At other times initial cavalry engagements screened troop movements or created confusion
among the enemy to aid advancing hoplites who followed.
(Thuc. 7.6.3; 6.69.2; Xen. *Hell.* 6.4.1; Polyb. 2.66.4) It was not

unusual to send skirmishers on ahead to probe an enemy phalanx (Diod. 15.32.4; Thuc. 4.33; 5.10), and there were also occasional retreats or collapses in toto before the battle had even commenced. (Thuc. 5.10; Xen. *Hell.* 3.2.17; 4.3.17; 7.1.31)

Still more baffling is the question why one side did not merely stay put, kneel down, cover with the shield, and extend the spear, anchoring its butt in the ground. This would have required the enemy to try his luck at crashing through such a virtually impenetrable wall of bronze and iron. The Persians had enjoyed some success with this tactic at Mykale, where their wall of interlocking shields blunted the Greeks' charge for a brief time until they were finally overwhelmed. (Hdt. 9.99.3) In battle between Greeks the first rank, low to the ground and reinforced with seven rows to the rear, should have presented great difficulty for both man and beast, even massed in a column and charging on the run. After all, a stationary wall was just that—a line of unbroken bronze far more dense than the usual shuffling and bobbing shields of a phalanx approaching on the move.

In rare cases we do hear of just such tactics where the phalanx is stationary, "dug in" so to speak, and not to be dislodged. Yet, often in such instances, troops who adopted such a posture were not even attacked by the suddenly timorous enemy column. Perhaps that is why vase paintings show hoplites apparently awaiting the enemy on one knee or simply resting on their haunches. With the spear extended, they cover their bodies with the shield, which is either resting on the ground or hanging on the shoulder. (Ducrey pl. 84; Snodgrass 1967: pl. 38) When Chabrias and his outnumbered defenders of Boiotia in 378 found good ground and remained still, they rested their shields and awaited the Spartans' charge. (Diod. 15.32.4–6) Wisely, Agesilaos and his Spartans backed off, apparently appreciating the difficulty of penetrating disciplined troops arrayed in such a secure position. At Pylos (425), too, the matchless Spartan army was confused when presented with an enemy that refused to advance; the Athenian heavy infantry "remained stationary" while their light-armed troops attacked the Spartan flanks, where the men finally became worn out without reaching the Athenian square. Thucydides' account suggests that the Athenian army had initially marched forth against the Spartans, then suddenly halted, and, finding a secure position, sent out skirmishers, while they waited confidently for the expected Spartan advance. (4.33ff)

The circumstances at the first battle at Mantineia in 418 were similar: the Argives had taken up a strong position and again waited for the Spartan onslaught. Here, rather predictably, the unsophisticated Spartans continued to approach until "an old man" in the army cautioned Agis, their general, against this ill-advised advance; at that point Agis had no other choice than to draw his Spartans back in retreat. (Thuc. 5.65) Again, this rather unusual incident shows men deployed in a strong though by no means unapproachable position, who confidently desire to stay put in order to receive the enemy charge; in such circumstances, they are more than a match for the superior troops arrayed against them. The key to their success, if that is the proper word for what amounts to an avoidance of battle, is in part favorable terrain and sound tactics but more certainly the willpower of men able to show determination in the face of a charge by column. (E.g., Thuc. 4.73)

Nevertheless, these incidents were the exception rather than the rule: most armies drew up as if by mutual agreement and attacked simultaneously. That this was the usual Greek practice is well illustrated by examples where one phalanx clearly holds the superior ground, certain to withstand any advance of the enemy, and yet chooses to abandon that advantage and meet the adversary on the move. The best instance is found at the battle of the Piraieus in 403. There, Thrasyboulos' outnumbered exiles were arrayed on a hill overlooking the superior forces of the Thirty Tyrants. His men were marshaled in column to the unusual depth of fifty shields, and had also brought along sufficient contingents of light-armed and missile-throwing troops. They then awaited the *uphill* charge of the enemy with grounded shields; before the engagement Thrasyboulos spoke to his troops of their numerous advantages, appropriately reminding them that men forced to advance uphill have difficulty in throwing the javelin and at the same time are easy targets for a shower of missiles that would inevitably rain down upon them. In short, it was an ideal situation for an army to stay put. Indeed, Xenophon's account suggests that this was at first exactly the plan: superior morale, favorable terrain, shields grounded, troops both stationary and massed in unusual depth to absorb an enemy already on a difficult uphill advance. What followed makes no sense at all unless it is considered as an illustration of the ever-present, natural impulse, however misguided and unwise, for any Greek phalanx to charge forward. For at this point, after reminding his troops of the advantages of their position, Thrasyboulos suddenly struck up the order to advance, leading his men *downhill* into the phalanx of the enemy, and so rushing into the middle of their column. (Xen. *Hell.* 2.4.11–20) If Thrasyboulos' behavior seems inexplicable, in that he exchanged a secure, stationary position for the dangers of breaking rank on a downward charge and therewith reduced the march for his tiring opponents, consider his enemies' posture. They compounded their initial mistake by exhausting their troops in an *uphill* run. That same type of misguided attack was also undertaken by the Athenians earlier at Delion in 424 when they, too, charged uphill against Boiotian hoplites, men who already were running *downhill* to meet them (Thuc. 4.96.1)—so much for Epameinondas' advice never to attack the enemy from an inferior position. (Xen. *Hell.* 7.5.8) If troops, then, were willing to risk defeat in an uphill charge, we can understand their normal desire to attack on the move when both sides shared the customary level ground.

The problems posed by an enemy who with grounded shields refused to advance, or who steadfastly held a superior position, may have bothered commanders, but did not usually deter most armies from trying to meet the enemy in motion. Four reasons, I think, account for this tendency of Greek hoplites to meet each other on the move if at all possible. The first, of course, still enshrined even now in Western military practice, is that the formation in column was designed specifically for attack, whatever

the circumstances; it reminds us of the origins of hoplite battle, when small landholders decided to leave the safety of their
walled cities and in concerted effort push the enemy off their
croplands. We should not underestimate the tradition of the advance, for it is this same urge to attack, to "do something," to
put men on the move that has led to so many suicidal disasters
like the charges at the Crimea, Gallipoli, and the Somme. To
the classical Greek hoplite, digging in and waiting for the enemy phalanx to make its way forward must have seemed as in-
glorious as archery, skirmishing, or the supporting work of the
light-armed trooper. All were a poor substitution for the pitched
battle where both sides met head-on. This explains why armies
seem somewhat taken aback by enemies who did not advance—
as if the rules had somehow been broken. Agis, for example, is
not sure whether he should charge uphill against the Argives
at Mantineia, and Agesilaos in 378 hesitates before Chabrias in
Boiotia, as if impelled to advance even under unfavorable circumstances in conformity with the comfortable old way of
fighting.

In Greek warfare, which by convention was battle for a day,
the prebattle environment—the yelling and singing that went
on within the phalanx, the drink of wine before battle, the expectation of a speech by their leader—was more conducive to
attack than to defense. This accustomed activity before battle
was aimed at rousing the hoplite to advance, rather than calm-
ing him in an effort to keep steady, stay put, and wait for the enemy's charge. The troops must have realized, too, that the lack
of forward movement once the battle commenced was para-
mount to defeat. In all combat, the key was to push ahead. The
first warnings of doom were not necessarily steps backward but,
rather, the lack of any progress *forward*, which would give rise to
the sinking apprehension that an inevitable, irresistible push
backward was on its way. For Greek infantry to adopt that posture in advance was, in a strange way, to acknowledge that battle was already half lost, that the troops had already given up the
initiative.

Thirdly, there were practical grounds for keeping men on the move. Experience taught the hoplites that the best way to push their iron through the bronze and wood of enemy shields and breastplates was to achieve momentum before both sides became entangled and the chance to drive home a running spear-thrust with real power was lost. This desire on the part of the spearmen to have one clear shot, to crash into the opposing side in one fell swoop, was an enticing narcotic; even the rational argument that the very momentum he gathered on the run might just as easily impale him on the propped spears of a kneeling enemy, or distort his advancing line of protective shields, would have fallen on deaf ears, since everyone knew that this was the best way to penetrate the enemy's armor.

Lastly, there was always the fear of missile attack. Most infantry knew of the damage inflicted even to armored men by well-trained slingers, archers, and javelin throwers. There was no desire to stay still and so allow the enemy to fix his aim on a stationary target; that meant essentially to suffer pitifully in a sea of arrows like the Spartan remnants at Thermopylai. Running the last two hundred yards of no-man's-land, as the hoplites at Marathon showed, limited such exposure to attack until the protective cover of the general mêlée could be reached. (Cf. Arr. *Anab.* 2.10.3)

After the troops had lined up into formation and the phalanxes had squared off on the agreed site of battle, Greek warfare suddenly lost the rigid conformity of finely tailored columns. The point of departure from the clear order of the battle squares did not begin—as most assume—when the two sides met together, but often much earlier at the very moment the men began to lumber forward at a trot of some four to six miles per hour.

Very rarely could the discipline of command extend down the line of allied contingents—a phalanx which might stretch on for nearly a mile. Consequently, as the tide of hoplites first surged forward, there was rarely uniformity in the moment of their departure, the rate of their advance, or the direction of their course.

Among most Greek armies, the attack resembled more the rush of an armed mob than the march of disciplined troops in careful formation, though it is true from both ancient and modern sources we receive a picture of an ordered, deliberate advance of the Spartans. With reference to the literary evidence, Pritchett, for example, remarks:

> The sequence of events seems to have been as follows. The commander-in-chief, whether general or king, gave the command to advance by beginning the paian. The trumpeter sounded the call. The soldiers joined in the song whether the advance was at normal or faster pace. All the evidence is that the paian was a sort of hymn or chant, and the use of the word "paian" in other connections favors this belief. . . . The song was begun when the armies were three or four stades apart. Once the battle was joined, the marching paian might be replaced by the war cry. (*1. 107*)

Thucydides' famous description of the Spartan advance at the first battle of Mantineia (418) may be the clearest picture of how the Spartans usually made their move forward.

> And after this battle was joined. The Argives and their allies for their part went forward eagerly and wildly, but the Spartans slowly and in time to the many flute-players who were at their side—not out of any religious custom, but rather so that they might march evenly and their order might not disintegrate—a thing which large armies are prone to do as they march forward to battle. (*5.70*)

This progression of events is said to have occurred in most battles in which the Spartans, the only true professional soldiers in Greece, took part; but in truth, it remains an idealized picture of even the Spartan army, which often did not follow such a textbook procedure. At the Pactolos River, for example, Agesilaos ordered the first ten age groups to charge the enemy on the run. (Xen. *Hell.* 3.4.23) And, as Thucydides himself notes, most other armies, the Argives in particular, tended to be much more disorganized. Perhaps few ancient Greek armies could match the charge of a Swiss phalanx of pikemen, a model of both speed and discipline—no doubt indicative of both their lighter body armor and the uniform composition of their columns:

> There was no pause needed to draw up an army composed of many small contingents in line of battle—a thing which led to so many quarrels and delayed feudal units. Each phalanx marched on the enemy at a steady but swift pace, which covered the ground in an incredibly short time. Reading the narratives of their enemies, we gather that the advance of a Swiss army had in it something portentous; the masses of pikes and halberds came rolling over the brow of some hill or out of the depths of some wood, and a moment later they were drawing near, and then—almost before the opponent had time to realize his position—they were on him, with four rows of pike-heads projecting in front, and the impetus of file on file surging up from the rear. *(Oman 2.256)*

The problems in the advance first originated because not all hoplites of the individual contingents—that is, the center and the two wings of the army—moved forward at the same time, nor were even the men in the same phalanx always aware that their own ranks ahead had begun to march. Of course, once the cohesion and uniformity of the army as a whole was disrupted, it could never be really restored, as the cautious, slow-moving Spartans knew so well. They apparently felt that increased exposure to aerial attack and the accompanying loss of impetus at the collision were not so important if the phalanx could at least arrive at the enemy line in its original formation. Their success on the battlefield until Leuktra (371) suggests that they may well have been right in their belief that a charge on the run was apt to create lethal gaps in the line of any phalanx. What gave the Spartans cause for concern were situations such as occurred at Miletos in 413. There, the Argives suddenly rushed their Milesian enemies across the battlefield, leaving the phalanx of the Athenians in the center of their allied battle line far behind, and thereby creating disorder in the planned attack. (Thuc. 8.25.3) Years later at Corinth, the Argives again went out ahead in frenzy, causing disruption in their own phalanx and in the line of advance of the entire army. Although they defeated a phalanx of Sikyonians stationed opposite, they were soon isolated in turn by the Spartans and overwhelmed. (Xen. *Hell.* 4.3.17)

Men of different allied city-states, encased in armor and separated by thousands of yards, even though they might fight on the same side of the battle, had their own particular views on the enemy contingents arrayed against them; many multistate armies were never more than a loose coalition and accordingly rarely coordinated their attack: they either did not hear, or deliberately neglected, the general trumpet signal to advance. Yet, even more importantly, men quite near each other in the same tribal contingent did not always know what was going on. That is what Thucydides implied when he remarked that large armies are not likely to march out evenly, but instead reach the enemy in disorder. The poor performance of the Syracusans in their first battle with the Athenian infantry in Sicily in 415 was caused by the initial confusion about the outset of battle; some men were not even in formation when the Athenians went ahead with their attack. Apparently, they ran up late, looking to find any place they could in the ranks as their phalanx moved on out. (Thuc. 6.69.1) Even the dreadful, chilling walk of the professional Spartans which so impressed Thucydides was known to disintegrate under the harsh reality of the battlefield. At Leuktra they never recovered their cohesion once they started off their advance in disorder. Xenophon relates that the Spartan king Kleombrotos led out his attack "before his own army even perceived that he was advancing." (Xen. *Hell.* 6.4.13) His Peloponnesian allies on the other end of his battle line, if not many of his own Spartans nearby, were not even aware their commander had signaled the charge. If the general shouting and background noise made the order to advance difficult for the helmeted hoplite to hear, the alternative was to pass the command to move out down the line by word of mouth, a procedure which would have ensured some disruption in continuity at the very outset. (E.g., Plut. *Arist.* 18)

The "Run"

Once the men were on the move, we hear from a variety of sources just how difficult it was to keep them marching at the same step all the while preserving their formation. Xenophon, for example, describes how the mercenary soldiers of the Ten Thousand shouted to one another to keep their order and not run out wildly as they went after the enemy. (*An.* 1.8.9) Philopoemen, the general of the Achaean League in the early second century, Polybius says, was "careful to watch his order" when he commanded his phalanx to charge on the run at Mantineia. (11.15.2) This is not all surprising since the march forward must have quickly exhausted most hoplites, and tired them at varying rates, without regard to the general advance of the columns, but rather depending on the limits of each man's own individual endurance — quite an uncertain process when we realize that there were some forty or so different age groups dispersed throughout the phalanx. We know now that Herodotus' story of the Athenian "run" for a mile at Marathon is just that, a story. Modern studies of physical endurance under similar conditions have found that about 220 yards is about all men in heavy armor can manage at a speed of five to six miles per hour, and still maintain their shields in the chest-high position with enough reserve energy for battle. In these modern tests, after three hundred yards even a simple two-file formation disintegrated in exhaustion. (Donlan and Thompson 1976; 1979) The picture we have, then, is that hoplites in formation approached the enemy at a walk until they felt they had closed the distance to the point (roughly two hundred yards) where a final trot was possible. If both sides advanced at five miles per hour, they would collide in less than two minutes. The battle at Koroneia in 394 provides a good example. Both Thebans and Spartans walked to within two hundred yards of each other, at which point the Thebans began their run. When they had narrowed the distance to a hundred yards, their Spartan adversaries also rushed forth to meet them. (Xen. *Hell.* 4.3.17)

The decision when to begin the final charge on the run was bound to be only guesswork; most commanders could not accurately estimate at which point to launch the full-speed attack, since the exact speed of the enemy, also on the move, was difficult to gauge. The terrain, the condition of the soil, the time of day, the emotional state of the troops, and the ability to get the word out quickly were additional factors. In short, while in some instances armies waited too long to begin the final dash and were faced with an enemy mass moving faster with greater momentum, more often hoplites began too soon, in their eagerness to reach the enemy at top speed. If this occurred, they soon found themselves tired, struggling, and at a decided disadvantage when they finally began fighting. Those less hardy, perhaps soldiers either over thirty or slowed by old wounds and ailments, quickly fell out of step as the younger and less experienced men rushed on ahead. Thus, Diomilos and his six hundred Syracusans were easily routed by the Athenians since, Thucydides tells us, they were advancing "as fast as each man was able, but they had nearly three miles to march before reaching the enemy." This poorly planned advance during the Athenian expedition to Sicily "in considerable amount of disorder" sealed their fate. (6.97.4–5) Thucydides makes it clear that when they finally reached the enemy the cohesion of their phalanx was long gone and they had become an army of individuals. This was an extreme case, but many armies reached their adversaries in some type of disorder. For example, at Amphipolis in 422, the Spartan general Brasidas remarked of the confused Athenian advance that troops in such a state "with heads and spears bobbing can never withstand the charge." (Thuc. 5.10) That prospect of a running, confused advance concerned the Greek mercenaries at Kunaxa, when their commander Klearchos marched them forth at about eight hundred yards, but held off their final run until they were within bowshot—probably two hundred yards or less. Diodorus explains that Klearchos was intent on both keeping his men fresh for battle and yet limiting their exposure to the shower of enemy Persian missiles. (14.23.1–2; Polyaen. *Strat.* 2.2.3) Surely, Klearchos had

seen many phalanxes break into a run too early, only to find themselves disorganized and worn out, without much of an offensive
punch when they reached the spears of the enemy.

There were problems not merely in the speed but also in the
direction of the advance. Only the men in the first three ranks
of the phalanx had a clear view of the enemy and thus of the general point at which they would soon collide. Of course, while there
was little chance that two phalanxes could ever miss each other
entirely, the evidence is, nevertheless, that each side rarely
charged straight ahead but came at each other obliquely. That
characteristic, along with the difficulty of the run and the uncertainty of the initial start, added yet another dimension to the
overall confusion. Most hoplites in the front ranks would realize
that the men directly opposite, on the other side of the battlefield, were probably not the hoplites with whom they would actually collide. In his rich description of the battle of Mantineia
of 418, Thucydides recalls the peculiar habit of most armies on
the move to drift rightward, sometimes radically so, each hoplite
wishing to shelter his own vulnerable right side within the protection of his neighbor's shield. So at Mantineia each side found
their left wing nearly enveloped by the enemy's right. Later, at
the battle of the Nemea River in 394, Xenophon tells us clearly
that both sides "veered to the right in their advance" (*Hell.*
4.2.18), so much so that the Spartan right wing caught only a portion of the Athenian phalanx. More than twenty years later, at
Leuktra, the Spartans apparently had moderated, or rather mastered, this natural drift and transformed it into a deliberate plan
of envelopment from the right. (Plut. *Pel.* 23.1)

Opposing battle lines were not necessarily the same length. An
army that was inferior in numbers or that had chosen to shorten
its line by massing in column might find itself facing an enemy
that stretched beyond both its wings. In most such cases, hoplites
were probably forced to move at an angle, whatever their rightward urge, natural or deliberate, just to meet the enemy: those
charging in superior numbers would have angled in on their outnumbered foe, while the outnumbered were forced to move in

mass to the right to prevent being outflanked on both wings, or to drift outward at both flanks and thus risk leaving a gap in the middle.

No-Man's-Land

At the moment of departure the silent, if not contemplative, lull before the storm was suddenly broken as the battlefield quickly was turned into a sea of dust and noise. Breathing and hearing were difficult enough for a bearded hoplite wearing the Corinthian helmet, and they worsened in the crowded ranks of the phalanx. Yet, once the march forward began, his senses would have been further limited and his own discomfort overwhelming, as thousands of feet shuffling under the weight of panoplies kicked up the dry ground of summer. Individual shouts crescendoed into the collective war cry, which was doubled by the similar sounds of the approaching enemy.

After the devastation of Attica by Xerxes' army, Demaratos was said to have seen a vision growing from out of Eleusis, a cloud, Herodotus says, "such as an army of 30,000 infantry might raise" (8.65)—apparently he knew of the dust a host of armored men kicked up. We know of nearly the same thing in a skirmish between the Athenians and the Corinthians at Solygeia in 425 during the Peloponnesian War; although most of the Corinthians could not actually see the battle between their own kinsmen and the Athenian invaders, they quickly found out what was going on by the cloud of dust that rose up into the air. Their view of the fight, Thucydides points out, was obstructed by Mount Oneion, so we get some idea here just how large a cloud must have been raised by a few thousand men on the move. (4.44.4) And in the final battle between Antigonos and Eumenes, the successors of Alexander, Plutarch would have us believe the fine white sand of the battlefield rose into a cloud "like lime" which blinded the vision of all, allowing Antigonos to sweep into the enemy camp. (*Eum.* 16) That must have been the normal scene any time armored men met on the dusty fields of summer. Under unusual conditions, such as at Pylos, where ash was ubiquitous, the dust and discomfort might become so severe that hoplites were actually blinded and stumbled aimlessly in confusion. (Thuc. 4.34.4; cf., e.g., Diod. 19.42.1–2; 19.61.1; Polyb. 5.85.12) Indeed, Homer first recorded the dust swirling over the Greek battlefield at the first engagement between the Greeks and Trojans:

> And as when under the screaming winds the whirlstorms bluster on that day when the dust lies deepest along the pathways and the winds in the confusion of dust uplift a great cloud, such was the indiscriminate battle. (Il. *13.334–37*)

It was impossible for men in hoplite armor to move without rubbing and jostling against their neighbors' breastplates, shields, and spears. These sounds of clashing metal created the background or the foundation noise in the strange, mixed cacophony of battle. That hoplites in motion were extremely noisy is clear from the story of the Plataians in 429 who escaped their besieged city soon after the outbreak of the Peloponnesian War. They were careful to keep apart from each other so that the jostling sounds of their arms would be dispersed, and the night wind would muffle the sounds of the bronze weapons from the ears of the Spartan sentries. (Thuc. 3.22.2)

The snorting of horses mixed together with the clatter of arms also added to the din of the battlefield. (Diod. 19.31.2) On rarer occasions, falling rain or hail against the bronze could do the same, as the Carthaginian invaders learned at the river Krimesos in Sicily: "and no small part of the problem was the sensation of the claps of thunder, and also the clatter of both the driving rain and hail on the men's armor, making it impossible to hear the orders of the battle commands." (Plut. *Tim.* 28.2) Elsewhere, we hear of the intentional clanging of spear against shield (Xen. *An.* 4.5.18), the thud of missiles landing among the armor of the infantry as they marched (Xen. *An.* 4.3.28); both created the same effect: tremendous, inhuman noise arising from their very equipment in motion.

A second level of sound came from the men themselves who, of course, talked, sang, and yelled at each other as they walked and then ran. Here, they bolstered their spirits with chatter among individuals or private warnings and exhortations to keep in formation as the enemy neared. Homer, for example, remarked that the sound of the Trojan advance was like wildfowl,

> as when the clamour of cranes goes high to the heavens,
> when the cranes escape the winter time and the rains unceasing
> and clamorously wing their way to the streaming ocean
>
> (Il. 3.3–5)

In obvious admiration, Thucydides describes the personal exhortation within the Spartan ranks at Mantineia; unlike the Athenians, the private conversations and singing of familiar war chants, rather than the usual battle general's harangue, were sufficient to steel their nerves for the advance. (5.69) The hero, Tyrtaios writes, "has well trained his heart to be steadfast and to endure, and with words encourage the man who is stationed beside him." (12.18–19)

The greatest noise was produced not by individual talking and shouting, but by the collective war cry that the army uttered in unison—the ancient equivalent of the rebel yell, which was designed to make each soldier forget his own fear as he sent a message of terror to the enemy. (E.g., Aesch. *Sept.* 270; Xen. *Ages.* 2.10–11; *An.* 4.2.12) Aristophanes suggests that among the Athenians it resembled the strange sound "eleleleu." (*Av.* 364) At Koroneia in 394, Xenophon tells us the Thebans finally moved against the enemy on the run, "yelling" as they went. (*Hell.* 4.3.17) And during the Spartan invasion of Arcadia in 365, after the troops of the Arcadian alliance had resisted the Spartan attack, they too went on the offensive; at this point in the battle, Xenophon says, "there was a great deal of shouting," as if their sudden boldness had created a surge in confidence and drawn forth a collective scream. (*Hell.* 7.4.22)

As the two sides approached each other, the sound of armor in motion, the shouting among those on the move, and the collective yells of both armies (e.g., Xen. *Hell.* 4.2.19), all mixed in from every direction, became deafening. At Kynoskephalai in 197 the shouts and war cry of both the Macedonians and Romans, as well as the general cheering of the noncombatants, created a sense of rampant disorder throughout the battlefield. (Polyb. 18.25.1) No wonder that Homer had described the war cry of the advancing Greeks mixed together with that of the Trojans as:

> Not such is the roaring against dry land of the sea's surf
> as it rolls in from the open under the hard blast of the north wind;
> not such is the bellowing of fire in its blazing
> in the deep places of the hills when it rises inflaming the forest,
> nor such again the crying voice of the wind in the deep-haired
> oaks, when it roars highest in its fury against them,
> not so loud as now the noise of Achaians and Trojans
> in voice of terror rose as they drove against one another.
>
> (Il. *14.394–401*)

At the Spartan debacle on Pylos in 425, Thucydides reminds us that "the loud shouting" of the enemy advance, along with the rising dust, destroyed the cohesion of their ranks. (4.32.2) The reasons for the Athenian collapse on the heights of Epipolai a few years later were not merely darkness and the terrain, but also the shouting of their victorious Sicilian attackers mixed in with the confused sound of their own men falling back in disorder. (Thuc. 7.45) In much the same way Polybius at one point describes the initial terror of the Romans when they were struck by the trumpets and wild war cries of the Greeks across the battlefield. (4.64.6–8) If we can believe Plutarch, the shouting and clashing of arms made it impossible for Dion's troops in Sicily to hear any of his commands. (*Dion* 30.6)

Once the signal was given to advance, the Greek hoplite—if he could hear it—had to pay attention not to be left behind, to stick close to the men around. In closing the final distance across no-man's-land, the formation of the phalanx was often disrupted as each man ran at a slightly different speed. And there were roars of men, animals, and equipment on both sides, as well as a general impairment of vision caused by the rising dust, the crests and

spears of the men ahead, and the mass of moving humanity in
general. In many instances the outcome of a hoplite battle was
decided right here during the first charge when some men simply caved in to the fright and ruined the unity of their columns
before they even reached the enemy. As we shall see, the key to
success in a battle between phalanxes was to create a lethal gap
in the enemy ranks, an initial hole through which troops could
push, destroying the cohesion of the entire enemy formation.
Some armies were rent before they even reached the spears of
the enemy, the battle ending before it had even begun. Indeed,
it is surprising that such a collapse in mass was not more common when we consider just how demanding, how awful that final move into the enemy actually was.

13 *A Collision of Men*

There is many a boy here today who looks on war as all glory, but, boys, it is all hell.
— *William Tecumseh Sherman*

I also say it is good to fall, battles are lost in the same spirit in which they are won.
— *Walt Whitman*

After the charge, the two sides at last met in what the poet Kallinos called the "first stage of confused battle." (1.11) What followed cannot be understood unless we first consider the peculiar spectacle of the collision, the sights and also the sounds of that frightening meeting of humanity.

True, the blast of rifle and cannon fire was absent, but there is no reason to suppose that the ancient battlefield was any quieter than the modern one; after all, men were not spread out over miles at the front, separated by rough terrain, fighting in hundreds of isolated skirmishes, but were now bunched together, giving and receiving hundreds of blows at close range. The entire noise of men and equipment was concentrated onto the small area of the ancient battlefield—itself usually a small plain encircled by mountains, which only improved the acoustics. In contrast, as Kellet has recently remarked, "not everyone would agree that the modern battlefield is a noisy place; Marshall viewed it as dominated by a 'great quiet which seems more ominous than the occasional tempest of fire.' Further on he implied that this situation mystified men who had fortified themselves with altogether different preconceptions." (223) It was not just that the decibel level of Greek battle increased as the two phalanxes neared and met. The *nature* of the sound also changed from that of recognizable human speech—the war cry or song— and the reassuring jostling of equipment on the move to a terrible cacophony of smashed bronze, wood, and flesh.

Very early on in Greek literature we learn that the ancients were well aware of this particular inhuman sound of death. In the *Iliad*, for example, there are over half a dozen onomatopoeic words for fighting or battle that can only be translated as "roar" or "thud," the sounds which arose after the two sides finally crashed together. (Cf. Pritchett 4.28—*kelados, phloisbos, ktupos, klonos, kydoimos*) The seventh-century poet Kallinos, too, wrote of that sound, the thud of colliding weapons (1.14–15)—a sound that his near contemporary Tyrtaios also said arose from the bashing together of rounded shields. (19.14–15) Since most wars involved only an hour or more of pitched battle, it is striking that very early on in Greek history a rich vocabulary arose for what was a relatively rare occurrence, but that collision of men must have made a singular impression. The sound of armored men in contact was not a fanciful image solely for the poets, but the reality of the battlefield. Nearly three hundred years after the Lyric poets, Xenophon, in his famous description of the battle of Koroneia in 394—a battle "like none other" in his lifetime— was clearly impressed by the initial meeting of the two armies: "There was not any yelling, but there was not silence either; instead that particular sound was present which both anger and battle tend to produce." (*Ages.* 2.12) That "particular sound," that "awful crash," as Xenophon knew, was not human, at least not entirely: "and then there was a great slaughter of men, and too, a great thud of all types of weapons and missiles, together with a great shout of men calling out for help among the rank, or urging each other onward, or praying to the gods." (Xen. *Cyr.* 7.1.35)

The Greeks recognized that the peculiar noise of this initial crash came from a variety of sources. First, there was the dull thud of bronze against wood as either the metal spear point made its way through the wood core of a hoplite shield, or as soldiers struck their shields against the bronze breastplates and helmets of the enemy, or as wooden shield was bashed into shield. To Aristophanes that sound was a synonym for war. (*Ach.* 588) Together with this, there was the sharp clatter of metal driven against metal as spear and sword met breastplate, helmet, and greave. Even breastplate might be driven into breastplate, as men in the front row lost control and were literally pushed into the enemy ranks, jammed together "chest against chest." (Tyrtaios 8.33) And repeated sharp sounds indicated when ash spears snapped under the pressure of contact in what Sophocles called "the storm of spears." (*Ant.* 670)

The live sounds were more animal-like than human: the concerted groans of men exerting themselves, pushing forward in group effort with their bodies and shields against the immovable armor of the enemy—grunts such as one hears around men sweating at work in field or shop, for battle, after all, as Homeric man knew, was "work" of the worst kind. Finally, whatever Tyrtaios advised about the hoplite "biting his lip," there were all too often the noises of human misery. Here arose a tortured symphony of shrieks as a man went down with a wound to the groin, the steady sobbing of a soldier in extremis, a final gasp of fright as the spear thrust found its way home. Ugly, indeed, Tyrtaios wrote, is the corpse in the dust. (11.19) Livy's famous description of the Roman disaster at Trasimene during the second Punic War and the utter confusion in the ranks must have been a common nightmare for all ancient soldiers:

> But owing to the very din and tumult neither any encouragement nor orders were able to be heard, so much so that the infantry could not recognize their maniples, centuries, or even their own assigned place—their minds were hardly capable of taking up their arms in battle. Indeed some found themselves more burdened by their equipment than protected. Also, there was such a cloud of fog that men relied on their ears rather than their eyes. They turned their faces toward the groans of the wounded, the blows of flesh and arms, and the mingled cries of both the frightened and panicked. *(22.5)*

We can understand why a witness of battle among the armored men in the medieval period wrote: "The din was so frightful that one could not have heard even God's thunder." (Verbruggen 166)

The visual aspect of the troops on the battlefield was now dras-

tically altered. True, the neat columns of the prebattle formations were already somewhat rent in the general, uneven surge
forward, but after the impact, both sides regained their density
as the ranks to the rear piled up behind their leaders and
bunched together laterally to seek protection in the line of
shields. Then the two armies became forever intertwined and
irrevocably mingled as man pressed into man at front, side, and
rear. The sea of dust was now stationary, and still more stifling
as men were shuffling but not really moving, at least at first.
Friend and foe were quickly becoming indistinguishable. Pockets of brave fighters must have soon made their way into the
ranks of the enemy phalanx, either to be absorbed and killed,
or to grow steadily into a fatal cancer as their colleagues in line
to the rear sensed a reward to their efforts and pushed them even
farther inside the depths of the enemy. Some idea of this confusion is reflected in Greek literature where we are repeatedly
told that those in the front ranks of hoplite battle are not merely
fighting "hand to hand" or "spear to spear" (e.g., Xen. *Hell.*
4.3.17; Thuc. 6.70.1), but touching "chest-to-chest" and "helmet-
to-helmet" as well:

> Let him fight toe to toe and shield against shield hard driven,
>   crest against crest and helmet on helmet, chest against
>   chest;
> let him close hard and fight it out with his opposite foeman,
>   holding tight to the hilt of his sword, or to his long spear.
>   *(Tyrtaios 11.31–34)*

These images also suggest that the rear ranks had been pushing
madly at the very instant the two sides collided, literally thrusting their friends ahead into the faces of the first ranks of the enemy. In both prose and poetry, ancient Greek battle was often in
these first few seconds understood as a "mixing together," as any
clear separation between the two sides was now lost forever.
(Thuc. 8.25.4; Kallinos 1.11; Hom. *Il.* 13.131; 15.510; 16.215–17)

We have spoken of the sight and sound which arose from this
initial collision, but only as would-be spectators; hoplites on the
battlefield never had this view. Sweating in earnest, their vision

obscured by the helmet, dust and bodies in motion everywhere, they were captives in confused humanity as hearing, bad to begin with, now was lost entirely amid the noise, much of it coming from the banging of enemy spear tips on their own armor. For the men in the initial three ranks the view of the fighting, then, would be the blurred shapes of the enemy at their face—and at their feet—their entire perception of the world reduced to a few feet of the ground ahead. Those to the rear would learn that they had reached the enemy phalanx only when they realized the backs of their friends in front had become immovable. There was also an increased smell of sweat from the thousands toiling in the sun, the odor of blood and entrails from fresh, open wounds, and the occasional scent of excrement among the fearful or recently killed—though possibly the sense of smell was dulled along with vision and hearing.

Some have suggested that the initial clash of many infantry battles is at times not literally a collision, there being a last-second avoidance of a real impact between the two bodies, a mutually understood step back on each side. Keegan, for example, in a discussion of Du Picq's views, has said that "large masses of soldiers do not smash into each other, either because one gives way at the critical moment, or because the attackers during the advance to combat lose their fainthearts and arrive at the point very much inferior in numbers to the mass they are attacking." (71) And yet a fair reading of the ancient accounts of hoplite battles suggests that in the case of the Greeks—and perhaps among the Greeks alone—the first charge of men usually smashed right into the enemy line: the key was to achieve an initial shock through collision which literally knocked the enemy back and allowed troops to pour in through the subsequent tears in the line. That is exactly what Arrian meant when he remarked that the idea of Greek battle was to force back the enemy during the initial charge. (*Tact.* 11.1–2) While in most cases such a crash was spontaneously transformed into a grinding, hand-to-hand struggle between two locked phalanxes, each striving to tear a gap in the battle line of the other, on occasion we do hear of an entire army demolished, simply rammed right off the battlefield in shambles because of the force of the initial crash of men on the move.

The collision must have been an unbelievable sight. The spears of both sides were nearing each other at some five miles an hour. At Koroneia in 394, Agesilaos' men "ran" to meet the enemy; when they came "within spear thrust," the enemy collapsed from the very shock. (Xen. *Hell.* 4.3.17) Indeed, the narratives of the battles of Mantineia, Delion, Nemea, and Leuktra, not to mention the accounts of earlier (often nameless) conflicts in the Lyric poets, make no sense unless we understand that both sides literally collided together, creating the awful thud of forceful impact at the combined rate of ten miles per hour. Perhaps the most notorious case was the second half of that same battle of Koroneia, where, Xenophon tells us, Agesilaos and his Spartans crashed "head to head" against the Thebans. There can be no doubt about the sequence of events. The enemy, wishing to "break through" to their friends, had "massed together tightly and advanced stoutly." Xenophon remarks that the wiser course might have been to let the charging mass pass by and take them in the rear. Instead Agesilaos "crashed" his phalanx right into the Theban column and was nearly killed. (*Hell.* 4.3.19)

There are at least four reasons why we must assume that ancient Greek battle within its first few seconds was a terrible collision of soldiers on the run. The first and most obvious was the great depth of the phalanx, a massive column of men lined up at least eight ranks deep. The function of those to the rear, presumably ranks four through eight, was literally to push their comrades forward, and for those in front there was, consequently, really no choice but to complete their run. If they hesitated or gave into any natural fear of physical collision, they would, nevertheless, be shoved onward—or else trampled by successive waves piling against their backs from the rear. Since the men in back did not yet have to face the line of enemy spears, they had less fear of pressing ahead, pushing the men at the front onward while there was still this protective wall of flesh between themselves and the spear points of the enemy. Indeed, the peculiar nature of hoplite battle at this juncture ensured that all except those in the last rank were *forced* to advance at the enemy ahead. We hear no reference to a repugnance for the killing—a common phenomenon on the modern battlefield, where infantry is divided into fighters and nonfighters, doers and nondoers, leaders and followers, and where some soldiers are present whose dislike for the bloodletting makes them passive actors who mimic, but do not engage in, the slaughter. Here, the vast majority in the first seven ranks of the phalanx, whatever their preferences, were forced by the men at their back either to participate (i.e., to fight) or not to participate (i.e., die or become wounded). (Cf. Asklepiodotos 5.2; Ael. *Tact.* 14.6) There could be no last-second flinching by either the men in front or their followers to the rear. The latter knew well that their own hope of survival lay in creating the greater impetus, forcing their own front line deeper into the belly of the enemy phalanx.

Secondly, the unusual size and bowl-like shape of the hoplite shield helped to create a feeling of absolute protection in the last seconds of the run; the running Greek infantryman found security in its concave, three-foot diameter—"his chest and his shoulders under the hollowed-out protection of his broad shield." (Tyrtaios 11.24) Perhaps he thought that, if he ran with his shield chest high and his head lowered, he might not even see the enemy upon impact. Surely, all of us have experienced this natural desire at the split second before an unavoidable crash to close our eyes, or better yet, shield our face and cover up—as if this made the frightful experience somehow more tolerable. Yet, those final moments of "blindness" ensure that the collision cannot be averted.

At this point the enemy line was not necessarily an absolutely impenetrable wall of shields, touching rim to rim. The men were, of course, running and thus had already distorted their original prebattle deployment. That vision of locked shields might not return until the general mêlée when the rear ranks piled behind their leaders and the entire phalanx massed down the line in an effort to keep out pockets of enemy attackers. Veterans of hoplite battle would have known that in the final rush into the enemy phalanx, they had a chance to miss the barrier of an enemy shield or spear, that rather than hitting a wall of wood and/or flesh, a point of iron, a plate of bronze, they might be forced in *between* the small gaps of running soldiers—a chance that they might smash their way through arms and legs, and begin stabbing at the second or third rank of the enemy phalanx. "Large armies," Thucydides reminds us, "break their order just as they meet the enemy." (5.71.1)

Finally, should we believe that men at this stage were rational? Were they capable of either sober reflection on the dangers of the situation, or even a clearheaded sense of the natural instinct to avoid a collision, to such a degree that they might hesitate, bunch up, step back, or run away? When the hoplite was in the final steps of a hundred-yard run, his adrenaline and the laws of motion made continued movement forward more likely than a sudden stop. Besides, his vision and hearing were poor and he no longer had a clear visual picture of the trouble awaiting him. Moreover, he was a member of the "group." He and the other men may have been drinking together in the morning before battle and may not have been sober but, rather, functioning in these moments on "automatic pilot." Very few of us, as we have learned in the twentieth century, can predict what close-knit groups of men on the run, their inhibitions dulled by drink, can and will do in any situation.

Oman, in his account of medieval warfare, presents a clear picture of the collision of a German phalanx and a square of Swiss pikemen which must have been similar to the clashes of antiquity between heavier armored Greek hoplites:

> The two bristling lines of pikes crossed, and the leading files were thrust upon each other's weapons by the irresistible pressure from behind. Often the whole front rank of each phalanx went down in the first onset, but their comrades stepped forward over their bodies to continue the fight. When the masses had been for some time "pushing against each other," their order became confused and their pikes interlocked. *(2.274)*

14   *Tears and Gaps*

> . . . the gigantic breach made in the French army; the
> English grape-shot and the Prussian grape-shot aiding
> each other; the extermination; the disaster in front; dis-
> aster in the flank; the Guard entering the line in the
> midst of this terrible crumbling of all things.
> — *Victor Hugo,* Les Misérables

The most common way to collapse a Greek phalanx on the field
of battle was to cause a collective loss of nerve that would sweep
through the enemy ranks and so result in a mad dash from the
rear. The key to that objective was to find gaps or, better yet, to
create breaches in the enemy line and to stop at all costs opposing men from "standing their ground and closing their ranks together." (Tyrtaios 11.11–12) If a space could be opened between
downed hoplites, men might pour in, attacking at the enemy's
sides and backs as they came on. Then the entire enemy column
would totter, in fear of a general collapse at the front. So, for example, in medieval warfare, the initial charge of the knights gave
way to close-in fighting in the midst of the enemy formation: "the
narrative sources reveal that the break-through occurred in two
distinct phases: first, the charge in closely serried formation, and
then the penetration into the enemy units." (Verbruggen 94)
Keegan has remarked on the similar aims of the French charge
in mass at Agincourt: "The object would have been to knock over
as many of them as possible, and so to open gaps in the ranks
and isolate individuals who could then be killed or forced back
on to the weapons of their own comrades; 'sowing disorder' is a
short-hand description of the aim." (99)

In most Greek battles there were essentially two methods of
sowing disorder, one psychological, the other physical. In the seconds before the advance, even as the enemy made its way across

the battlefield, a sudden disintegration of unity could occur when men suddenly realized that they were outnumbered, exposed on the flank, or poorly deployed. Perhaps, too, they discovered that they were supported by untrustworthy allies or had suffered disheartening losses of prebattle skirmishers and horsemen, or that the enemy arrayed against them consisted of frightening professionals (i.e., the Spartans), or simply that they had already lost order in a haphazard, reckless march. In such cases, when the army not merely lost its formation but was transformed into a mob of individuals, gaps and rents in the phalanx opened immediately and randomly along the entire face of the column. Then everyone knew that a battle of the classic type was now impossible, and the engagement was over before the two sides had even met. Men simply turned and fled (e.g., Xen. *An.* 4.8.38; *Hell.* 3.2.17; 4.3.12; 4.3.17; Thuc. 5.10), in what the Greeks sometimes termed a "tearless battle." (Plut. *Ages.* 33.3; Xen. *Hell.* 7.1.28ff)

Usually, however, Greek battles were not so easily won; here my concern is with the breaches in the enemy line that had to be made by hard fighting and occasional dying. This was now the work of the first, second, and third ranks of the phalanx—men whose spears had reached the enemy at the first collision and who had survived the crash—to create holes like those the Macedonians ripped open at Chaironeia in 338, when the entire Greek line that faced them was "constantly turned open and exposed" (Diod. 16.86.3–4), or like those later at Pydna in 168, when the Macedonians themselves were "ripped open and torn" by their Roman adversaries under Aemilius Paullus; Plutarch remarks that initially breaches in the phalanx originated because of the differing success of the combatants: one segment presses ahead in success, while not far away others are forced to fall back. (*Aem.* 20.4–5) Chabrias' attack in 388 on Aigina caused a Spartan-led phalanx to collapse when the front line of the enemy, no longer resembling "any dense mass," quickly disintegrated. (Xen. *Hell.* 5.1.12) In other words, the front two or three rows of the Spartan phalanx allowed Chabrias' men either to create or exploit gaps in their line, and the unity of the entire formation was quickly destroyed. How, in these first few seconds of battle, was one side able thus to penetrate the enemy line, making or finding gaps between the shields of the enemy infantry?

As the hoplites on each side began their final run in the last two hundred yards, they lowered the spear and carried it at the side in an underhand grip; this is clear from the literary evidence as well as scenes on vase paintings and sculpture. (Anderson 1970:88–89) Momentum and power could be maximized through such an underhand thrust while on the move, and, of course, it was easier this way to maintain both speed and balance. Perhaps, too, there was less chance of accidental wounding, as the spear tip was kept well below the shield and breastplate of the man ahead. The idea must have been to penetrate the enemy's groin or unprotected upper thighs which were exposed under the lower lip of his shield: the groin was the area which Homer called "beyond all places where death in battle comes painfully to pitiful mortals." (*Il.* 13.567) That such blows were favored in the initial collision may be apparent from Tyrtaios' sad description of the old man who holds his groin bloody from a spear thrust (10.25); that unfortunate man, he reminds us, had been fighting admirably in the first ranks. The advantages of such thrusts were that they might force the front-line fighters immediately to drop the shield and spear to cover up such a painful wound, and thus to withdraw from the active fighting within a few seconds. That seems to be the circumstances portrayed by some vase paintings where hoplites in various encounters thrust their spears at the groin with an underhand grip, attempting to direct a blow under the edge of the shield. (Cf. Anderson 1970: 294 n. 12)

Another alternative was to strike the legs above the greave where a deep wound could stop a hoplite just as quickly. Archidamos, who commanded the Spartan phalanx that invaded Arcadia in 365, as soon as his troops were attacked, fell wounded in the thigh among the first ranks, suggesting that he was such a casualty of the initial charge by the Arcadians. (Xen. *Hell.* 7.4.23; cf. Hom. *Il.* 8.306) Elsewhere in Greek literature we hear of many who suffered wounds to the knee or thigh, which confirms that this unprotected area was a favored target for the initial underhand thrust. (E.g., Plut. *Arat.* 27.2) A vase from Syracuse pictures a hoplite collapsed in convulsions with a terrible, gaping wound down the entire side of his thigh (Lorimer pl. 8); in fact, on several ceramic representations we see soldiers on the ground with large, fresh tears along their unarmored, exposed thighs, the blood gushing out, the victim with grimaces of pain on the face, or simply his eyes closed in a near comatose state. (E.g., Ducrey pl. 28) The advantage of striking beneath the shield was that this was the first—and the last—chance to drive home the spear thrust into an unarmored area with enough power to take the hoplite instantly and completely out of battle. Moreover, these initial spear attacks would not only cripple these front-rank fighters but, more important, sometimes drive them backward, propelling their stunned bodies right into the faces of those to the rear, and so temporarily keeping others at bay as well. Again from vase paintings, we see that a spear thrust toppled the victim *backward,* while blows from less effective missiles or swords at times left the hoplite tottering or even falling *forward.* (E.g., Ahlberg 15, 32, 33)

Occasionally in these initial attacks there were successful thrusts to the chest—fatal blows that pierced right through the breastplate. Jabs of sufficient force to penetrate bronze or wood armor probably could only be delivered on the run during the final dash. In these cases, as the hoplite covered with the shield in the seconds before the collision, the spear would be angled slightly upward and driven at great speed into the large target of the chest. Unlike a javelin, sling, or arrow, a spear did not lose momentum upon contact, as a man's arm continued to impel it forward. That must be the point of Tyrtaios' reference to the soldier who "sustains the beating wall of assault" and perishes "with wounds to his chest, where the spear that he was facing has transfixed that massive guard of his shield, and gone through his breastplate as well." (12.25–26) The great Theban general Epameinondas perished thus in the initial phase of the battle of Mantineia; although his charge against the Spartan right wing had been successful, he fell with a spear shaft in his chest, leaving his men unable to capitalize on their victory. (Diod. 15.87.6) Agesilaos, too, at Koroneia probably suffered a similar type of spear wound during the initial crash, since Xenophon says he was wounded "right through his armor." (*Ages.* 18.3)

This first clash of spears was the very beginning, rather than the climax, of battle, a means of gaining an entrance into the belly of the enemy phalanx, rather than of causing a general collapse. Aeschylus, remember, wrote of battle "where knees sink in the dust and spears shatter *at the very outset.*" (*Ag.* 64–66) The key was to follow up an initial inroad by hard fighting at close range, and it is then that battle must have become fiercest, as each side tried to be the first to create a fatal spot of disorder in the ranks of its adversary. Such a furious effort was at the center of the battle of Solygeia in 425, which Thucydides says was "difficult and completely hand-to-hand." (4.43.3) There is no reason to doubt his statement, since men could go at it face-to-face once their spears had splintered upon impact. Most were broken as soon as they hit the round wooden shield, or else they simply snapped off after penetrating the breastplate and flesh of the enemy. "Most of the spears were shattered" is almost a stock phrase in Greek literature, and perhaps another sure indication that the initial collision was between running, rather than standing, hoplites. (Diod. 15.86.2; 17.11.7; 19.83.4–5; Xen. *Hell.* 3.4.14; and cf. too Hdt. 7.224.1; 9.62.2; Plut. *Eum.* 7.3; *Alex.* 16.4)

Once most of the spear shafts were destroyed within the initial line of hoplites on both sides, many of the survivors would recover their senses and now go at it, inches apart, to seek out any weaknesses in the formation created by the crash, and they probably used any weapon still at their disposal to knock away the men in their faces. For all who still had their eight-foot spears intact, a switch to overhand grip was now essential to gather enough power from a stationary position to force the point downward into the neck, groin, shoulders, or face of the enemy. Vase paintings show this clearly: standing hoplites jam their spears downward with the overhand grip in an effort to go over the top edge of the shield of their adversary. For example, on an Attic red-figure calyx crater of the early fifth century, a hoplite, despite a feeble parrying blow with his sword, is nearly knocked off his feet by a single, overhand, downward thrust to the groin which is left unprotected by the shield. (Lazenby pl. 12; Ducrey 284) Head and neck wounds were also a frequent occurrence in the general mêlée, and we know that the downward spear thrust from the standing hoplite must have at times caught the helmet and unprotected portions of the neck. (E.g., Lorimer pl. 8)

Once the spear was gone, the first choice of the hoplite was his secondary short sword—a weapon notorious for its diminished range and associated with the Spartans, who "fought close to their enemies." (Plut. *Mor.* 191 E; 216 C; *Lyc.* 19.2) Usually hoplite battle reached this unusually brutal point within seconds, if no clear momentum had been established through the collision, and instead both sides were now butchering each other with their secondary weapons. Diodorus, for example, relates of the second battle at Mantineia in 362 that both sides engaged with swords after their spears were shattered during the collision: "At the beginning they struck each other with spears; because of the sheer density of the blows most were broken and they continued the battle with swords." At that point men became literally interwoven with each other by the very crowd of the phalanx and unceasingly inflicted wounds as they "persisted in this terrible work." (15.86.3) The desperation of that stage of close-in fighting must explain why Archilochos could remark of battle, "It will be the mournful work of swords." (3)

Yet, we hear even of closer, more savage fighting, if it were possible, when the press of bodies made the use of either spear or even sword impossible. Often men are said to have used their bare hands to grab the shafts of the enemy spears in an effort to wrestle their opponents down or knock them over; that is what occurred among the desperate Persian troops at Plataia (Hdt. 9.62) and Aemilius' Romans at Pydna. (Plut. *Aem.* 20.2; cf. Polyaen. *Strat.* 2.29.2) Even broken spear shafts might be used:

they still offered men a short stub with a jagged edge that had enough point to penetrate exposed flesh. Together with its reduced length (ideal for this type of free-for-all brawling) and the ever-present, ever-lethal butt spike, these remnants may have become most effective, though improvised, weapons. (Plut. *Arist.* 14.5; Polyb. 11.18.4; 16.55.2–4)

Some idea of the fighting at this point is found in the literature, where battle is described not merely as "hand-to-hand" but in greater detail, as if such a generic phrase was insufficient to capture the desperation of the situation. Hoplites grabbed at the beards, hair, or helmets of their opponents in an effort to pull them down with their bare hands (Plut. *Thes.* 5; Polyb. 4.3.2); Alexander was said to have urged his men to shave closely to prevent such enemies from bringing them down by their facial hair. (Plut. *Mor.* 180 B 10) In the frantic struggle at Thermopylai, Herodotus reports, at the end of the day after the Spartans had finally lost their spears and swords (in battle with unarmored men the spears of the Greeks must have survived the initial collision), they went on fighting "with their hands and teeth." (7.225.3) Plutarch describes the final brawl between Neoptolemos and Eumenes of Cardia as ending up in a sort of wrestling match as they ripped at each other's helmet and breastplate. (*Eum.* 5.5)

That there must have been wild slashing and a frenzy of desperate grabbing more often than careful tactical jabs or rehearsed movements is suggested by Herodotus' story of the blind Eurytos, who was led into the battle of Thermopylai by his servant. (7.229) His similarly blind colleague Aristodemos, however, claimed his disability and escaped the final annihilation. Yet once he returned to Sparta alive he was considered by all a coward; apparently in the Spartan way of thinking, for this type of hand-to-hand, close-in fighting, where there was no lack of targets, blindness was not necessarily deserving of an exemption. Indeed, occasionally even cripples were expected to fight, since "in war there's need not of men who run away, but of those who stay put." (Plut. *Mor.* 210 F 34; 217 C) It seems understandable, then, why Plato felt weapon-training not to be so crucial for hoplite battle

(*Lach.* 182 A–B); how could you teach the martial arts to men in armor forced forward constantly by the ranks to the rear?

Plutarch remarked that once the fighting became desperate and hand to hand, hoplites struggled to push and overturn each other in an effort to find a gap in the enemy line. He thought that the Thebans' skill in wrestling, transferred to the battlefield, at least in part explained their success at Leuktra. Clearly, much of the fighting in the first ranks was desperate grabbing, tripping, and overturning among men who were constantly under pressure—fighting where wrestlers who knew how to use their bare hands were just as important as hoplites skilled in the use of shield and spear. (*Mor.* 639 F; cf. especially Pritchett 4.64) Xenophon was of course correct, if not understating the case somewhat, when he remarked that in hoplite battle there was little chance of missing a blow (*Cyr.* 2.1.16): the real aim was to find a way, any way, to hit the target with enough force to knock him out.

Sometimes clever fighters could take advantage of the steady pressure that forced their enemies forward. One ancient source describes a move where the hoplite takes a step backward to draw his onrushing opponent off balance and expose him to a sudden sword thrust. (Cf. scholiast to Eur. *Phoen.* 1407–13 and Pritchett 4.64) One wonders how this was accomplished when there was pressure at his back as well. The references to pulling and grabbing suggest that not only the right hand was free of its offensive weapon, but also the left arm was now without the hoplite shield. The shield may have been cracked, or transfixed with a spear or sword. In any case, the frequent references to shields falling off in battle may explain why a hoplite would have both hands free to wrestle.

We must not forget that hoplite battle, even at this crucial desperate stage, was still a group struggle; those brawling in the hand-to-hand fighting had to give their constant attention to the men at their side. Remember, they not only had to find a way through the enemy line, but also had to keep the foe out as well. If a hoplite could not find protective cover within the shield of his neighbor, then he had to be sure to do his fighting right next to the man at his side, where the sheer density of their flesh might keep out the enemy as they pressed forth. That close attention to order saved the Phocian phalanx at Plataia: initially surrounded on all sides by their Persian captors, they stood firm in the face of the Persian advance, "drawing themselves close and packing their ranks as densely as possible." (Hdt. 9.18.2) The men to the rear had to be ready constantly to rush up a rank and block any penetration that threatened to tear the phalanx apart. This general tendency of hoplites to bunch together is a recurring theme in most battle descriptions, where we are told that the successful side somehow maintained close order all down the line, advancing with locked shields into the tears in the enemy column without leaving even a small gap in their own. To endure that onset at close quarters, Tyrtaios wrote, the warrior must "close the ranks together" and thereby "protect the army behind him." (11.13) The need for men to maintain their assigned places in the face of attack explains Sophocles' reference to the man who must "stand firm in his place during the storm of spears." (*Ant.* 670)

Any reckless departure from the line by individuals in quest of personal success was of little value: the resulting penetration in the enemy line was hardly worth the gap left behind. Aristodemos apparently was the most courageous of the Greek hoplites at the battle of Plataia, yet after the victory the Spartans passed him over in awarding the prize for valor, since "in a frantic state he left the formation to show all his brave deeds." (Hdt. 9.71.3) Indeed, such a departure from the formation to meet the enemy in a single display of martial prowess was the worst thing any soldier might do. Herodotus reminds us that the Persians suffered from such recklessness; at Plataia they sealed their own fate when they ran out to meet the Spartans "in groups of ten or so, sometimes more, sometimes less." (Hdt. 9.62.3) The ephebic oath, required of young Athenians, described the ideal battle conduct: each swore, "I will not leave my comrade wherever I'm stationed on the battlefield." (Tod 2.204)

From repeated allusions throughout Greek literature to the advantages of keeping the shields locked (e.g., Polyb. 4.64.6–9; Hdt. 9.99) and the battle line unbroken (e.g., Polyb. 10.22; Diod. 23.2.1; Xen. *Hipp.* 2.7; *Mem.* 3.1), we might gain contradictory, even baffling images of hoplite battle. Once the two phalanxes met, success always required that fighters in the van, fighting bare-handed if need be, force an inroad among the enemy, an entry-way for the rear ranks to push through—all the while maintaining a physical closeness with those at the side and rear. Hoplite battle, like other aspects of Greek culture, must have then required a unique duality of spirit in the warrior: at once a reckless barroom fighter who would brawl his own way through the flesh and bronze of the enemy in his face, and yet, mindful all the while to do so in orchestrated effort with those at his side. He was thus asked to accomplish two difficult and almost mutually exclusive tasks: to unleash a wild fury in the initial crash, and then to maintain complete mastery of this savagery, to guide each step into the enemy columns with complete discipline.

In most hoplite battles, it is true, the initial collision of men and subsequent hand-to-hand fighting soon gave way to the *othismos*, the "push" of shields, as one side eventually achieved a breakthrough, allowing its troops to force their way on into and through the enemy's phalanx. On occasion we hear that neither side could open up the requisite tear, and thus both sides simply butchered each other right where they stood, the dead discovered after the battle with "all their wounds to the front." (Diod. 15.55.2) In these rare cases, the soldiers in the rear could not push their way to victory, but were forced to step up a rank over the fallen corpses and take their own turn in the stand-up killing. (E.g., Diod. 20.12.7) For example, at the battle at the Nemea River, when men of Pellene crashed headlong into the phalanx of the Thespians, both sides fought and perished in their ranks. (Xen. *Hell.* 4.2.20) That the push of shields in hoplite battle might not lead to a quick collapse soon after the crash is clear also from the second stage of fighting at Koroneia, where the Theban and Spartan phalanxes met head-on: "throwing up their

shields against each other, they pushed, fought, killed, and died."
(*Hell.* 4.3.19) Such battles were often longer, and certainly more
brutal. The writers realized the anomaly in such fighting where
two locked phalanxes simply ground away at each other in constant slaughter without the expected advance. Had something
gone drastically wrong in Greek warfare? When one side did not
disintegrate, there is a certain trace of awe as well as sadness in
the telling. It can be seen in Xenophon's famous remark on the
battle of Koroneia, that "it proved to be such as none of the battles of our time" (*Hell.* 4.3.16), and in his account of the Nemea
River, where the Thespians and the men of Pellene "died in their
places." (*Hell.* 4.2.20)

15 The Push and Collapse

To advance is to conquer.

—*Frederick the Great*

Hard pounding this, gentlemen; let's see who will pound longest.

—*Duke of Wellington*

The men stationed behind in ranks four through eight of most standard phalanxes were not idle as their comrades ahead met the enemy; they were in no sense "rear-echelon" troops as conceived and despised by modern fighting men. Indeed, often the best troops were placed at the rear, where they kept watch on the very pulse of battle. If there was no initial advance after the collision, their role was to stand firm, maintain their station, and resist any wave of back pressure that might come from jittery hoplites in the middle who saw little chance for forward motion and now had ideas of escape. (E.g., Polyb. 18.30.4; Asklepiodotos 5.2) Even in modern battle, where there is not the closeness in rank of the ancient phalanx, Kellet points out that:

> Another condition that deters a soldier from fleeing is momentum. Frederick the Great, for example, would make his squadrons charge at a fast gallop so that a coward's very fear would carry him along; if he hesitated, he would be crushed by the remainder of the squadron. Momentum was also a feature of Napoleon's columns, and it may be even more characteristic of modern battles as a result of mechanization. *(304)*

With spears extended skyward, hoplites kept their own deadly points away from the backs of their friends ahead; if enemy missile troops attempted to target the phalanx as it lumbered through no-man's-land they could deflect the attack somewhat with their raised shafts. Other tasks also kept them busy. Spear shafts might be brought down hard in a vertical stab into enemy

troops lying wounded between the ranks, the spear butt penetrating the armor and shield of any such fallen. Also friends from
the first ranks who had been stunned, wounded, or knocked
down could be helped to their feet and absorbed in the formation or passed back to the rear. Obviously, such consideration was
difficult to accomplish: it required an armored man to bend over
and raise a fellow soldier (himself weighing nearly two hundred
pounds with his equipment)—all the while maintaining steady
pressure, and without breaking formation. There must more
likely have been frequent "walking"—if that is the word—over
the bodies of wounded friends.

The real importance of these men in the rear was simply to
push those in front with their shields—in Asklepiodotos' words,
"to exert pressure with their bodies." (5.2) Of course, from the
moment of impact they had been doing essentially just that, as
they piled up behind their file leaders; increasingly, their pressure grew stronger or more desperate, since they were striving to
force back the entire enemy mass which was itself trying to press
forward. It is surprising how many ancient authors saw the crucial phases of hoplite battle as "the push," where each side
sought desperately to create the greater momentum through the
superior "weight" or "mass." (Cf. Xen. *Hell.* 2.4.34; 6.4.14; 7.1.31;
Ages. 2.12; *Cyr.* 7.1.33; Thuc. 4.96.2; 4.35.3; 6.70.2; Hdt.
7.224–25; 9.62.2; Polyb. 18.30.4; Arr. *Tact.* 12.10.20; 14.16; Paus.
4.7.7–8; 13; Plut. *Ages.* 18.2) In Aristophanes' *Wasps* the veterans are made to say, "after running out with the spear and shield,
we fought them . . . each man stood up against each man . . . we
pushed them with the gods until evening." (1081–85) At Koroneia, Xenophon wrote, the Spartans "crashed against the Thebans face to face, and throwing up their shields, they pushed,
fought, killed, and died." (*Hell.* 4.3.19)

The ancients took it for granted that the deeper the column,
the greater its thrusting power and momentum; what the opti-
mum number of additional rows was, we do not know. Surely, phalanxes with more than sixteen ranks must have also had other
considerations in mind—at times perhaps they may have wished

to shorten their exposed front (selfishly) in an effort to force reluctant allies to accept greater exposure along the battle line. In
any case, most phalanxes were generally described not as rows,
or ranks, or spears, but rather as "shields" in depth, which may
indicate that the main idea for the ranks in the middle and rear
was to push ahead with their shields and bodies. On occasion hoplite battle could be summarized simply an *othismos aspidon,* "the
push of shields." (Thuc. 4.96.2) The goal was to break the dead-
lock in those precious few minutes before exhaustion set in; the
perception of success, of movement forward, must have been
nearly as important as any actual progress ahead, since it kept
men hopeful that their strenuous efforts were not wasted.

Of course, there was never uniform pressure all down the line
of any phalanx. One wing, or even a small segment of an individual contingent, might sense a tremor of weakness in the specific group of enemy hoplites facing them and, so, a chance of
forward motion into their ranks. Yet, as they began to redouble
their efforts, they likewise had to be wary lest somewhere along
their own line their fellow warriors were like their yielding foe,
giving ground, being torn away from the phalanx, allowing the
enemy in the process to press in on their own sides and rear. We
hear two contrasting cries of exhortation in Greek battle that ex-
press these extremes: the shouts of exultation as men suddenly
believed that they had found success and merely needed additional effort, a last concentrated push, to crack the tottering enemy wide open—"Grant me one step forward and we shall have
victory" (Polyaen. *Strat.* 2.3.2–4; 3.9.27; 4.3.8); or, alternatively,
a call to the beleaguered to stand firm and not give in to the press
of bodies, not to be pushed off the field of battle:

> No, no, let him take a wide stance and stand up
>   strongly against them,
> digging both heels in the ground, biting his lip
>   with his teeth
>
> *(Tyrtaios 11.21–22)*

In some descriptions of hoplite battle it is evident that one wing
has its eye constantly on the other, worried (or perhaps sus-

picious) that its own successful push forward might be endangered by less successful or less trustworthy allies, who have no intention of following along, or even protecting their rear and sides,
during the rapid advance. For example, at the first battle of Mantineia in 418, the Mantineians broke the Peloponnesians' left
wing and routed them all the way back to their camp; at that
point, they were forced to break off the pursuit because they suddenly saw their own friends on the battle line, the Argives and
the Athenians, "defeated and the Spartans now coming against
them at full speed." (Thuc. 5.73) In the same manner, Xenophon
said the Peloponnesian left wing at Leuktra held its own until
they looked across at the crack Spartan troops on the right wing,
and then "saw that their own right wing was falling back," at which
stage, no doubt in horrified disbelief, they, too, collapsed. (*Hell.*
6.4.14)

How exactly was this mass pushing accomplished? References
to the great "weight" or "mass" of one phalanx must be to the
physical energy that row upon row of men generated; the infantry in the column behind the third rank—that is, rows four
through eight in most phalanxes—doubtless leaned with their
own bodies into the men ahead in the initial moments after the
two sides collided. In other words, each hoplite pressed with the
center of his shield against the back of the man to his front,
probably steadying his balance at times with his upright spear
shaft as he leaned forward. The shaft in this way served as a staff
of sorts—used to push off, it provided extra momentum as well
as balance. Xenophon had this image in mind when, in his
fictionalized account of battle, he noted that Egyptians were especially well suited for fighting in column since their peculiar
body-shields allowed the infantryman to rest the shoulder while
he pushed. (*Cyr.* 7.1.33) From reconstructions of the hoplite
shield, evidence of vase painting, and suggestions in Greek literature, we know that the lip of the top rim of the hollow Greek
model was ideal for precisely that steady pushing; the hoplite
supported the shield on his shoulder as he drove it against the
backs of his friends ahead. That way the weight was distributed

over the entire body rather than the left arm alone, while the shield's broad surface ensured that such pressure would be distributed evenly across the back of the man in front, neither tripping him nor forcing him off balance. Polybius simply declared that men push by "the weight of their bodies" (18.30.4); that same image of pushing is found again in many varieties of authors and can only confirm our belief that men in fact shoved everyone forward as they dug their bodies into the spacious dish of their own shield. (Thuc. 4.96.2; Asklepiodotos 5.2; Arr. *Tact.* 10.12; Ael. *Tact.* 14.6) The poet Theocritus describes how Castor urged Hercules "to put his shoulder behind his shield" (24.125), and the technique carried over into later warfare: Livy said of the famous battle at Zama that the Romans pushed their own men ahead by thrusting at their backs with the centers of their shields. (30.34)

One indication of the tremendous force generated by this mass of shields was the nature of the casualties inflicted after the initial impact: there are many references to men who either were trampled down or literally suffocated as they stood. Any man who stumbled or fell wounded was in danger of being ground up as the men in the rear lumbered forward, blinded by dust and the press of bodies, and ignorant of the exact sequence of events at the flash point of the battle. Fully armed hoplites found it difficult to scoop up a fallen warrior, to do much more than awkwardly sidestep his body. A Greek general could not call off the push even momentarily; to do so would suggest to the men in the rear that the fighting ahead was going poorly, causing them to think in terms of escape. While there were cases where those who fell could regain their feet, like Sphodrias' son, who went down three times at the battle of Leuktra (Xen. *Hell.* 5.4.33), such recoveries were probably rare and largely confined to the battle line at the front of the phalanx in the very few seconds following the collision, for at that time only there was still present in the killing zone a degree of fluidity in the combat which allowed some individual mobility. More commonly we hear of the trampling and even smashing of bodies on the ground, as if the

breastplates were no protection against marching feet. At the battle of Corinth, for example, the Argives were forced back against
a stockade by the advancing Peloponnesians. Not only were they
bowled over by the enemy advance, but the lack of any escape
ensured that many were flattened from the rear by their own men.
After the battle, Xenophon remarked that so many had fallen in
such a brief period that the pile of corpses looked like "stacks of
wheat, wood, or stones." (*Hell.* 4.4.12) In other words, there were
layers of dead men, suffocated and piled on top of one another.
Xenophon fails to tell us how high the pile was. Diodorus and
Thucydides both record such trampling of bodies in either the
general advance or retreat (e.g., Diod. 16.86.3; Thuc. 5.72), and
from Herodotus we receive a vivid description of the carnage that
could be caused by the steady pressure from the rear. At the last
stage of the battle of Thermopylai, the Persians, he says, "fell into
heaps," some into the ocean, but even more "were trampled to
death by their own infantry." (7.223) The Roman poet Lucan
could envision a battle where the pressure was so great that "every
corpse remained standing" (4.787), an image that was perhaps
not creative fantasy if men were caught and suffocated from pressure at both front and rear. Even in Roman battle, where there
was much greater fluidity, Ammianus claims he saw combat
where the dead remained upright, so dense had the fighting apparently become. (18.8.12)

When vase painters attempt the difficult portrayal of the
group effort, they usually show one or two Greek hoplites stumbling, about to go under the feet of the general mêlée. (Lorimer
pl. 11) In sculpture, we see similar evidence of the pressure: for
example, the frieze of the Siphnian treasury at Delphi depicts a
downed warrior about to be trampled by the oncoming enemy.
(Ducrey pl. 174) Some of those who first went down in the trampling may have been the elder hoplites, or those with less skill at
or appetite for the fighting. But since the maintenance of ranks,
beating off the attack while keeping in formation, was just as important as inflicting casualties on the enemy, even a hoplite of
the middle ranks possessing little skill or strength with the spear

and shield, or even little desire to kill, served his comrades well by keeping in position as he was pushed forward—his body occupying until his death a crucial link in the preservation of the entire formation. S. L. A. Marshall points out that the maintenance of a unit in modern battle often depends not merely on those who lead the way, but also on those who follow:

> The inaction of the passive individuals does not have a demoralizing effect on those who are making tactical use of their firepower. To the contrary, the presence of the former enable the latter to keep going. Every potential effective along the line who is within sight of any other soldier adds moral strength to the line. It is only when men begin to give ground that courage wavers all along the line. And while it is clear beyond challenge that the true defensive strength of the position is in those men who use their weapons, there is no proof that the soldier who will not take the initiative in firing against the enemy will quit the ground any sooner, under pressure, than his more aggressive comrade. *(65)*

At some point, on one side or the other, a portion of the phalanx could withstand the pressure no longer and began to be pushed back. At that point, the unity of the entire column was endangered and all men—both those who had advanced into gaps along the enemy line and those to the rear who were pushing ahead—began to think for the first time of their own individual survival. In other words, the final rout began. Sometimes there was a dramatic, sudden collapse at one particular point in the phalanx; the Greek word *pararrexis* and its cognates (the "breaking" of the line) best capture the meaning of such a disaster. While the progression of events that followed is easily imaginable, we are more interested in the peculiar *environment* within the phalanx at this, the last desperate stage of Greek hoplite battle.

First, there would have arisen on one side of the battle line the element of self-interest: each hoplite, in varying degrees depending on his position relative to the point of the collapse and on his own physical status, confronted the ever-growing danger posed by remaining in rank within the phalanx, fighting to the bitter end, and choosing to "stand his ground and fighting hard for his children and land." (Tyrtaios 12.33–34) In a matter of seconds, each soldier, sensing that the battle was lost and that rank after rank was falling away from the rear, would have to decide when, how, and if he could make good his escape. For some there was never any dilemma, only the choice made by the old war poets Kallinos and Tyrtaios, or of the Three Hundred at Thermopylai: to die in one's tracks as the enemy poured in now from the side and rear, and to avoid at any cost the disgrace of flight. So, for example, Xenophon recounts the violent last seconds of Anaxibios, who chose in 389 to die along with his fellow Spartan officers, while his men made a run for it: " 'Men, it is a fine thing for me to die right here, but you get to safety before you get caught up with the enemy.' Thus he spoke and taking up his shield from his shield-bearer he died fighting on the spot." (*Hell.* 4.8.38) Likewise, during the awful flight after the Athenian disaster at Amphipolis in 422, some of Kleon's beleaguered troops—far better men than their commanding general—kept their formation and repulsed the attack, many ending their lives in a last stand beneath a sea of missiles. (Thuc. 5.10.9) Surely, their courage was just as remarkable as that displayed in the earlier, more famous, slaughter at Thermopylai.

After the localized breakthrough there followed the wide-scale collapse (*trope*). Despite the admonitions of Homer and the Lyric poets, for many men retreat seemed preferable to glorious annihilation; it was simply a question of finding a suitable avenue of escape. The choice depended on various factors: the desperation of the situation, the availability of routes to safety, the degree to which panic and fear had overcome reason, the shame and personal disgrace felt by the more self-possessed. If the phalanx had retained any cohesion, an improvised fighting withdrawal was still possible, if difficult. True, initially to step backward away from the enemy, re-form the ranks, turn around 180 degrees, and establish a credible rear guard was not easy, but it offered the best chance for saving both reputation and lives. During the Peloponnesian disaster at Olpai in 426, Thucydides describes how most of the men, in the panic and disorder, suffered terribly in the wild retreat; the exceptions were the Mantineians, "who kept their ranks and made good their escape." (3.108.3) Likewise, at the battle of Solygeia, the Corinthians retired in order from their initial setback, formed up again on higher ground, and stood ready once more for another Athenian onslaught. (Thuc. 4.44.2) Later, in a battle against the Arcadians in 365, the Spartans gave way before the multitude of their attackers. Yet, as we would expect, they did so in mass, their formation intact until they had room to re-form their phalanx properly and try once more to withstand the enemy. (Xen. *Hell.* 7.4.24) Once again, nothing in Xenophon's account suggests that the Spartans, singly or even in small groups, chose to run for safety. Even at Leuktra in 371, the greatest military catastrophe in the history of Sparta, the smashed columns, despite significant losses, somehow managed to retire in order to their camp, ground their shields, and re-form their men again into battle formation; indeed, they brought out the body of their dead king Kleombrotos from the midst of the victorious Thebans. (Xen. *Hell.* 6.4.14) We receive a similar picture of such courage and discipline from the steadfastness of the Swiss pikemen of the fifteenth century, whose calm resembled the Spartans' in defeat:

> The battle of St. Jacob, mad and unnecessary though it was, might serve as an example to deter the boldest enemy from meddling with men who preferred annihilation to retreat. Possessed by the single idea that their phalanx could bear down any obstacle, the confederates deliberately crossed the Birs in face of an army of fifteen times their strength. . . . It was no light matter to engage with an enemy who would not retire before any superiority in numbers, who was always ready for the fight, who would neither give nor take quarter. (*Oman 2.264*)

Most armies, however, lacked the skill and nerve of Spartan or latter-day Swiss troops, and so the fear of death was an overriding concern: they had neither the chance nor perhaps even the will to re-form ranks and face the enemy spears again. In such circumstances only two choices remained. One was to seek out

small pockets of brave men who might retreat in groups of twos
and threes, or fives and tens, and make the enemy pay dearly for
any incautious pursuit. This was the most rational alternative under desperate circumstances, but it occurred infrequently. After
all, at this stage of the final collapse, it required an uncommon
degree of courage for a hoplite to hold onto his shield and move
laterally at a fairly slow pace across the battlefield in search of the
few who still were in control of their senses—all the while fending off at a disadvantage repeated attacks of the pressing enemy.
The Syracusans, defeated in their first encounter in 415 with the
Athenian hoplite army of invasion, seem to have maintained such
semblance of order, for Thucydides says that, although their phalanx was "broken in two," they still managed to fall back into some
type of group in their retreat. We get the impression that small
bands, perhaps aided by cavalry protection, drifted back on their
own until they could arrive together in sufficient numbers to re-
form the ranks. (6.70)

The best examples of such a fighting withdrawal of like-
minded individuals banding together to save themselves during
a general panic are found in a series of anecdotes that surround
the military career of the philosopher Socrates. From Plutarch
we learn that after the Athenian collapse at Delion in 424, Socrates led a small company back to safety at Oropos. (*Mor.* 581 D)
Plato, in his *Symposium,* describes that same incident in Alcibiades'
recollection that Socrates "calmly looked around at both his
friends and the enemy, all the while making it clear even from a
distance that if anyone were to attack such a man as he, he would
put up a considerable resistance. Accordingly, he made his way
back without harm along with his comrades." Alcibiades finishes
his account with an especially interesting observation on the behavior of hoplites during a phalanx collapse: "Indeed, in war the
enemy will not dare to press home their attack against men such
as this; instead, they go after the ones who are fleeing away in
complete disorder." (221 B) Apparently, in a similar rout later,
after the Athenian defeat at Amphipolis, Socrates in like manner
had saved Alcibiades and brought him out alive: "Both Socrates

and Alcibiades distinguished themselves in the fierce battle. Yet, once Alcibiades fell wounded, Socrates stood over him, defended him, and with manifest courage saved him and his armor. . . . " During the flight of the Athenians after the battle of Delion, Alcibiades rode up and saw Socrates retreating on foot with a small company; he rode close by and helped to defend him although "the enemy was pressing them hard and killing many." (Plut. *Alc.* 7.3) Plato, again in his *Laches,* must be referring to this resistance of like-spirited brave men when he suggests that the skill of fighting in armor, while of some value in the general mêlée, is of utmost importance "when the ranks have been broken, and there is a need for one-on-one fighting either in pressing home the attack against one who is offering resistance during his flight, or in fending off the pursuers." (182 A) Here Socrates, no doubt recalling his combat experience, is made to say that in the confused collision and subsequent pushing between phalanxes, skill in arms is not so important. Once the rout begins, however, the fluidity in battle requires hoplites to duel it out as individuals, if they are to save their lives.

The other alternative open to a man in a defeated phalanx was simply to throw away his weapons—his shield, spear, and helmet—and, like the poets Archilochos and Alkaios, to make a run for it on his own. Besides the odium attached to such a perfectly human response, this simple, reckless flight offered perhaps the worst chance of survival. Even in modern battle running away has been often about the most dangerous thing a man could do. "In the First World War it was often as dangerous (sometimes more so) to retreat, to surrender, or simply to remain *in situ* as to push on to the objective or to continue the fight." (Kellet 304) Not only did a hoplite endanger his friends by diminishing whatever chance still existed to re-form ranks, but more importantly, he offered his back as an easy target for a pursuer. The enemy were likely to target such easy "kills" first, since these men were now unarmored and equipped only with short swords, if anything. Obviously, they offered a much better opportunity than the pockets of stout resistance made up of those like Socrates and his friends. To gang up in a group effort against such scattered, defenseless targets might bring some strange pleasure in an easy killing that bore no real accompanying risks:

> We, a thousand, are the murderers of the seven men who fell
>   dead. We overtook them with our running feet.
>
> (Archil. 101)

So might sing Archilochos when he was on the offensive against unarmed, running men—the same poet who bragged that he, too, on one occasion had thrown away his own shield and run away from battle. In much greater detail Tyrtaios aptly described the pathetic scene of slaughter when men turned their backs and fled in terror:

> For once a man reverses and runs in the terror of battle,
>   he offers his back, a tempting mark to spear from behind,
> and it is a shameful sight when a dead man lies in the dust there,
>   driven through from behind by the stroke of an enemy spear.
>
> (11.17–20)

That "shameful sight" of the trapped hoplite is a favorite theme on both vase painting and sculpture, where we see the fallen soldier, in vain drawing forth his short sword before the final coup de grace of spear thrusts from a victorious enemy. (Anderson 1970: pl. 10)

Perhaps the reason why mob flight rather than the ordered withdrawal of the columns was the more frequent end to hoplite battle lies in the utter vulnerability of the entire phalanx to the weakness of a very few individuals. If a mere one or two hoplites for some inexplicable reason broke rank, that sudden departure to the rear was perceived immediately by everyone around, men who might not stop to question their decision but follow instinctively, as if the fainthearts had discovered some unknown mortal danger. Besides, few could stomach the idea that their continued resistance to the enemy, their bravery in attack, served only to allow the safe flight of the cowardly while risking their own eventual destruction. S. L. A. Marshall saw nearly the same phenome-

non among modern infantry during the Second World War—
among troops who fought in line (rather than in the close physical proximity of the ancient phalanx) and should have been far
less vulnerable to the panic of a few:

> In every case this something could have been avoided. That was the
> common denominator, that the trouble began because somebody was
> thoughtless, somebody failed to tell other men what he was doing. I
> think it can be laid down as a rule that nothing is more likely to col-
> lapse a line of infantry in combat than the sight of a few of the num-
> ber in full and unexplained flight to the rear. Precipitate motion in
> the wrong direction is an open invitation to disaster. *(145–46)*

Perhaps the best example of such a disaster was the so-called tearless battle between the allied Peloponnesians and the Spartans
in 368. The allies could not endure the prospect of the Spartan
charge and simply turned and ran away before their very eyes.
In their wild panic they were butchered unmercifully by Archidamos and his various contingents. Diodorus claims that nearly
ten thousand men were cut down from the rear. (15.72; cf. Xen.
Hell. 7.1.31)

Besides the pursuit of hoplites, there was even greater danger
from the entrance of both cavalry and light-armed skirmishers.
During the initial battle these auxiliary corps were kept largely
out of the fighting since they had no chance of pressing an attack against their betters who held the firm line of hoplite
shields. But now for the first and only time since the minor prebattle skirmishing, it was possible for them to enter the battlefield and demonstrate that they were, after all, effective fighters
as they rode or ran down the helpless prize troops of the enemy.
After the Athenian collapse at Delion, for example, Thucydides
singled out the efforts of the Boiotian and Locrian cavalry who
had the best success against the fleeing enemy. (4.96.8–9) The
same thing happened in 429 during the Athenian retreat to Poteidaia. There Chalcidian cavalry and missile throwers caused more
than four hundred casualties among the fleeing Athenians and
killed all their generals. (Thuc. 2.79) Xenophon, in his *Cavalry
Commander*, is speaking of such ideal occasions when he bluntly

urges that horsemen should be sure to attack an enemy fleeing in disorder:

> Always the pursuer must be stronger than the prey. If you think about it, it is easy to see the point. Even animals without any of the intelligence of humans, such as hawks, snatch anything that is left unguarded and then withdraw into safety before they can be caught. (*4.18*)

16 *Confusion, Misdirection, and Mob Violence*

> Mon centre cède, ma droite recule, situation excellente. J'attaque!
>
> —*Marshal Foch*

There was generally a certain regularity to Greek battle: charge, collision, hand-to-hand combat, push, and eventual rout. This sequence of events is borne out by ancient observers who developed a vocabulary to describe what they saw or heard: the charge (*ephodos* or *epidrome*), the clash of spears (*doratismos*), the hand-to-hand struggle (*en chersi*), the push (*othismos*), and the collapse (*trope*). Yet, to consider hoplite battle in such stages may be misleading if one assumes that there were always such "segments" of distinct action rather than a continuous blur of movement, uninterrupted and always somewhat unsure of its next course. The hoplites on the battlefield probably never had a clear idea whether their phalanx had moved onward from the collision to successful penetration of the enemy, or was on the verge of being pushed into fatal disorder. They could have only the vaguest sense, mostly through the contact of bodies and the press of flesh rather than through vision or hearing, that the battle was turning toward victory or defeat. Infantrymen saw only flesh in motion everywhere, bodies at their front, rear, and side, corpses at their feet, disorder and chaos, not a progression of predictable events.

Also when both sides were intertwined so that there were no lines of advance and retreat, no clear demarcation between sides, it was hard to be sure of who was an enemy, who an ally. A Greek hoplite did not wear a uniform, and only the insignia on his shield indicated which force he belonged to. The professional soldiers of Sparta might be distinguished by their peculiar, if not frightening, red tunics, but otherwise, once the two sides met, the uniformity of helmet and breastplate throughout the Greek world made soldiers nearly indistinguishable. And in the general fighting at close quarters, the letter or emblem attached to each shield was simply not enough to distinguish friend and foe, especially after the shields had been struck repeatedly in the collision and subsequent fighting. At one point, for example, in Aristophanes' *Acharnians* (1180), the emblem on Lamachos' shield simply breaks off. Moreover, we often hear of individual rather than national shield devices, and at times none at all. Because of the confusing, ever-changing alliances of the small city-states of Greece, there was not always a sure way of recognizing a "friendly" soldier. Also there might be no guarantee that troops necessarily were carrying their own shields. Xenophon relates such an incident when the Spartans in 392 came to the aid of their hard-pressed allies the Sikyonians at a small battle near Corinth. Pasimachos, the Spartan commander,

> took their shields away from the Sikyonians, and then attacked the Argive enemies with a force of volunteers. The Argives, however, since they saw the *Sigmas* [the Greek letter "s" for Sikyon] on the shields, were not at all afraid since they believed these men to be Sikyonians. At that point Pasimachos was supposed to have proclaimed: "By the twin gods, men of Argos, these *Sigmas* will trick you." (Hell. *4.4.10*)

Not only could hoplites not necessarily be identified by their dress, but their speech offered little clue either. Speakers of Doric or Attic Greek might find themselves facing each other across the battle line as their city-states allied themselves with those of another dialect. At the engagement on Epipolai in the heights above Syracuse, when the Athenians heard the Doric war cry they were confused as to whether it emanated from their own allies, the Argives and the Corcyraians, or from the enemy Peloponnesians and Syracusans. (Thuc. 7.44)

So hoplite battle was frequently enough a free-for-all of sorts between infantry who looked, dressed, fought, and spoke alike, and there is little wonder that often men had no idea whom they were fighting once their phalanxes had crashed and merged. Since the pressure of advancing and retreating lines varied, men might find their own colleagues out in front and nearly in their faces, while pockets of the *enemy* were at their side and perhaps already to their rear. Two consequences of such confusion are obvious: either the tragic, accidental wounding of friendly troops—also the scourge of modern high-tech warfare—or the sudden attack of an unseen and unexpected enemy. Keegan describes the accidental wounding that was common during the final hours of Waterloo:

> there are numerous authentic accounts of losses by "friendly fire"— and even "friendly" swordcuts—at Waterloo. Mercer describes at length how he suffered from a Prussian battery which mistook his men for French, inflicted on them more casualties than they had suffered throughout the day's fighting and were only silenced by the arrival of a Belgian battery—"beastly drunk and not at all particular as to which way they fired"—who in their turn mistook the Prussians for the enemy . . . Tomkinson, of the 16th Light Dragoons, reveals in an aside of his own how woundings could occur even between people well known to each other: a Frenchman had feigned surrender and then fired; "Lieutenant Beckwith . . . stood stiff and attempted to catch this man on his sword, he missed and nearly ran me through the body." *(193)*

We see such chaos clearly among the Athenians during the debacle on Epipolai. Thucydides remarks, "and thus at last all over the battlefield they fell into disorder with each other, once they were completely disoriented, friends among friends, citizens among citizens, not only did they frighten one another, but they even began fighting hand to hand, and scarcely could be separated." (7.44.8) The danger here, of course, was that the fighting might take on a life of its own between "former" friends who now had good cause to continue the killing. In our times, at the end of the Second World War, Allied planners feared comparable results on a theater level if they penetrated too far into Germany and linked up with the Russians on the move, in the heat of bat-

tle. The supreme allied commander "was reluctant to enter into
a contest with the Russians for Berlin. That might prove not only
embarrassing for the loser but—in the event of an unexpected
meeting between the onrushing armies—catastrophic for both
forces." (Ryan 209)

Certainly, the same general confusion occurred often enough
on the ancient battlefield, as can be seen in Thucydides' description of the initial Athenian success at the battle of Delion in 424.
There at one point, the Athenian right wing overwhelmed and
then virtually encircled the left side of the Boiotian alliance stationed opposite them, trapping hundreds of enemy Thespians
in the process who were unable to make good their escape. Soon
the Athenians had enveloped the entire Thespian wing, so that
when both sides of the Athenians, now crescent-shaped, met up,
they became "confused in the encirclement, mistook and thus
killed one another." (4.96.4) Although the Athenians and the
Boiotian confederates spoke different dialects and may have had
different insignia, the Athenians must nevertheless have been so
caught up in the spirit of the killing, or so disoriented, that they
continued to strike at anything which appeared in their faces—
until they ended up fighting their own kinsmen. Indeed, Thucydides' matter-of-fact description assumes that this was a perfectly
understandable occurrence among men who could hardly see
or hear and thus could distinguish an enemy only by his relative
position on the battlefield. When the sense of direction was lost,
hoplites must have had no real idea whom they were attacking.
Later in that same battle, the Athenians wrongly surmised that a
mere two regiments of enemy cavalry that appeared suddenly
over a hill were, in fact, an entire fresh army; they senselessly
broke in panic and fled the battlefield altogether. (4.96.3–7; cf.
1.50.1–2)

It is understandable that once hoplites became turned around
and lost their direction, they were liable to kill anyone in their
face, friend or foe. Yet, even beyond that confusion there was no
doubt a considerable amount of accidental wounding and killing
within the phalanx itself. During the push, hoplites in ranks two

through four were liable to catch the sharp butt spike of their colleagues ahead as they pressed against their backs. After all, front-line troops in the first three rows were fighting for their lives with leveled spears against the enemy. They could hardly worry about the danger of their own butt spikes to the men behind. At the same time, the men in the front row or two might themselves be wounded on the flank from the spear tips of those in the rank behind. Since the spear was a double-pointed weapon, lethal at both ends of the shaft, and extended far beyond the reach of its holder in both directions, there must have been frequent, unavoidable accidents as men struggled to keep on their feet during the push. Perhaps, on rarer occasions, a sword or spear might wound its owner if he was suddenly shoved off balance. Even more commonly, tripping and a subsequent trampling of friendly hoplites occurred. How could those to the rear know exactly the conditions of battle around the men in file ahead? If a hoplite in the initial rows slipped, he could soon be trampled, despite his breastplate, by the feet of his own oncoming, unknowing men of the rear. If his spear snapped and shield fell, he might be driven back by the enemy into his own troops, becoming wedged, if not suffocated, while standing, between these two sources of pressure. At Mantineia in 418 King Agis smashed the allied center and left wing at the first onset; right away men began to trample each other in their desperate attempt to back away from the oncoming Spartans. (Thuc. 5.72.4)

Although panic among those removed from the fighting usually caused most columns to collapse from the rear, in rare cases the phalanx disintegrated right at the front. As those in the first three ranks found their situation desperate, they might begin to step back or attempt to turn around and force a path out through the oncoming men behind—men who, at first, in ignorance of the growing disaster ahead, probably continued to push forward for a time. The result was a collision in the middle of the column: front and rear met head-on in fear. (E.g., Diod. 14.104.4; Eur. *Andromache* 1136–47) Livy envisioned the same scene at the Roman disaster at Lake Trasimene in 217, where during the general panic, he relates, men turned and fell, and then were trampled by their own legionnaires. (22.6)

In the general mêlée there was often no clear idea of whom a man might actually be attacking. Instead, much of the fighting consisted of random slashing and stabbing. Three hoplites, for example, might center their spears on one enemy who happened at that second to be caught as the battle line undulated and changed. Again, two hoplites might find themselves enveloped by ten or more, cut off and entrapped by an advancing pocket of adversaries. On vase paintings we often see such small groups of hoplites in threes and fours advancing against each other, as if the artists saw these pockets of fighters as the best (and only) way of capturing combat between two phalanxes. (Lorimer 84; Greenhalgh pl. 44) And since the spear tips of the first three ranks of each phalanx initially protruded into the killing zone, there was always an anonymous wall of points, "the swarm of spears," into which the enemy advanced. Two-thirds of these weapons were held by men who were at least one rank removed from the first collision; with their helmets on, given the dust and reduced vision, they perhaps had no idea at all whom or what they had targeted, no sense whether they had wounded their adversary, or, in fact, killed one or more men outright. In most descriptions of hoplite battle, there are rarely any references to individual claims of specific "kills." Men who boasted of their victims usually referred to the one-on-one skirmishing, cavalry attacks, or the death of some notable person—like Anticrates' claim that he had speared the Theban commander Epameinondas at Mantineia. (Plut. *Ages.* 35.1–2) Individual rewards for bravery and valor in battle were determined by such criteria as maintenance of order in the ranks under extreme difficulty, the rescue of the wounded in the face of the enemy (Pl. *Sym.* 220 D), extraordinary daring in leading the advance, or becoming the first to mount a wall or reach the enemy camp. (Diod. 14.53.4; Polyb. 6.39; Thuc. 4.116.2) Rarely, as we would expect in this type of group effort, do we hear of recognition given to those who have claimed the most enemy killed. Outside of epic poetry, soldiers perhaps might have really no idea how many men, if any, they had killed.

Battle quickly exhausted those in the phalanx, both physically and psychologically—perhaps in little less than an hour's time. The killing was face-to-face; each blow required a maximum physical effort to drive the weapon through the bronze of his opponent, all this to be performed while the hoplite carried armor and was pushed constantly by the ranks to the rear. Since there was no real distance between the men who gave and received such blows, a sea of blood was everywhere. Hoplites were soon covered by the gore of those whom they met, struck, and were pressed on into. References to the blood of battle in literature are meant to be taken literally as firsthand, eyewitness descriptions from men who knew what the killing at close quarters was really like. For example, Tyrtaios says that only the true warrior can "endure to look upon the bloody slaughter." (12.11) Mimnermos had that same image in mind when he wrote of a great anonymous warrior of the past who made his way through the clash of the "bloody battle." (14.7) So, too, after the conclusion of the battle of Pydna in 168, Scipio was said to have come off the field "covered with the blood" of his enemies, "carried away by the pleasure" (Plut. *Aem.* 22.4); here, it seems the Roman commander had nearly become "blood drunk" from the killing.

Much of the psychological shock also came from the loss of relatives and friends right before each infantryman's eyes; he must have been abundantly aware that lifelong companions were being butchered a few feet away. Xenophon gives us a glimpse of such slaughter when he describes the casualties in the Spartan right wing at Leuktra in 371. First, the Spartan king Kleombrotos fell wounded, then Deinon, his chief officer, and, by him, Sphodrias, another top aide, and Sphodrias' own son. In other words, within a few seconds many of the elite of the Spartan army, lifelong friends and relatives, were killed under the thrust of Epameinondas' Theban mass. At that point the rest of their comrades suddenly gave way and were pushed off the battlefield. Perhaps the shock of seeing so many of their own top fighters wiped out in a single stroke was too much to endure. (Xen. *Hell.* 6.4.14) Kellet writes of the effect of such casualties on modern troops:

> The effect on the unwounded of seeing men hit around them must have been particularly trying in the close-order formations of the eighteenth and nineteenth centuries. Any advance or retreat involved passing over a carpet of dead and wounded, both enemy and friendly, and simply remaining in position required men largely to ignore death and injury of comrades close around them. Captain Grenow wrote of the Grenadier Guards' square at Waterloo: "It was impossible to move a yard without treading on a wounded comrade or upon the bodies of the dead." *(264)*

Throughout Greek battle a number of men not only became confused and disoriented under the strain of the killing, but also lost their senses to such a degree that they no longer may have even known what was going on, suffering from what we might call "battle fatigue" or "battle shock." In nearly every Greek battle we hear of *epiphanies,* stories of gods and heroes who at a certain moment descend to fight alongside a particular contingent. (E.g., cf. Pritchett 3.11–46) Most are described as occurring either before or after the battle, and thus can be explained as faked prebattle stratagems to encourage morale, or postmortem mythmaking to explain some superhuman or unbelievable achievement of arms. Yet a few seem almost hallucinatory and may not be later, deliberate creations of fantasy. Rather, under the stresses of battle, men claimed to have seen images before their eyes during the actual fighting. Perhaps the best known is the reported vision of Epizelos, an Athenian at the battle of Marathon, who "saw" an enormous hoplite pass by to kill the man at his side:

> At this engagement the following strange thing occurred: a certain Epizelos, the son of Kouphagoras, as he fought in the ranks and proved himself a brave fighter, suddenly lost sight in both eyes. Yet, he had neither been struck or pierced in the body by any weapon. From that moment on he remained blind for the rest of his life. I have

heard that Epizelos used to attribute his misfortune to the following cause: a great armed hoplite had appeared opposite him, whose entire shield was by his beard. This phantom had passed him by, but had killed the soldier stationed at his side. *(Hdt. 6.117)*

At the same battle others were sure they had seen an armed Theseus who led them on against the Persians. (Paus. 1.15.4; Plut. *Thes.* 35)

Other signs of battle shock and depression are seen in random stories of hoplites irrationally exposing themselves to danger or deliberately choosing to die in battle. For example, Xenophon relates that in 365 after Andromachos, commander of the Elean cavalry, led his men in a disastrous attack against the Arcadians, he killed himself on the spot. (*Hell.* 7.4.19) Deliberate exposure in battle was nearly the same as suicide, and on occasion we hear of hoplites who intentionally exposed themselves in such a way as to ensure their own demise. That was the course which the blind Eurytos took at Thermopylai when he ordered his servant to lead him toward the last stand of the Three Hundred. (Hdt. 7.229) Likewise, Anaxibios, the Spartan commander who faced the Athenian Iphikrates in 389, once he saw his men caught in a hopeless slaughter, ordered everyone to flee. But he intended to perish there as well; twelve other Peloponnesians chose the same fate. (Xen. *Hell.* 4.8.38)

V

Aftermath

17   *The Killing Field*

At dawn the next morning the Carthaginians applied themselves to collecting the spoils and viewing the carnage, which even to an enemy's eyes was a shocking spectacle. All over the field Roman soldiers lay dead in their thousands, horse and foot mingled, as the shifting phases of battle, or the attempt to escape, had brought them together. Here and there wounded men covered with blood, who had been roused to consciousness by the morning cold, were dispatched by a quick blow as they struggled to rise amongst the corpses; others were found still alive with the sinews in their thighs and behind their knees sliced through, baring their throats and necks and begging who would to spill what little blood they had left. Some had buried their heads in the ground, having apparently dug themselves holes, and by smothering their faces with earth had choked themselves to death.

—*Livy, on the aftermath of Cannae (Selincourt trans.)*

The fearful spectacle of the battlefield, heaped with dead and wounded, in conjunction with the heaviness of his head, the news that some twenty generals he knew well were among the killed and wounded, and the sense of impotence of his once mighty army, made an unexpected impression on Napoleon, who was usually fond of looking over the dead and wounded, proving thereby, as he imagined, his dauntless spirit. On that day, the awful spectacle of the battlefield overcame this dauntless spirit, which he looked upon as a merit and proof of greatness.

—*Tolstoy*, War and Peace

Unlike modern battle, fighting in the ancient world ceased after a few hours, and the field of conflict fell silent. Ground was not fought over again and again. The bodies of the dead were left in peace for a few hours—spared the indignity that our "civilized" age visits upon the fallen of being ground up by artillery and motorized transport. The field of the past hours' killing had an eerie appearance as men viewed the carnage in the immediate aftermath. Given the formalized nature of Greek hoplite fighting, the battle itself might be reconstructed from the position of the dead.

Of course, the scene of the initial collision and subsequent push was a sickening spectacle, for there the killing had been brutal, confined, and intense. The bodies were piled, perhaps as many as two or three high, as each side had been driven into the spears of its adversary in a desperate effort to create some type of forward advance. It was here that nearly everyone had died "with all the wounds in front" (Diod. 15.55.2); they had been "climbing" over the corpses of their friends to find some inroad ahead. Xenophon remarked of the dead after Koroneia: "where they had fallen in with each other the earth was red with their blood, corpses of both friend and enemy were lying with each other, shields smashed, spears snapped, swords drawn from their scabbards, some of which were thrown to the ground, some fixed in bodies, others still in the hands of the dead." (*Ages.* 2.14–15) And where the trapped Argives at Corinth were forced to face the onslaught of the Spartan phalanx, they likewise fell into heaps; once rigor mortis set in, they were like "stacks of wheat, wood, or stones," Xenophon says. (*Hell.* 4.4.12) It was such a "pile" of dead friends and enemies into which Pelopidas fell wounded in battle near Mantineia, where he lay "buried among the pile of dead friends and enemies" until he was pulled out alive by Epameinondas. (Plut. *Pel.* 4.5) So, too, Herodotus tells us, the Persians who ran into the spears of Leonidas and his Spartans at Thermopylai "fell in heaps"; unable to advance beyond this line of enemy spears, they simply piled on top of one another, row after row. (7.223) And the late Roman historian Ammianus saw the same thing in a struggle between Illyrians and Persians:

> So crowded together were the dead that the corpses of the slain, propped up by the sheer mass, were not able to find space to fall over. One soldier in front of me, with his head cleaved—a strong sword

thrust had sliced it into equal parts—pressed in on all sides, stood erect like a tree stump. (*18.8.12*)

At Pydna in 168, Marcus, the son of Cato, at some point lost his sword; once he had regained that ground he found it buried "under a great pile of weapons and corpses." (Plut. *Aem.* 21)

Very early in Greek vase painting we see a clear attempt to depict this "stack" of men on the battlefield; these images suggest that the pile of corpses was known as a traditional part of any Greek battle. (E.g., cf. Ahlberg pls. 6, 57, 87, 88, 89, 90) Keegan describes a similar picture of the French dead at Agincourt:

> Brief reflection will, moreover, demonstrate that the "heap higher than a man" is a chronicler's exaggeration. Human bodies, even when pushed about by bulldozers, do not, as one can observe if able to keep one's eyes open during the film of mass burials at Belsen, pile into walls, but lie in shapeless sprawling hummocks. When stiffened by rigor mortis, they can be laid in stacks, as one can see in film of the burial parties of a French regiment carting its dead from the field after an attack in the Second Battle of Champagne (September 1915). But men falling to weapon-strokes in the front line, tripping over those already down, will lie at most two or three deep. For the heaps to rise higher, they must be climbed by the next victims: and the "six-foot heaps" of Agincourt could have been topped-out only if men on either side had been ready and able to duel together while balancing on the corpses of twenty or thirty others. The notion is ludicrous rather than grisly. . . . The mounds thus raised were big and hideous enough to justify some priestly-rhetoric—but not to deny the English entry into the French positions. (*107*)

Once the phalanx had collapsed, trails of corpses led away on one side from the pile in the center of the field toward one periphery; many of them were probably the remains of men who had been trampled in the mad rush to the rear. The field of carnage would have been asymmetrical: a mountain of mixed dead roughly in the center of the plain, but, except for a random missile casualty, a near-complete absence of bodies on one side of the pile, where men had marched in victory on into the territory of the enemy phalanx; on the other side, the ground of the defeated was sometimes thick with bodies of dead and wounded who had been run over by both friend and foe; men run down in retreat or perhaps trampled as they tried in vain to free themselves from the confines of their formation. Here, most were probably from one side—fathers and sons, brothers, boyhood friends lying together. These were not the bodies of soldiers who had fallen face forward in a final give-and-take, with wounds in their faces and chests, their hands still grasping their weapons. Rather, they were the remains of frightened, terrified men who had been butchered anonymously from the rear by unseen foes, easy targets of slaughter in their final seconds of confused panic, and then trampled by a succession of heavy feet. No wonder that Tyrtaios wrote of these figures:

> For once a man reverses and runs in the terror of battle,
> he offers his back, a tempting mark to spear from behind,
> and it is a shameful sight when a dead man lies in the dust there,
> driven through from behind by the stroke of an enemy spear.
>
> (11.17–20)

Finally, there were random corpses of men who had made their way clear of the phalanx and had run free, only to be ridden down by cavalry or light-armed pursuers. For example, Plutarch says of the Macedonian debacle at Pydna in 168 that "the slaughter of those who had fled was tremendous, so much so that both the plain and the foothills were filled up with corpses." (*Aem.* 21.3) Yet, more commonly there were smaller, scattered scenes of individual battle, one-sided and brief, all the way to the rough terrain. The bodies of the slain, then, were probably scattered for thousands of yards, if not several miles. Xenophon, for example, during the retreat of the Ten Thousand, retraced the final steps of his panicked troops by a long trail of strewn corpses of those who had been butchered by the Babylonian cavalry of Pharnabazos. (*An.* 6.5.5–6) Not much later, in the aftermath of Kynoskephalai in 364, Pelopidas' Thessalians chased the routed enemy for a "great distance" and then "filled the entire countryside with their corpses, killing more than three thousand of them." (Plut. *Pel.* 32.7) We can be sure that bodies were strewn out in twos and threes for miles on end.

The dead told yet another story, for there was a more human side to the wreckage: the sight of corpses of relatives and friends who had been stationed and stood by each other throughout the battle, or on rare occasions, men of the same tribe who perished together in toto—like the Athenian dead at the battle of Plataia, all from the single tribe Aiantis. (Plut. *Arist.* 19) When the phalanx of Thespians at Delion in 424 were surrounded by the Athenians in the first stages of battle, they were cut off and annihilated. As a result, the Thebans invaded their territory sometime later and dismantled the walls of their small city, for too few men had returned from Delion to resist them. Thucydides adds in explanation that this exercise could take place because "the flower of the [Thespians'] youth had all been destroyed in the encounter with the Athenians." (4.133.1) From this angle, the piles of corpses told not of collision, push, turning, and rout, but rather of the joint fate of entire groups of kin, families, and comrades—a small holocaust, so to speak, of closely connected men who lay beside each other dead, just as they had fought side by side while alive. A similar picture arose after the Spartan debacle at Leuktra in 371. There, an entire veteran cadre of friends and relatives had perished on the spot within a few minutes of each other, some four hundred elite of the seven hundred Spartiates who fought in the phalanx of Peloponnesians. (Xen. *Hell.* 6.4.15) Not much earlier, at the Nemea River in 394, there must have been a similar slaughter. Most of the Spartans' allies gave way, but at one point along the line the men of Pellene collided with the Thespians. Both sides "fought it out and fell in their places" (Xen. *Hell.* 4.2.20), as if these small contingents had chosen annihilation rather than flight. But the best-known instance was the sight of the Theban Sacred Band, every one of whose members lay massacred on the field of Chaironeia in 338 after their fatal encounter with the Macedonian pikemen of Philip:

> After the battle, as Philip was looking over the dead, he stopped at the spot where the three hundred lay: all slain where they had met the long spears of the Macedonians. The corpses were still in their ar-

mor and mixed up with one another, and so he became amazed when
he learned that these were the regiment of lovers and beloved. "May
all perish," he said, "who suspect that these men did or suffered anything disgraceful." *(Plut.* Pel. *18.5)*

Often a macabre fascination with the dead is illustrated in the
many accounts in Greek literature where there are references to
a postmortem "viewing" by a host of onlookers. Indeed, there was
almost an urgent need to look upon the dead as they lay, before
the bodies were carted away and the enormity of the scene was
lost. We see perhaps the same interest with the battlefield dead
in early Greek art where a great effort is made to portray the deceased with haunting realism. Of all the figures in early vase painting and sculpture, corpses seem to draw the most detailed treatment—limp arms, hands with fingers extended, head in a
dropped position. (Ahlberg pls. 87, 88, 89) Of course, it was a
standard practice for the victorious commander to view the
dead, to examine closely the remains of those who had killed
many of his own men and were now for the first and last time to
be approached with impunity. The custom lasted for millennia—
it was known to Napoleon. So, for example, Philip of Macedon
surveyed the Greek dead after his victory at Chaironeia just as
Xerxes had done after the final Greek defeat at Thermopylai
when he hunted out the body of the Spartan king Leonidas. (Hdt.
7.238) There are indications that the battlefield was also visited
by others who may have had no part in the fighting. After the
Athenian victory at Marathon, the two thousand Peloponnesians
who arrived too late to join in the fighting nevertheless marched
on past Athens to the battlefield. Herodotus explains, "they went
out of a desire to look upon the Persian dead." (7.120)
Xenophon illustrates that same curiosity when he writes of the
aftermath of Koroneia that "there was now the chance to view
the spectacle" (*Ages.* 2.14); apparently the carnage was unbelievable where the Theban phalanx collided head-on with the
Spartans. Finally, we must not forget Xerxes' pathetic attempt to
hide his disastrous losses at Thermopylai by burying the dead

quickly in concealed trenches. He apparently expected a multitude of curious onlookers who would converge on the scene, eager to walk among the corpses, and he was not disappointed. So
predictable was this practice that the Persians offered to supply
boats to ferry the curious over to the battlefield to examine the
slaughtered Greeks; nevertheless, "so large was the number of
those who wished to look that it became difficult to find any"; no
wonder that Herodotus rightly called it a "sight-seeing" tour.
(Hdt. 8.24–25; 8.66.1)

Besides the sheer concentration of bodies, the most common
sight to these onlookers would have been the quantity of spilled
blood and gore. In some of the larger battles—Delion, Leuktra,
or Plataia—thousands of corpses lay with huge, gaping wounds
from the spear and sword. Since the flesh was never incinerated
as it came to be in modern battles by the explosion of bomb and
shell, and because the entry and exit wounds created by double-
edged iron spearheads tend to be larger than those caused by
small-arms fire, the bodies would have drained much of their
body fluids upon the ground. Walking among the pile of corpses
entailed treading everywhere over stained earth and pools of
blood. Polybius says that after Zama the battlefield was so thick
with bloody corpses that it was nearly impossible to advance over
the ground (15.14.1)—which suggests that many had attempted
to do just that. In his famous description of Koroneia, Xenophon
recalls that the very earth "had turned red," a phrase that was
probably no exaggeration. (*Ages.* 2.14) And in Sicily at the final
slaughter of the Athenians in 413, the bodies of the dead lay piled
on top of each other in the water, their spilled blood turning the
very current red. (Thuc. 7.84.5–7.85.1) Plutarch recorded a similar picture after the death of some 25,000 Macedonian pikemen
at Pydna. The entire plain there, he says, was filled with corpses
and the river Leukos ran red with their blood. Again, this seems
likely: if each of the fallen men lost a mere third of his six quarts
of blood, either during the final moments of death or after the
corpse lay in the dust, there could have been more than ten thousand gallons to soak the field. (Plut. *Aem.* 21.3)

The removal of this human debris was especially trying. Thousands of men had marched forth and collided in mass attack. Now, there might be thousands of those same men who lay dead, and the disposal of their bodies required prompt attention. Panoplies of bronze armor, difficult under any circumstance to cart away given their unusual weight and size, even without the problems of rigor mortis, were scattered for miles about and had to be removed from the stiffened corpses as quickly as possible. Shields, greaves, helmets, spears, swords, and breastplates could be sold on the open market or, if in good condition, reemployed by any of the victors whose own equipment was either damaged or inferior. More importantly, they were often used as dedicatory offerings to be presented as part of the battlefield trophy, to be shipped off to local temples and shrines, or hoarded and given over to the gods at the major Panhellenic sanctuaries. After the Athenian disaster at Epipolai in 413, for example, Thucydides remarks that the Syracusan victors found far more weapons on the field than could be accounted for by the corresponding number of corpses. (7.45) No doubt, in nearly every battle, many survivors, like the Lyric poet Archilochos, threw away their arms once they began running in earnest. It was not the sheer number alone of the panoplies that posed problems, but the more mundane task of unbuckling these arms from a dead corpse, which was initially rigid but soon was bloated and swelling. The Roman commander Lucullus did not exaggerate when he said it would be easier for his men to slay their Greek opponents than strip away their heavy armor once they were down. (Plut. *Mor.* 203 A 2)

Other concerns were the location and identification of the fallen as well as the ever-growing stench arising from the decomposing rotting flesh, which made removal and burial especially difficult and unpleasant. After a few hours, for example, the very process of picking up or dragging the corpses off the battlefield became nearly impossible, especially in the heat of a Greek summer. Xenophon, in recounting a particularly macabre incident during the march of the Ten Thousand, explains that some of the Greek dead who had fallen some five days earlier had to be buried right "where they lay" since the remains were in no condition to be removed (*An.* 6.4.9); in other words, the bodies had become rotten, bloated, and decomposed to such a degree that they could not have been kept intact. Robert Graves describes the phenomenon from his own experience in the First World War:

> After the first day or two the bodies swelled up and stank . . . ones we could not get in from the German wire continued to swell until the wall of the stomach collapsed, either naturally or punctured by a bullet; a disgusting smell would float across. The colour of the dead faces changed from white to yellow-grey, to red, to purple, to green, to black, to slimy. *(200)*

Homer at the very dawn of the hoplite age knew well of that quick process of decay once a warrior fell in battle. In the twenty-fourth book of the *Iliad,* Hermes assures Priam, the aged Trojan king, that the corpse of his son Hektor was preserved by the gods: "he has lain there, nor does his flesh decay, nor do worms feed on him, they who devour men who have fallen in battle." (413–14)

Thucydides presents a picture of the rotting corpses of Athenians killed at Delion; in a dispute over the return of the fallen, the Thebans released the dead only after some seventeen days. (Thuc. 4.101) In an extremely rare instance in Greek battle, the three thousand Sicilians who fell at Himera in 409 were not buried for nearly two years—until Hermokrates returned later to collect what remained of the corpses. Likewise, Plato's mystical account of the myth of Er in his last book of the *Republic* begins: "Er, the son of Armenius, and a Pamphylian who had perished in war, after ten days when the other decayed bodies were taken up, his alone was found uncorrupted." (614 B) Diodorus relates that the bad air arising from Arbela made Alexander move his army quickly away from the battlefield. (17.64.3; Curtius 5.1.11) Perhaps a more graphic scene of the battlefield dead in Greek literature is found in Menander's *Aspis:*

His body I could not identify for sure
They had been out in the sun for three days, their faces were
Bloated.
Then how could you be certain?
There he lay, with his shield, buckled and bent.

(Arnott trans. 69ff)

Even without decomposition, other factors made for problems
in identifying the dead, given the type of wounds inflicted in
Greek hoplite battle. True, the damage did not resemble the mu-
tilation of modern war, where artillery and bombs shred flesh
and torso and extremities may lie yards apart. But hoplite armor
tended to focus many of the sword and spear thrusts to the unprotected face, as we see on many Greek vases. Together with
the general tendency to trample over any fallen warriors, and
the occasional decapitation from an especially powerful spear
or sword thrust, many hoplites received on occasion facial
wounds so grotesque that their features were distorted beyond
recognition. Oman graphically describes the damage that could
be inflicted by the halberd which the men of a Swiss phalanx
wielded. Eight feet in length, it was like a hoplite spear, but with
a wider hatchetlike blade:

If the most ponderous, it was the most murderous of weapons.
Swung by strong arms it could cleave helmets and plate-armor as no
sword could do. It was the halberd whose edge dashed in the skulls
of Duke Leopold's knights at Sempach, and struck down Charles of
Burgundy—all his face one gash from temple to teeth—in the frozen
ditch by Nancy. *(2.254)*

It is thus no surprise that when the Trojans collected their
dead, "they found it hard to recognize each individual dead man;
but with water they washed away the blood that was on them."
(*Il.* 7.423) Fear of terrible disfigurement probably lies behind
the strange account of Polyaenus, who relates that on one occasion the Spartans inscribed their names on their own shields "so
that when it came time to collect the dead they might be known
to their friends." (1.17) Presumably, they felt the shield grip
would ensure that they fell still clasping their shield; such iden-

tification would serve as "dog tags" should they suffer some hideous wound to the head. Diodorus also records nearly the same story when he states that the Spartans sometimes inscribed their names on wooden bracelets. (8.27.2)

We also hear of dead who were never recovered—either mangled beyond all chance of recognition, or who wandered off into the underbrush and were never found. After Solygeia in 425, for example, the Athenians were not able to find two of their dead. Later, the corpses were found and returned by the Corinthians. Apparently, they had either been discovered far from the initial clash or, after a careful examination of the battlefield dead of both sides, been determined to be Athenians after all. (Thuc. 4.44.5–6) Xenophon in his description of the cavalry engagement before the battle of Mantineia in 362 relates that (only) "some" of the Thessalian dead were given over by the Athenians. Were others lost and unaccounted for? (Xen. *Hell.* 7.5.17) Even those who perished right in the midst of the clash between the two armies might not be found for a time, so great was the density and intermingling of bodies within the pile. Only later after the corpses had become untwined may identification have been possible. With that in mind we can understand why Stryphon took over command of the trapped Spartans of Pylos; his predecessor Hippagretas had been left for dead, Thucydides tells us, "though still alive out among the bodies of the slain." (4.38.2) He had been either knocked unconscious, left in a state of shock, or buried alive under the mass of bodies and found later during the general cleanup of the battlefield. Thucydides recalls that before the funeral oration of Pericles, the Athenians in wagons bore the bones of each tribe in cypress coffins; one empty coffin was offered up for those bodies of the men who were never found. (2.34.3) Were these soldiers whose bodies had not been found after hoplite infantry battles, or exclusively sailors lost at sea? This custom seems different from the modern idea for a Tomb of the Unknown Soldier, since in the latter case the bodies, destroyed beyond any chance of identification, are usually recovered in some form.

All these difficulties, together with the sorry state of the survivors, many of whom were in no condition to toil long hours in the days after the battle (e.g., Diod. 14.105.2; 19.31.2–3; Xen. *Hell.* 4.3.20), explain why so many of the dead and much of the equipment were never found. The first efforts would have been directed toward carrying off, dragging, or loading the wagons with the wounded who still had some chance of survival. No wonder, then, that many battlefields were never cleared of the debris and that an archaeology of battlefields grew up around most sites. For years to come, visitors and locals might walk about picking up old and damaged weapons and armor, as well as the skeletal remains of lost or dismembered hoplites. Later on, as peasants plowed and turned over the soil, or as the spring runoff rushed down from the hills, new souvenirs, so to speak, would be unearthed.

We usually associate remembrances of past battle with modern war, where artillery changed the very landscape and there is a horde of accompanying metal artifacts—shell casings, ration tins, cans, abandoned vehicles, and the like. But in the ancient world, too, a considerable amount of debris remained; perhaps the concentration of battle onto such a confined area may help to explain the survival of so much material. Herodotus claims that he viewed the very field where Cambyses and Psammenitus had fought more than a hundred years before his own time. The locals pointed out to the famous inquirer the bones of the dead, and also the peculiar differences in the thickness of Persian and Egyptian skulls, and Herodotus adds that he had observed the same thing at Papremis, where once more he had looked upon the bones from a past battle. (3.12) Years after the battle of Plataia in 479, he remarks, Plataians found numbers of items on the battlefield—a skull without a seam, a jaw with fused teeth, an entire skeleton that measured some eight feet in length—and adds that those were only the most recent discoveries: in the years right after the battle they had dug up gold, silver, and other treasure. (9.83) From his account we get the impression that local dwellers hunted out lost coins and jewelry, and only when that was largely exhausted did they gather together skeletons which they might show off to wandering tourists like Herodotus.

Perhaps the best ancient account of the "living" battlefield comes from Plutarch's life of Sulla, where he writes that nearly two hundred years after Sulla's great victory in 87 over Archelaos at Boiotian Orchomenos (and during his own lifetime), bows, helmets, fragments of iron, breastplates, and swords continued to be uncovered. (*Sulla* 21.4) Indeed, arrow and lance heads, skeletons, and other small finds have been unearthed at the major battle sites in Greece—Marathon, Thermopylai, and Chaironeia—even in modern times.

Although Greek battle between heavily armored men in the classical age was not catastrophic in terms of the total fatalities of the entire army, there was, nevertheless, an unusually large number of corpses within such a confined area. Krentz has reported (1985: 18) that the number of dead among the victorious side in hoplite battles averaged 5 percent of the original force, while the defeated usually suffered around 14 percent of their forces killed. In some of the larger battles, then, such as those at Acragas (472) or the Nemea River (394), there may have been four thousand or more combined dead from the two sides. Nearly all those killed on the winning side fell during the charge or the subsequent hand-to-hand mêlée before the rout; *at least* a corresponding 5 percent figure (of the 14 percent total average losses) of the losers fell there too. If both sides were roughly the same size, 10 percent of all the men who marched out on the morning of the battle would lie piled together in heaps at day's end in the middle of the battlefield along a line usually not much longer than one to three thousand yards. No wonder their equipment would continue to be unearthed within that space for years to come.

18   *The Wounded*

The bodies of the dead lay unburied. Whenever any one recognized the corpse of a friend among them, he was struck with grief, along with fear. And there were also the wounded and sick to be left behind alive; they were even more pitiful to the eyes of the living than the bodies of the dead, more wretched than those who had already perished.

— *Thucydides, on the Athenian disaster in Sicily*

Casualties are one of war's grimmer realities. In a way perhaps its most important element. An army that cannot take casualties cannot fight. And an army that takes too many will lose.

— *James Jones*

After the battle there may have been more wounded men, more "near dead," than bodies of the slain. The disabled comprised roughly two general categories, the first being those who had suffered relatively minor flesh wounds, contusions, or simple fractures, who could be helped off the battlefield by friends (e.g., Ducrey pl. 146), be bandaged and treated right on the spot (Lazenby pl. 4), or perhaps walk home under their own power. All had a good chance of surviving at least a few days or weeks after the battle if not longer. Indeed, on vase paintings we often see soldiers attempting to remove a spear or arrow from their wounds, which suggests that on many occasions the injured had a reasonable chance of eventual recovery. (E.g., Ahlberg 7, 12, 13, 15)

The more seriously wounded who lay out on the ground would need prompt attention, but the outlook for them was less hopeful if they could not rise under their own power. Most had fallen during either the initial clash or the subsequent rout, the two stages of battle when fluidity of combat best allowed lethal blows and thrusts. For those struck down during the running collision of spears at the onset the outlook was bleak: these would be most likely to have suffered fatal penetration wounds (probably to the large target of the chest) as their undergarments were driven right into their flesh along with the weapon, once their bronze breastplates were pierced. Tyrtaios wrote of that scene:

> And he who falls among the champions and loses his sweet life,
>   so blessing with honor his city, his father, and all his people,
> with wounds in his chest, where the spear that he was facing
>   has transfixed,
> that massive guard of his shield, and gone through his
>   breastplate as well.
>
>   (*12.23ff*)

Excavation at the Athenian Kerameikos has revealed the corpses of thirteen Spartans who probably fell in an attack on the city in 403. One such skeleton was found with an iron lance-head lodged in the rib cage, in situ after some 2,400 years. (Cf. Van Hook) And in iconographic representations we often see large wounds as the spear is pulled back out of the victim by the attacker. (Ahlberg B7) The immediate likelihood was of a quick death within a few minutes from widespread damage to the branches of the circulatory system surrounding the pulmonary artery; there was also the later danger of widespread infection in the flesh and subsequent sepsis of the chest cavity. Epameinondas, for instance, died soon after being carried off the field of Mantineia, a broken spear shaft still lodged in his chest. (Diod. 15.87.1) Collapse of either lung or destruction of the airways in the respiratory system often resulted from these chest-high blows; a strong thrust to the ribs, even if it somehow missed the major vessels, could also fracture the bone, driving it back into the lungs and thereby quickly collapsing the breathing channels. True, the ancients had some knowledge of treating pleurisy and collapsed lungs through the use of syringes and bladders. Yet survival rates were dismal and in any case most "doctors" would be too overwhelmed in the first critical hours after a battle to attempt a critical, complicated procedure. Frolich, whose nineteenth-century work examined the wounds recounted in Homer's *Iliad*, found that of 147 incidents, 106 were said to have been inflicted by the spear (58–62), and more significant, 80 percent of them resulted in the death of the hero. In Frolich's view, by far the greatest number of these fatal thrusts were to the chest. Homer, then, sang of battle where blows were delivered at close range, the target was most often the chest cavity, and the results were usually fatal. One wonders whether he knew of early hoplite battle firsthand, or whether his descriptions of wounds simply followed identifiable formulaic structures of oral poetry, corresponding more to the thematic patterns of an aristocratic duel than to the reality of the battlefield.

These initial running spear thrusts could also penetrate lower down through the bronze breastplate well into the abdominal cavity, or possibly, missing the edge of both the shield and breastplate, arc up from an underhand attack into the groin. Such "belly wounds" in the lower stomach and groin were almost always fatal, leading in a few days, if not hours, to death from shock, peritonitis, or other infections, as the contents of the intestines spilled out into the abdominal cavity and the hoplite collapsed from blood and fluid loss. Tyrtaios remarks of the sight of the old warrior who struggles with his wounded groin:

> For this is indeed disgraceful, that at the very forefront
>   an older man falls and lies down in front of the
>   younger,
> his hair white and his beard grey,
> breathing out his last strong spirit amidst the dust,
> holding in his hands his testicles all bloody.
>
> *(10.21–25)*

Apparently the poet had seen or heard of battle where the front-rank fighter was knocked off his feet by a tremendous running thrust which caught the hapless victim right between the legs, unarmored and, at that second, unprotected by the shield. We hear of a number of such fatal battle wounds in the Hippocratic corpus. One Aenos suffered a javelin wound deep into the lower back which resulted in the usual peritoneal inflammation.

Though initially not painful, by the third day he was in severe agony and suffering constipation. Twenty-four hours later, constantly vomiting and convulsing, the victim became dazed and dehydrated. He passed away, five days after the original wound. (*Epidemics* 5.61)

The other fatal target during this collision of spears was the cranium. In the famous Hippocratic treatise "On Wounds in the Head" there are rich descriptions of the variety of injuries caused by edged weapons to the head; apparently the ancients were able to distinguish trauma caused by missiles, smooth-surfaced or elongated weapons, and tripping and trampling. (11.20–40) At times, the initial thrusts of the enemy could make their way between the cheek pieces into the face, like the blow of Ajax which killed Akamas the Thracian: "the spear point fixed in his forehead and drove inward through the bone." (*Il.* 6.6–8) On other occasions, the sheer momentum of the lance head ensured the penetration of the bronze helmet, or its being dented to such a degree so as to kill the hoplite anyway: in these cases the spear probably drove the sides of the helmet against the skull, injuring the cerebral arteries and causing massive subsequent hemorrhaging. In other words, a man might die of a head wound even without apparent damage to the skull, indeed, without any visible trauma at all. Extant examples of Corinthian helmets show numerous extensive dents, cracks, and caved-in sides, suggesting that such blows, while not actually breaking the metal surface, might have caused considerable brain damage to the wearer. Nearly all such traumas were likely to be fatal. Even if the wounded survived the initial forty-eight hours they still faced dim prospects: the accounts of ancient Greek efforts to relieve cerebral edema caused by concussion, whatever their fascination to the medical community, nevertheless make nightmarish reading and give little indication of long-term success. (E.g., cf. Majno 168–69) And even when the Corinthian helmet protected the hoplite against serious brain injury, the sheer force of the running spear thrust could snap the head radically backward or downward, fracturing the cervical vertebrae altogether. This ei-

ther severed the spinal cord, causing paralysis or perhaps sudden death, or induced hemorrhaging within the spinal canal, and
that could lead to intolerable pressure and eventual death or a
wasting quadriplegia—a condition that was probably fatal in the
ancient world, due to accompanying infection and problems of
care. There are no instances either in literature or on vase painting depicting paralyzed men in chairs or in beds. Such spinal
trauma or accompanying head wounds must have been a common occurrence in Greek battle (e.g., Hom. *Il.* 11.350–56; Ar.
Ach. 1180 ff; Plut. *Arist.* 14.5) and indeed in any battle between
armored men who were desperately trying to knock their enemy
out as quickly as possible. Pyrrhus was struck unconscious by a
blow which hit him on the vertebrae below the helmet; at that
point one of Antigonus' men decapitated the near-comatose general. (Plut. *Pyrrh.* 34) The excavation at the medieval battlefield
of Wisby (A.D. 1361), for example, indicates that 44 percent of
all injuries were to the skull. (Thordeman 179–85)

Great slaughter also occurred in the rout when one phalanx
collapsed in panic and was cut down or trampled by friend and
foe alike. Wounded men who lingered on after the battle, cling-
ing to life, most likely suffered from either deep spear wounds
to the back or an assorted array of compound fractures. In the
Iliad, for example, Phereklos is chased down by Meriones and
"struck in the right buttock, and the spear head drove on and
passing under the bone went into the bladder." (5.65–68) Fractures must have been especially common here, as soldiers stepped
on hands, arms, legs, and even backs in a desperate effort to be
free of the mob. True, simple fractures, sprains, or even severe
lacerations were usually treatable. (E.g., Hdt. 3.129.1) The success of ancient medicine arose from the Greek physicians' remarkable knowledge of anatomy; for the most part, they easily
handled wound trauma where the fractures were simple and the
bleeding was caused by tissue damage or the breakage of the
smaller veins. Doctors had acquired such a thorough knowledge
of the various types of wounds created by the blow of sword or
spear that Plutarch could relate that a rare self-inflicted wound

could be easily distinguished from true battlefield injuries. (*Dion* 34.3–5) Yet many of the men who had been run over from the rear had fractures of a more severe type, compound breaks where the bone pierced the skin, causing relentless bleeding beyond treatment, and generally guaranteeing fatal infection to the marrow itself. Here, the outlook was uniformly grim: the wounded hoplite either perished from blood loss in a matter of hours, or survived beyond that period only to meet a painful death due to infection.

But not all battle wounds were fatal. We often hear of men who survived "dozens of blows," veterans of hoplite battle who are said to have had a body full of old scars and injuries of various types, men like Pelopidas, who was carried away from a battle near Mantineia after receiving "seven blows to his front" (Plut. *Pel.* 4.4.5), or Agesilaos, who lived through Koroneia, "even though he had wounds in every part of his body from every type of weapon." (Xen. *Ages.* 2.13) The hoplite most likely took non-lethal injuries to the chest or head during the general mêlée of hand-to-hand pushing and thrusting, since blows delivered at this point in the battle were not necessarily strong enough to penetrate bronze armor or to tear major organs and arteries. Instead the combatants desperately slapped each other with the remnants of the spear shaft, slicing and hacking with the short sword from a standing rather than a running position. In such circumstances, the injuries to the chest or abdomen were not necessarily penetration wounds and so did not always turn out to be fatal. Perseus, the Macedonian general, for instance, escaped from the battle at Pydna with a deep bruise from an oblique blow which did little more than tear away his tunic and leave a few sore ribs. (Plut. *Aem.* 19.4–5) The helmet, too, could withstand the shock of blows delivered by an off-balance opponent who had little chance in the close-in brawling to develop any momentum behind his attack. This was the situation in the *Iliad* at one point: Diomedes hits Hektor directly in the head "but the bronze from the bronze was driven back, nor reached his shining skin, the helmet guarded it, three-ply and hollowed-eyed." (*Il.* 11.350–53) Antiochos in Bactria suffered a wound to the mouth and the subsequent loss of his teeth, but nevertheless made a full recovery. (Polyb. 10.49.13–15) The Persian Intaphernes, Herodotus tells us (3.78.2), lost his eye after suffering a spear wound to the socket, but eventually regained his health. The ancients were also knowledgeable about the extraction of missiles and spears and sometimes saved the injured soldier if blood loss was not excessive. Alexander the Great recovered from a deep arrow wound to the ribs after the shaft was sawed off, his breastplate removed, and the head extracted. At that point Alexander lost consciousness and nearly died, yet recovered after a lengthy convalescence. (Plut. *Alex.* 63)

Less serious secondary wounds to the arms, legs, hands, and feet were even more frequent, since these body parts were not always protected by body armor; in most cases, they, too, were not necessarily fatal. There is that strange incident in Herodotus (7.181.2) of the Aiginetan Ischenous who fell into the hands of the Persians off Skiathos. After a valiant resistance he was nearly "cut to pieces" by his captors. However, once his numerous wounds were treated with myrrh and bound with cotton, he lived on. Most likely, these were nonpenetration wounds of close hand-to-hand fighting; blood loss could then be prevented by prompt treatment as long as the major arteries and organs were spared. Some idea of the frequency of these blows to the exposed extremities is conveyed by a passage in Xenophon's *Cyropaedia*. After Cyrus's men had engaged in a mock, practice battle with fennel sticks in the place of real spears, they all complained of sore hands, necks, and even bruises to their faces. (2.3.17–20)

We assume that many of the wounds in the stand-up pushing and brawling were severe cuts and slices from the slashing and parrying of spear and sword, since the opportunity for truly deeppenetrating trauma from a running spear thrust had largely passed. Hoplites are often described as suffering from secondary cuts to the arm (Diod. 16.12.4; 17.61.3), hand and foot (Plut. *Dion* 30.6; *Mor.* 241 F 151), or thigh. (Plut. *Arat.* 27.2) The possibility of treating these injuries successfully was good since, from Homer on, the Greeks were remarkably adept in binding torn tissue to prevent fatal blood loss. We know, for example, that linen or cotton bandages were regularly applied to open wounds (e.g., Ar. *Ach.* 1176; Hom. *Il.* 13.599–600; Hdt. 7.181.2), and myrrh, fig juice, or even wine was often used to lessen hemorrhaging. There are also references to wool or lint plugs, or even plasters of gum and wheat used as sponges to soak up blood and cleanse the wound. (Majno 150) In most cases, however, such treatment of simple surface wounds or uncomplicated fractures marked the limit of the expertise of the medical corpsmen who accompanied the army. (Xen. *Cyr.* 6.2.25–3.4; *Hell.* 4.5.8; *An.* 3.4.30; *Lac. Pol.* 13.7; Arr. *Tact.* 2.1) Medical treatment was also undertaken by the fighting men themselves. On some vase paintings a hoplite on the battlefield applies a field dressing of sorts to the wounded arm or finger of a friend. (Ducrey pls. 142, 143) Suturing and stitching with bronze needles were also known and employed in cases of simple cuts and tears of the flesh where mere bandaging was less effective in preventing loss of blood. The crucial factor, again, was the noninvolvement of major arteries and vessels, since the ancients had no way to replace large quantities of lost blood. The brother of the poet Aeschylus, for example, bled to death during the battle of Marathon once his hand was severed at the wrist. (Hdt. 6.114)

Even the walking wounded who left the battlefield alive, and thus were not considered a part of the day's actual casualties, sometimes eventually succumbed to "minor" wounds. Warriors might die a few hours or days later from deeper, internal injuries where blood seepage was unrelenting (Plut. *Artax.* 11.6), or a large vein had been damaged too severely to prevent steady blood loss. Most important, of course, was the specter of infection. Most hoplite weapons were good collectors of bacteria commonly found in the soil and animal feces on the ground, specifically clostridial infections such as tetanus or gas gangrene—diseases that arise even from superficial injury where initial blood loss may have been managed. In most such instances, death was inevitable given the absence of an appropriate antibiotic or antitoxin. So, for example, a writer often remarks on the unexpected demise of a soldier days or even weeks after the battle, often from a wound considered not at all serious at the time. (Diod. 20.23.2–8) That may have been the reason for the death of the Persian king Cambyses, who never recovered from an apparently nonlethal, accidental stabbing from his own spear tip; Miltiades also succumbed to gangrene weeks after he had suffered a thigh wound on Paros. (Hdt. 3.64.3; 6.136) Hannibal also was said to have perished from a slight scrape from his own sword after infection set in. (Paus. 8.11.11) We see a vivid picture of the course of events from incidents described in the Hippocratic corpus. One patient who suffered from an arrow wound "barely worth noting" later was torn by the convulsions of tetanus to such a degree that "the jaws locked; if he took some fluid into the mouth and tried to swallow it, it came back through the nostrils." (Cf. Majno 199) It was here that ancient medicine was woefully inadequate, for Greek doctors did not understand infection and the lethal dangers involved with even simple trauma. In place of an antiseptic cleansing of the injury and prompt effort to prevent further blood loss, the ancient physician was guided by the well-known idea of a "balance" of the four humors, a view of human health that almost always resulted in exactly the wrong course of treatment for battlefield injury: "In every recent wound it is expedient to cause blood to flow from it abundantly." (Hippocrates *On Wounds* 2.796) Majno best sums up the degree of success of the ancient physician on the battlefield: "All in all, Greek care for the wound itself probably did little harm and some good. It is quite another story when one comes to the general treatments, aimed at 'helping the wound' more indirectly. They range from bad to hair-raising." (188) Perhaps, the lingering casualties explain why occasionally additional names are added in different hands to yearly casualty lists on stone of the battlefield dead. (E.g., *IG* I² 929 62–70)

19 *Epilogue*

And we are here as on a darkling plain
Swept with confused alarms of struggles and flight
Where ignorant armies clash by night.
—Matthew Arnold

Ils ne passeront pas.
—Marshal Pétain, at Verdun, 1916

The Citizen and the Battlefield

At one point in Plato's *Laws,* the Cretan lawgiver is made to say that among the Greeks, peace "is merely a name; yet in truth, an undeclared war always exists by nature between every Greek city-state." (1.626 A) If the relentless warfare found throughout Greek tragedy, history, and epic is any clue to either the writers' own interests, or the general concerns of their audiences, then the Cretan's way of thinking accurately reflected the common Greek view toward the armed conflict they saw in their small world. Yet, we should not make a fundamental error here: the state of near-perpetual hostility between city-states, well-recognized as it was by both ancients and moderns, had little to do with actual infantry fighting on a battlefield: "war" and "battle" were two very different concepts to the Greeks. Even during the dark years of the Peloponnesian War, a continuous twenty-seven-year struggle on both land and sea, the hour or so of brutal killing and dying in phalanx battle on land was still a rare phenomenon for most men. The only two encounters of infantry of any magnitude in that war were the terrible battles at Delion (424) and Mantineia (418). For the Athenian and Peloponnesian losers of those engagements, the sum total of the battle dead and wounded was shocking for a day's work. Nevertheless, they were probably insignificant in comparison with either the great plague at Athens or the subsequent Athenian military catastrophe on Sicily. Indeed, if we were to total all the moments of a man's lifetime in which he actually attacked an enemy with spear and shield in the phalanx, it was surely a minuscule amount—sixty, three hundred, six hundred minutes—not even comparable to one week of combat for an infantryman on patrol in Vietnam. Even during the time a hoplite spent away from home while on duty— taken up with the mechanics of the campaign, marching with his sack of provisions and his servant at his side—he was secure in the knowledge that there was little chance of battle until he lined up in column and faced a similar enemy across the field.

It was precisely because the fighting in the phalanx was so brief that the Greeks developed such an interest in warfare. Battle became an obsessive image in the minds of those who saw very little of infantry combat. Still, the experience of battle is always qualitative—if we dare use such word in this context—rather than merely quantitative. And a citizen of a Greek city-state understood that the simplicity, clarity, and brevity of hoplite battle defined the entire relationship with a man's family and his community, the one day of uncertain date that might end his life but surely gave significance to his entire existence. The power of Medea's cry in Euripides' play that she would "rather stand in battle three times than give birth once" derives not merely from its novelty or even its sensitivity, but surely for the audience of Athenian males, from its very absurdity: the awkward burdensome armor that hung unused and tarnished above the hearth was a daily reminder both of how infrequent and unusually savage those few minutes were and would be in the perennial wars still to come.

The sheer number of kin in this personal drama—fathers, sons, grandfathers, cousins, uncles, and lifelong friends—also accounts for the general emphasis on war in Greek society: all men were initiates in that most awful of the many rituals in their culture, and the bonds forged during the few minutes of collective fighting gave new definition to the older idea of "family" and "friend." Since there was very little drill, daily weapon training, or collective messes outside of Sparta, militarism in most Greek states was insignificant in the life of the citizen. Instead, donning the panoply and marching out only called to mind a time for killing and dying in the nightmarish world of the phalanx; it did not invoke any mystique of "the cult of the warrior." For all the recent anthropological attempts to understand classical Greek battle, at least in part, as an initiation rite of passage from adolescence to adulthood, there is little evidence at least in Greek literature that the Greeks themselves viewed it this way, for many of them fought for most of their life, and fought well into middle and old age. The peacetime fascination with the use of shield and spear, the hoplite's ritualistic dance, the competitive race in armor—and the interest of vase painter, sculptor, and poet—were, I believe, symptomatic of the anticipation and the anxiety that gnawed in the heart of each man, growing large in inverse proportion to the relatively few moments of actual fighting on the battlefield. Because the classical Greeks saw their infantry fighting ultimately as economical and practical—a manner of battle that was left to later generations to find romantic— there exists a morality in their legacy: the idea that war's image must never be anything other than that of falling bodies and gaping wounds.

The actual battle environment for men who served in the phalanx was nearly identical wherever and whenever they fought: this allowed each citizen-soldier to know exactly why the poet called Greek warfare "a thing of fear." The simplicity and clear order of hoplite combat ensured that the fighting would be roughly the same at any one spot or at any given moment in the battle: the experience of the one was also that of the many. This unusual uniformity in both arms and tactics, in a wider dimension, guaranteed that the killing and wounding were largely familiar to many generations—whether they had fought one summer day in the mid-fifth century in a valley in Boiotia, or on a high plain in the central Peloponnese one hundred years earlier. For men aged twenty through sixty—uninitiated and veteran alike—the charge, the collision of spears, the pushing,

trampling, wounding, panic, confusion, even the pile of the battlefield dead, were all similar events to be experienced one awful, fatal time, or perennially until a man could fight no more.
The presence especially of old men in the ranks also ensured that
battle was not seen as a youthful frolic where both sides lined up
in some strange game of chicken. Instead, the elders taught the
younger men that such decisive fighting was the only way to end
the ordeal as quickly as possible. Unlike later generations of infantry veterans in the West, there was rarely talk of vast, separate
theaters of battle; of nightmarishly protracted long campaigns;
of differing (and nearly always competitive) tales of bravery witnessed in either artillery, armor, or infantry, as spotter, sapper,
rifleman, flamethrower, machine gunner, or messenger. For the
Greek citizen of every age, there was one image alone of hoplite
spearman, imprinted in the mind like the warriors on the frieze
courses of so many Greek temples, a picture that each man shared
with every man he knew.

The Evolution of Greek Battle

The steady economic and social progress made throughout
Greece from the seventh to the late fifth century B.C. attests to
the singular genius of hoplite warfare: it was a system that prevented the constant and inevitable internecine struggles from
having any harmful lasting influence on the culture of the Greek
city-state. But the means of limiting losses in civilian lives and
property from such continual warring required that battle be
demonstrably decisive to all involved—and therefore sometimes
unusually brutal. Hoplite armor was so burdensome, so poorly
suited to the summer climate, so uncomfortable to its wearer,
that its very existence now seems to us absurd. But the panoply
accomplished one and only one crucial task: it gave thirty minutes or more of relative protection in which a fighter could close
with his enemy and strike savagely with the spear, often allowing
a man at least to face and to kill before he himself died. Unlike

cavalry armor or the lighter defenses of the targeteer, hoplite body protection was often offensive rather than purely defensive; it was designed to allow a hoplite a chance to carve out a path for those behind him in the phalanx before he was overcome by the swarm of enemies around him. At times men literally bashed each other with the "defensive" armor of shield, helmet, and breastplate as those to the rear pushed these human "rams" inexorably onward. The tactics of such fighting were equally brutal, consisting of little more than a mutually, face-to-face, destructive collision.

That the Greeks relegated horsemen, archers, and light-armed missile troops to a minor role in the fighting clearly indicates that for the first time in the history of armed conflict, their value was only incidental, rather than essential, to the warfare, which was exclusively infantry battle. Maneuver and the application of overwhelming force against a weaker opponent were also not welcome, since battle was "by convention," a reciprocal agreement on both sides to draw everyone down from the hills and out from the walls to confront each other in a battle that would result in a decisive victory. If it spelled certain death for hundreds involved, at least the intent was to limit, rather than glorify, war, and thereby save rather than destroy lives. The postmortem viewing of the dead, the exchange of bodies, the erection of the battlefield trophy, the lack of organized pursuit and further slaughter, and, above all, the mutual understanding to abide by the decision achieved on the battlefield—these were all rituals designed to reinforce the idea that further killing was not merely senseless but unnecessary as well. Surely, any continued fighting was a reproach to traditional values and to those who had gone down hours before and lay still on the battlefield.

There were no conscientious objectors in the Greek city-state in the great age of hoplite battle, few self-inflicted wounds, and no exemption for middle age or even physical impairment. Such issues would have been an abstraction for the Greeks; in fact, they were rarely discussed by either philosophers or military analysts. Tactical deployment and the art of marshaling men were

designed solely to bring the mass of humanity on both sides
quickly and efficiently together for the resulting slaughter. To win
a battle before it had even started was to allow a commander too
much influence over the infantrymen on the battlefield, to elevate the one above the many, and thus allow one side to "cheat"
in a victory achieved by some means other than their own bravery in the battle.

The succession of innovations and constant changes in the classical manner of battle which arose in the fourth century B.C.
should not be seen as improvements over an "obsolete," ineffective way of fighting. The introduction of integrated cavalry
forces, light-armed troopers, siege engineers, and organized
corps of highly skilled bowmen does not indicate the prior martial inadequacy of the older hoplites, but is, rather, indicative of
their very success. For these "new men" of the Hellenistic and
Roman ages, the traditional collision was too efficient, too predictably brutal; they believed (wrongly) that too high a proportion of the victors in classical Greek battle died even in their conquest. (Once they shed the body armor of their forefathers they
learned only too well how many more men could fall when larger
armies collided.) As the fragile equilibrium among the small, independent Greek city-states deteriorated, most men were no
longer willing to endure the hoplite battle only to have to abide
by a "decision" that they saw as intrinsically arbitrary.

The outcome of hoplite pitched battle left the property and
culture of the defeated intact, robbed only of some 15 percent
of their male citizens, many of whom were already past the prime
of life. In the best modern spirit, the successors to the Greeks
sought ever ingenious ways to lengthen, to expand, to glorify,
and to continue the fighting until their very social structure was
brought out onto the battlefield itself. They had forgotten or indeed not understood that the old style of hoplite conflict was by
deliberate design somewhat artificial, intended to focus a concentrated brutality upon the few in order to spare the many. The
idea had developed in Greece ever since the seventh century B.C.
that battle should be a particularly hellish ritual for all soldiers

involved, men of every age, if war was to be excluded from the daily life of their families back at home. Indeed, is there not, ultimately, a moral statement inherent in such a frank appraisal of conflict? Later Westerners sought a greater complexity and "science" to warfare, as if the introduction of such skills could somehow make battle more controllable or predictable and perhaps thereby more humane; instead, all they really accomplished was to allow the killing to intrude into the very lives of the citizens or subjects they sought to protect, as they created a cult of youthful heroism out of something so mundanely simple and brutal.

What survived as the legacy of classical Greek battle during Hellenistic and Roman times and thence throughout the history of the West was not the form or morality so much as the *spirit* of Hellenic warfare. Pitched infantry battle between columns of armored men was no longer always a realistic means of efficiently deciding an entire war, but such fighting nevertheless retained its usefulness: it provided a decisive (and glorious) conclusion to actions in a wide theater of operations, or a yearly campaign among armies who were both willing—if the chance of a clear victory was possible—to draw up their infantry forces for such a final solution. The Greek manner of infantry fighting, at its most basic, had always offered an effective means of concentrating warfare, and thereby killing and wounding combatants most efficiently, given the constraints of time and space. The key ingredient had not changed from classical times—the risk of a brutal fighting in exchange for the singular opportunity of eliminating large numbers of the enemy. For these men, the purpose was now to settle the entire business, if not fairly, then at least decisively.

Some may object that, in my emphasis on the misery of Greek hoplite battle, I have exaggerated the savagery in the fighting between the armored men of the classical age, an experience unrivaled in its brutality by the modern firefight in the jungle, or the week of shelling in the trenches—places where soldiers are forced to endure even greater suffering. Of course, there is terrible anguish in modern infantry campaigns: combatants during a year of active duty are constantly exposed to unpredictable fire from both soldier and civilian of any sex and age, even when enemy infantry are nowhere to be seen. However, battle was frightening for the Greeks precisely because killing was *not* random. Fighting without artillery barrages, the surprises of a jungle or urban ambush, or the anonymous bullet from a distant sniper, the Greeks could know that in battle, after all, very little is left to chance. They knew with certainty the sequence of events on the horizon: charge, collision, hand to hand, push, trampling, and rout. Also, there was a primitive animality in the use of edged weapons by men in armor, especially when, unlike in later times, the javelin thrower, archer, slinger, and their accompanying missile weapons were kept out of the bloodletting. A physical and psychological exertion of energy was required by men who killed with hand tools and then watched one another struggle, bleed, and go down beneath their feet. And because the casualties of such fighting were generally predictable and unchanging—10 to 20 percent among the defeated, 5 percent or less for the victors— battle became increasingly and more predictably terrifying as a man aged and went out again and again on these awesome missions. It was a course of events that was an inescapable part of his very life: in a sense, for the hoplite, battle was more of a death verdict rather than the indeterminate sentence of recent conflict. Now a tour of duty comprises both a beginning and an end to the exposure of death.

The notification of intent—at once a revolutionary and frightening precedent on the part of the Greeks, which has survived in the modern Western military mind—also explains the horror: once the respective phalanxes lumbered forth, all the men were sure exactly of what would soon occur, and knew that both victory and also defeat were the sole responsibilities of the men at their side. There was no solace in the hope of reinforcement from reserves or from a relief battalion. Preliminary aerial bombardment of the enemy and artillery "softening-up" were likewise unknown. The Greek soldier also even lacked the confidence that derives from knowing one may have an overwhelming numerical superiority or firepower or will fight with original tactics and superior generalship. Success or defeat depended only on the fighters' ability to stand upright in bronze armor for the next hour or so, resisting the temptation to fall back or even to shy away from the lance head at his face and groin. Nor was the manner of death unexpected, unimagined, or unknown: men knew precisely how they would die in battle—driven through by spear or sword, crushed by shield and foot, right in the midst of family and friends.

The End of the Greek Legacy

That the heritage of Greek hoplite battle now lives on in the West is especially surprising when the mechanics of pitched infantry battle, despite advances in technology, are now nearly obsolete, and with them the very tenets of the doctrine that justified them: notification of intent, mutual acknowledgment of the upcoming collision of forces, and obedience to the decision of the battlefield dead. There is a terrible danger in the nuclear age to all of us who see this very legacy of the Greek manner of warfare surviving and living on well past the demise of actual infantry battle and the moral climate of its birth, a climate with which it was once so uniquely designed and integrated. Clearly, we are no longer an agrarian society of independent small landowners. We have inherited only the idea of Greek battle as a heroic notion, we have detached it from the real fighting, and we have ignored its real lessons, transferring the Greeks' way of thinking to an entirely different—and dangerous—set of circumstances and a foreign theater of operations.

For example, we must not delude ourselves into thinking that an exchange of even tactical nuclear weapons is somehow justified because, like the Greeks, we finally have no recourse other than to notify the enemy of our intent, to signal both the time and manner of our attack, to array our forces upon the "battlefield," and then to advance—as if the acknowledgment of direct conflict, openly giving and receiving blows without guile, might somehow justify the enormity of the collision. Unlike the Greeks, we could not possibly abide by the decision of any such "battle," exchange the dead, content in the knowledge that in meeting and facing down the enemy we had minimized, rather than increased, the killing. The daylight collision of armed soldiers was originally for the Greeks a grim resolution to have the fighting done quickly and effectively with a minimum of fatalities, not a romantic stage to showcase brave resolve. But any nuclear conflict would of course be final and induce the end of civilization as we have known it. It is fearsome to think that Americans (who alone have employed the nuclear bomb in wartime use) could claim a heroic purpose in such a scenario. How can there be satisfaction on our part if we have led ourselves to our final slaughter?

Have we not seen then, in our lifetime, the end to the Western way of war?

Abbreviations of
Ancient Authors and Their Works
Used in This Book

Ael.	Aelian	*Pol.*	*Politica*
Tact.	*Tactics*	Arr.	Arrian
VH	*Varia Historia*	*Anab.*	*Anabasis*
Aesch.	Aeschylus	*Tact.*	*Tactica*
Ag.	*Agamemnon*	Ath.	Athenaeus
Cho.	*Choephoroi*	Dem.	Demosthenes
Eum.	*Eumenides*	Diod.	Diodorus Siculus
Pers.	*Persae*	Eup.	Eupolis
PV	*Prometheus Vinctus*	Eur.	Euripides
Sept.	*Septem contra Thebas*	*Bacch.*	*Bacchae*
Supp.	*Supplices*	*HF*	*Hercules Furens*
Alk.	Alkaios	*Phoen.*	*Phoenissae*
Amm.		Frontin.	Frontinus
Marc.	Ammianus Marcellinus	*Str.*	*Strategemata*
Anac.	Anacreon	Hdt.	Herodotus
Andoc.	Andocides	*Hell. Oxy.*	*Hellenica Oxyrhynchia*
App.	Appian	Hom.	Homer
BCiv.	*Bella Civilia*	*Il.*	*Iliad*
Archil.	Archilochos	*Od.*	*Odyssey*
Ar.	Aristophanes	*IG*	*Inscriptiones Graecae,* 1873–
Ach.	*Acharnians*	Isae.	Isaeus
Av.	*Aves*	Just.	Justinus, *Epitome*
Eccl.	*Ecclesiazusae*	Luc.	Lucan
Eq.	*Equites*	Lycurg.	Lycurgus
Lys.	*Lysistrata*	*Leoc.*	*Leocrates*
Nub.	*Nubes*	Lys.	Lysias
Plut.	*Plutus*	Men.	Menander
Ran.	*Ranae*	*Asp.*	*Aspis*
Thesm.	*Thesmophoriazusae*	Nep.	Nepos
Vesp.	*Vespae*	*Att.*	*Atticus*
Arist.	Aristotle	*Epam.*	*Epaminondas*
Ath. Pol.	*Athenaion Politeia*	Paus.	Pausanias

Pind.	Pindar		Thes.	*Theseus*
Pl.	Plato		Tim.	*Timoleon*
Ap.	*Apology*		Polyaen.	Polyaenus
Cri.	*Crito*		Strat.	*Strategemata*
Lach.	*Laches*		Polyb.	Polybius
Leg.	*Leges*		Soph.	Sophocles
Menex.	*Menexenus*		*Aj.*	*Ajax*
Resp.	*Respublica*		*Ant.*	*Antigone*
Sym.	*Symposium*		*El.*	*Electra*
Plut.	Plutarch		*OC*	*Oedipus Coloneus*
Aem.	*Aemilius Paullus*		*OT*	*Oedipus Tyrannus*
Ages.	*Agesilaos*		*Phil.*	*Philoctetes*
Alc.	*Alcibiades*		*Trach.*	*Trachiniae*
Alex.	*Alexander*		Strab.	Strabo
Arat.	*Aratos*		Theoc.	Theocritus
Arist.	*Aristides*		*Epigr.*	*Epigrammata*
Artax.	*Artaxerxes*		*Id.*	*Idylls*
Cim.	*Cimon*		Theophr.	Theophrastus
Dem.	*Demosthenes*		*Char.*	*Characteres*
Demetr.	*Demetrios*		Thuc.	Thucydides
Eum.	*Eumenes*		Xen.	Xenophon
Flam.	*Flamininus*		*Ages.*	*Agesilaos*
Kleom.	*Kleomenes*		*An.*	*Anabasis*
Lyc.	*Lycurgus*		*Ap.*	*Apologia Socratis*
Lys.	*Lysander*		*Cyn.*	*Cynegeticus*
Mor.	*Moralia*		*Cyr.*	*Cyropaedia*
Nic.	*Nicias*		*Eq.*	*De Equitandi ratione*
Pel.	*Pelopidas*		*Hell.*	*Hellenica*
Per.	*Pericles*		*Hipp.*	*Hipparchicus*
Phil.	*Philopoemen*		*Lac. Pol.*	*Respublica*
Phoc.	*Phocion*			*Lacedaemoniorum*
Pyrrh.	*Pyrrhus*		*Mem.*	*Memorabilia*
Sol.	*Solon*		*Oec.*	*Oeconomicus*
Them.	*Themistocles*		*Symp.*	*Symposium*
			Vect.	*De Vectigalibus*

Select Bibliography

Abbreviations of classical journals follow the pattern found in the Oxford Classical Dictionary. Titles are confined almost exclusively to those cited by last name of author in the text.

GREEK WARFARE IN GENERAL

Adcock, F. E. *The Greek and Macedonian Art of Warfare.* Berkeley, Calif., 1957.

Anderson, J. K. *Military Theory and Practice in the Age of Xenophon.* Berkeley, Calif., 1970.

Connolly, P. *Greece and Rome at War.* London, 1981.

Delbrück, H. *Geschichte der Kriegskunst im Rahmen der politischen Geschichte.* Vol. 1. Berlin, 1920.

Droysen, H. *Heerwesen und Kriegführung der Griechen.* Freiburg, 1888.

Ferrill, A. *The Origins of War.* London, 1985.

Garlan, Y. *La Guerre dans l'Antiquité.* Paris, 1972. Translated as *War in the Ancient World.* London, 1975.

Grundy, G. B. *Thucydides and the History of His Age.* London, 1911.

Hanson, V. D. *Warfare and Agriculture in Classical Greece.* Pisa, 1983.

Harmand, J. *La Guerre antique de Sumer à Rome.* Paris, 1973.

Humble, R. *Warfare in the Ancient World.* London, 1980.

Köchly, H. A. T., and W. Rüstow. *Geschichte des Griechischen Kriegswesen.* Arau, 1852.

Kromayer, J., and G. Veith. *Heerwesen und Kriegführung der Griechen und Römer.* Munich, 1928.

Pritchett, W. K. *The Greek State at War.* Vols. 1–4. Berkeley, Calif., 1971–85.

———. *Studies in Ancient Greek Topography.* Vols. 1–5. Berkeley, Calif., 1965–85.

Tarn, W. W. *Hellenistic Military and Naval Developments.* Cambridge, Eng., 1930.

Vernant, J. P., ed. *Problèmes de la guerre en Grèce ancienne.* Paris, 1968.

Warry, J. *Warfare in the Ancient World.* London, 1980.

Yadin, Y. *The Art of Warfare in Biblical Lands.* London, 1963.

HOPLITE BATTLE: STRATEGY AND TACTICS

Ahlberg, G. *Fighting on Land and Sea in Greek Geometric Art.* Stockholm, 1971.

Andrewes, A. "The Hoplite Katalogos." In *Classical Contributions: Studies in Honor of Malcolm Francis McGregor.* Locust Valley, N.Y., 1981, 1–3.

Armstrong, A. M. "Trial by Combat among the Greeks." *GR* 19 (1950): 73–74.

Arnould, D. *Guerre et paix dans la poésie grecque.* New York, 1981.

Borthwick, E. K. "The Trojan Leap and Pyrrhic Dance in Euripides' *Andromache* 1129–1141." *JHS* 87 (1967): 18–23.

———. "Two Scenes of Combat in Euripides." *JHS* 90 (1970): 15–21.

Cartledge, P. "Hoplites and Heroes: Sparta's Contribution to the Technique of Ancient Warfare." *JHS* 97 (1977): 11–28.

Cook, R. M. "Dogs in Battle." *Festschrift Andreas Rumpf.* Cologne, 1950.

Donlan, W. "Archilochus, Strabo, and the Lelantine War." *TAPA* 101 (1970): 137–42.

Ducrey, P. *Guerre et guerriers dans la Grèce antique.* Freiburg, 1985.

Fenik, B. *Typical Battle-Scenes in the Iliad* (*Hermes Einzelschriften* 21 [1968]).

Ferguson, W. S. "The Zulus and the Spartans." *HAS* 2 (1918): 197–234.

Frazer, A. D. "The Myth of the Phalanx Scrimmage." *CW* 36 (1942): 15–16.

Frost, F. "The Athenian Military Before Cleisthenes." *Historia* 33 (1984): 283–88.

Greenhalgh, P. A. L. *Early Greek Warfare.* Cambridge, Eng., 1973.

Griffith, G. T. *The Mercenaries of the Hellenistic World.* Cambridge, Eng., 1935.

Holladay, A. J. "Hoplites and Heresies." *JHS* 102 (1982): 94–104.

Krentz, P. "The Nature of Hoplite Battle." *CA* 4.1 (1985): 50–61.

Lammert, F. "Katalogos." *RE* 10 (1919): 2470–71.

Lazenby, J. F. *The Spartan Army.* Warminster, Eng., 1985.

Lorimer, H. L. "The Hoplite Phalanx." *BSA* 42 (1947): 76–138.

Rahe, P. "The Military Situation in Western Asia on the Eve of Cunaxa." *AJP* (1981): 79–98.

Ridley, R. T. "The Hoplite as Citizen: Athenian Military Institutions in their Social Context." *AC* 48 (1979): 508–48.

Salmon, J. "Political Hoplites?" *JHS* 97 (1977): 87–122.

Shefton, B. B. "Some Iconographic Remarks on the Tyrannicides." *AJA* (1969): 173–79.

Siewert, P. "Ephebic Oath in Fifth Century Athens." *JHS* 97 (1977): 102–111.

Snodgrass, A. M. "The Hoplite Reform and History." *JHS* 85 (1965): 110–22.

Trumy, H. *Kriegerische Fachausdruck im griechischen Epos.* Basel, 1950.

Vidal-Naquet, P. *Le chasseur noir: Formes de penseé et formes de société dans le monde grec.* Paris, 1981.

Whatley, N. "On Reconstructing Marathon and Other Ancient Battles." *JHS* 84 (1964): 119–39.

Wheeler, E. "*Hoplomachia* and Greek Dances in Arms." *GRBS* 23 (1983): 1–20.

———. "The *Hoplomachoi* and Vegetius' Spartan Drillmasters." *Chiron* 13 (1983).

Woodhouse, W. J. *The Campaign of Mantineia in 418 B.C.* London, 1918.

ARMOR AND WEAPONS

Anderson, J. K. "Shields of Eight Palms Width." *CSCA* 9 (1976): 3–8.

Andronikos, M. "Sarissa." *BCH* 94 (1970): 91–107.

Borchhardt, J. *Homerische Helme.* Mainz, 1972.

Chase, G. H. *The Shield Devices of the Greeks.* Cambridge, Mass., 1902.

Hageman, A. *Griechische Panzerung.* Leipzig, 1919.

Hammond, N. G. L. "Training in the Use of the Sarissa and Its Effect on Battle, 359–339 B.C." *Antichton* 4 (1980): 53–63.

Hoffman, H. *Early Cretan Armorers.* Mainz, 1972.

Markle, M. "The Macedonian Sarissa, Spear, and Related Armor." *AJA* 81 (1978): 483–97.

———. "Use of the Sarissa by Philip and Alexander of Macedon." *AJA* 82 (1978): 484 ff.

Reichel, W. *Homerische Waffen.* Vienna, 1901.

Robinson, H. R. *The Armour of Imperial Rome.* London, 1975.

Rolley, C. *Les Bronzes grecs.* Freiburg, 1983.

Snodgrass, A. M. *Arms and Armour of the Greeks.* London, 1967.

———. "Carian Armourers: The Growth of a Tradition." *JHS* 84 (1964): 107–18.

———. *Early Greek Armour and Weapons before 600 B.C.* Edinburgh, 1964.

Thordeman, B. *Armour From the Battle of Wisby, 1361 AD.* Stockholm, 1939.

THE CHARGE AND PURSUIT

Alfoldi, A. "Die Herrschaft der Reiterei in Griechenland und Rom." *Antike Kunst IV.* Berne, 1967: 13–47.

Anderson, J. K. *Ancient Greek Horsemanship.* Berkeley, Calif., 1961.

Best, J. G. P. *Thracian Peltasts and Their Influence on Greek Warfare.* Groningen, 1969.

Blyth, P. H. "The Effectiveness of Greek Armour Against Arrows in the Persian War." Ph.D. diss., University of Reading, 1977.

Donlan, W., and J. Thompson. "The Charge at Marathon." *CJ* 71 (1976): 339–43.

———. "The Charge at Marathon Again." *CW* 72 (1979): 419–20.

Hijmans, J. "Archers in the *Iliad.*" *Festoen A Zadoks-Joseph Jitta.* Groningen, 1976: 243–352.

Lippelt, O. *Die griechischen Leichtbewaffneten bis auf Alexander.* Jena, 1910.

McLeod, W. "The Bowshot at Marathon." *JHS* 90 (1970): 197–98.

———. "The Range of the Ancient Bow." *Phoenix* 19 (1965): 1–14.

Plassant, A. "Les archers d'Athènes." *REG* 26 (1913): 151–213.

THE WOUNDED
AND THE DEAD

Beebe, G., and M. DeBakey. *Battle Casualties: Incidence, Mortality, and Logistic Considerations.* Springfield, Ill., 1952.

Bradeen, D. "The Athenian Casualty Lists." *CQ* 63 (1969): 145–59.

Brophy, R., and M. Brophy. "Death in the Pan-Hellenic Games II: All Combative Sports." *AJP* 106 (1985): 171–98.

Frolich, H. *Die Militarmedecin Homers*. Stuttgart, 1879.

Hartwell, S. *The Mechanism of Healing in Human Wounds*. Springfield, Ill., 1954.

Krentz, P. "Casualties in Hoplite Battles." *GRBS* 26.1 (1985): 13–20.

Majno, G. *The Healing Hand: Man and Wound in the Ancient World*. Cambridge, Mass., 1975.

Major, R. W. *A History of Medicine*. Springfield, Ill., 1954.

Smith, G. "Athenian Casualty Lists." *CP* 14 (1918): 361–64.

Toynbee, J. M. C. *Death and Burial in the Roman World*. Ithaca, N.Y., 1971.

Van Hook, L. "On the Lacedaemonians Buried in the Kerameikos." *AJA* 36 (1932): 290–92.

Vernant, J. P., and G. Gnoli eds., *La mort, les morts dans les sociétés anciennes*. Ischia and Paris 1982.

Weiss, C. "An Unusual Corinthian Helmet." *CSCA* 10 (1977): 195–207.

Whipple, A. O. *The Story of Wound Healing and Wound Repair*. Springfield, Ill., 1963.

MISCELLANEOUS WORKS

Davies, J. K. *Athenian Propertied Families*. Oxford, 1971.

Earle, M., ed. *Makers of Modern Strategy*. Princeton, 1971.

Freeman, D. S. *Lee's Lieutenants*. Vol. 2. New York, 1944.

Graves, R. *Goodbye to All That*. London, 1933.

Herr, M. *Dispatches*. New York, 1977.

Horikoshi, T. *Zero*. New York, 1977.

Horne, A. *The Last Battle*. New York, 1966.

Keegan, J. *The Face of Battle*. New York, 1976.

Keegan, J., and R. Holmes. *Soldiers*. New York, 1986.

Kellet, A. *Combat Motivation: The Behavior of Soldiers in Battle*. Boston, 1982.

Manchester, W. *Goodbye Darkness*. New York, 1979.

Marshall, S. L. A. *Men Against Fire*. New York, 1947.

Oman, C. *History of the Art of War in the Middle Ages*. New York, 1924.

Prescott, W. H. *The Conquest of Mexico*. Philadelphia, 1893.

Ryan, C. *The Last Battle*. New York, 1978.

Shirer, W. L. *The Nightmare Years: 1930–1940*. New York, 1984.

Stouffer, S. A., et al. *The American Soldier: Combat and Its Aftermath*. Vol. 2. Princeton, 1949.

Tod, M. *A Selection of Greek Historical Inscriptions*. Vol. 2. Oxford, 1948.

Verbruggen, J. F. *The Art of War in Western Europe During the Middle Ages*. New York, 1977.

Weigley, R. F. *Eisenhower's Lieutenants*. Bloomington, Ind., 1981.

Wise, T. *Medieval Warfare*. New York, 1976.

Supplementary Bibliography

The following pages discuss relevant books and articles that have appeared since the manuscript of The Western Way of War *was first submitted for publication in 1987.*

CHAPTER 1. ORDINARY THINGS, ORDINARY PEOPLE

Recent research on ancient Greek agriculture as it related to warfare is found in the updated bibliographical commentaries to the new University of California Press editions of *Warfare and Agriculture in Classical Greece* (Berkeley and Los Angeles 1998) and *The Other Greeks: The Agrarian Roots of Western Civilization* (Berkeley and Los Angeles 1999). In the decade since the appearance of the first edition of *The Western Way of War* there has been an unprecedented amount published on ancient Greek agriculture in general. Some of the more specialized journal articles have now been summarized in a series of excellent introductory books; see for example T. W. Gallant, *Risk and Survival: Reconstructing the Rural Domestic Economy* (Stanford 1991); Robert Sallares, *The Ecology of the Ancient Greek World* (Ithaca 1991); B. Wells, ed., *Agriculture in Ancient Greece* (Stockholm 1992); A. B. Burford, *Land and Labor in Ancient Greece* (Baltimore 1993); and S. Isager and J. E. Skydsgaard, *Ancient Greek Agriculture: An Introduction* (London 1993).

The current status of classical scholarship concerning ancient Greek agriculture and the countryside is admirably reviewed by G. Davies, "Economic Geography of the Ancient Greek Countryside: A Re-examination of Monumental Rural Sites on the Island of Siphnos" (doctoral dissertation, Oxford 1998), especially 2–13. In addition, Paul Cartledge has analyzed the recent scholarship on ancient Greek agriculture during the last decade in two long review articles: "Classical Greek Agriculture: Recent Work and Alternative Views," *Journal of Peasant Studies* 21.1 (1993), 127–36, and "Classical Greek Agriculture, II: Two More Alternative Views," *Journal of Peasant Studies* 23.1 (1995), 131–39. For concise and updated synopses of ancient agriculture and controversies, see also now A. Burford, "Greek Agriculture in the Classical Period," *Cambridge Ancient History*, 2d ed., vol. 6 (Cambridge 1994), 661–77; and R. Osborne, "Classical Landscape Revisited," *Topoi* 6.1 (1996), 49–64.

If the neglect of ancient agriculture has been admirably addressed by classical scholars in the last ten years, unfortunately the discipline of classics in general has still lost ground both in and outside the university since my warnings in the first edition of *The Western Way of War*. The problems of contemporary classical scholarship and its increasing irrelevance for the general public are now discussed in Victor Davis Hanson and John Heath, *Who Killed Homer? The Demise of Classical Education and the Recovery of Greek Wisdom* (Berkeley and Los Angeles 1999).

CHAPTER 2. A WESTERN WAY OF WAR

Since the first appearance of this book, the term "Western way of war" has becoming increasingly popular. I have outlined the tenets of classical armies and their successors in more detail in *The Wars of the Ancient Greeks* (London 1999), 18–26, and the Greek military legacy in *Who Killed Homer? The Demise of Classical Education and the Recovery of Greek Wisdom* (Berkeley and Los Angeles 1999), 62–72. The recent *Cambridge Illustrated History of Warfare* (Cambridge 1995), edited by Geoffrey Parker (chapters on classical Greece and Rome by V. D. Hanson), is subtitled *The Triumph of the West*, and seeks to explain why the power of the past and present Western military has been far out of proportion to either the population or the territory of Europe and America. See also Parker's more recent "What Is the Western Way of War?" in *Quarterly Journal of Military History* 8.2 (1996), 86–97; and John Keegan's *A History of Warfare* (New York 1993), especially 239–81.

There is now a fine discussion of Western warfare, with ample attention paid to the philosophers, in D. Dawson, *The Origins of Western Warfare: Militarism and Morality in the Ancient World* (Boulder 1996). Dawson would give more emphasis to the Roman concept of total war as the catalyst for later Western military practice, but I think the Greeks by the late fourth century were quite aware of the natural evolution of the deadly warfare that they had created. By the same token, Stephen Mitchell ("Hoplite Battle in Ancient Greece," in A. B. Lloyd, ed., *Battle in Antiquity* [London 1996], 87–106) suggests that I do not realize that the modern European idea of horrific frontal assault as part of total warfare is a legacy of the postclassical Greeks. But see *The Western Way of War* (1st ed.), 217–28, where I emphasize how the discovery of Western warfare changes with the demise of the city-state, as the Hellenistic Greeks and Romans transformed pitched battles and frontal assaults fought by disciplined civilian soldiers under strict protocols into horrific battles for hegemony and imperialism. See now the excellent account by A. Santosuosso, *Soldiers, Citizens, and the Symbols of War: From Classical Greece to Republican Rome* (Boulder 1997), who attempts to explicate the success of Greek and Roman armies in terms of larger Western values such as freedom, technology, and egalitarianism.

The literature concerning the rise of the West itself is enormous and far too large to cite here. It has grown astronomically in the last decade as scholars have attempted to explain the end of the Cold War and the global spread of capitalism and constitutional government. In passing, I will remark that any attempt to suggest that Western military prowess has mostly resulted from privileged natural resources, microbes, or geographical and environmental conditions (e.g., J. Diamond, *Guns, Germs, and Steel: The Fates of Human Societies* [New York 1997]), rather than values and ideas, is unconvincing. By the same token, we should not believe that Western influence has been largely the result of military capability. (Cf., e.g., S. Huntington, *Clash of Civilizations: Remaking of World Order* [New York 1996].) Western armies do not exist in a vacuum; their lethal nature and dynamism are logical results of a preexisting system that has allowed free scientific inquiry, often kept religion out of politics, involved civilians in the management of armies, championed notions of personal freedom, consensual government, and self-critique, and drawn from the fruits of free markets and private property. All those values were known to the polis Greeks, and that tradition, altered and forgotten in part as it often was, explains the long success of Hellenic and later Roman military forces.

CHAPTER 3. NOT STRATEGY, NOT TACTICS

The battle experience—investigation of the graphic conditions under which men fight—is now a growing part of ancient military history. After the appearance of *The Western Way of War,* I edited a volume, *Hoplites: The Ancient Greek Battle Experience* (London 1991), in which nine classicists sought to recreate the environment of battle, ranging from noise and music to arms and armor, treatment of the dead, wounds, sacrifice before battle, dedications, and the role of generals as hoplites. More recently, see also A. B. Lloyd, ed., *Battle in Antiquity* (London 1996), for recreations of what Greek, Roman, and Near Eastern battles were like—especially S. Mitchell's excellent "Hoplite Warfare in Ancient Greece," 87–106; and (on Rome) A. D. Lee, "Morale and the Roman Experience of Battle," 199–218. A. Goldsworthy, *The Roman Army at War, 100 BC–AD 200* (Oxford 1996), has also applied a more detailed Keeganesque approach to the Roman army that at times discusses past Greek practice. R. Gabriel and K. Metz's *From Sumer to Rome: The Military Capabilities of Ancient Armies* (Westport 1991), though drawing exclusively from either translated or secondary sources, nevertheless provides some fascinating speculations on the lethality of ancient arms, the nature of wounds, and ancient medical care. Robert Cowley in *The Experience of War* (New York 1992) has collated and edited those essays from the *Quarterly Journal of Military History* that concern the battle experience, including articles on the ancient world.

Since *The Western Way of War* first appeared, W. K. Pritchett's monumental work on the military practices of the city-states has at last been completed: *The Greek State at War,* volumes 1–5 (Berkeley and Los Angeles 1971–91). In addition, there are fascinating discussions of hoplite battle at various places throughout his final volumes on the topography of battles and campaigning; see *Studies in Ancient Greek Topography,* parts 1–6 (Berkeley and Los Angeles 1965–89) and parts 7 and 8 (Amsterdam 1991–93).

CHAPTER 4. THE HOPLITE AND HIS PHALANX: WAR IN AN AGRICULTURAL SOCIETY

I have replied at length to L. Foxhall ("Farming and Fighting in Ancient Greece," in J. Rich and G. Shipley, eds., *War and Society in the Greek World* [London 1993], 134–45) in the revised edition of *Warfare and Agriculture in Classical Greece* (Berkeley and Los Angeles 1998). The origins of hoplites, the nature of the Homeric evidence, and the historicity of fighting in the *Iliad* remain controversial. I discuss all those issues in Chapter Six ("The Ways of Fighters," 221–44) of *The Other Greeks.* An updated bibliography of Homeric battle is found in K. Raaflaub, "Soldiers, Citizens, and the Evolution of the Early Greek *Polis,*" in L. Mitchell and P. J. Rhodes, eds., *The Development of the Polis in Archaic Greece* (London 1997), 49–59.

A. M. Snodgrass ("The 'Hoplite Reform' Revisited," *Dialogues d'Histoire Ancienne* 19.1 [1993], 47–61) offers a rejoinder to critics of his earlier work, and reminds us that the iconographic and literary evidence suggests a slow evolution to full hoplite warfare, perhaps encompassing most of the seventh and sixth centuries. H. Van Wees ("The Homeric Way of War," *Greece and Rome* 41 [1994], 1–18), despite differences with those who argue for an early phalanx in Homer, agrees that the poem represents fighting methods contemporary with the late eighth century B.C. See also his *Status Warriors: Violence and Society in Homer and History* (Amsterdam 1992), and "Homeric Warfare" in I. Morris and B. Powell, eds., *A New Companion to Homer* (Leiden 1997), 668–93;

and my "Hoplite Technology in Phalanx Battle," in V. Hanson, ed., *Hoplites: The Ancient Greek Battle Experience* (London 1991), 63–84. J. Rich and G. Shipley, eds., *War and Society in the Greek World* (London 1993), also have some interesting essays on Homeric and early polis fighting (cf. especially H. Bowden, "Hoplites and Homer: Warfare, Hero Cult, and the Ideology of the Polis," 45–63) that reach conclusions similar to those advanced in *The Other Greeks*—hoplite technology represents the efforts of a new (agrarian) class to improve their preexisting efforts at fighting in mass. See also R. Osborne's *Greece in the Making, 1200–479 BC* (London 1996), 170–75; and the cautionary words of W. K. Pritchett, *Studies in Ancient Greek Topography,* part 7 (Amsterdam 1991), 181–90.

An especially valuable article on the rise of hoplites is J. Bryant's "Military Technology and Socio-Cultural Change in the Ancient Greek City," *Sociological Review* 38.3 (1990), 484–516. For the protocols of hoplite battle of the early city-state, see R. Connor, "Early Greek Warfare as Symbolic Expression," *Past and Present* 119 (1988), 3–29. Josiah Ober has presented a more formal review of these rules in "The Rules of War in Classical Greece" (now republished in *The Athenian Revolution: Essays on Ancient Greek Democracy and Political Theory* [Princeton 1996], 53–71), which emphasizes the ritualistic aspects of hoplite fighting. Compare also Ober's "Hoplites and Obstacles," in V. Hanson, ed., *Hoplites: The Ancient Greek Battle Experience* (London 1991), 121–72. In this regard, consult the general account of R. O'Connell, *Of Arms and Men* (New York 1989), 45–68. There is no better concise synopsis of the nature of hoplite warfare as practiced at Sparta than that found in P. Cartledge's *Agesilaos and the Crisis of Sparta* (Baltimore 1987), especially 43–48. See now also the well-written, well-illustrated introduction of John Lazenby, "Hoplite Warfare," in J. Hackett, ed., *A History of War in the Ancient World* (London 1989), 54–81.

I think most scholars would now acknowledge that to understand hoplite battle without knowledge of ancient Greek agrarianism is simply impossible.

CHAPTER 5. SOURCES OF INQUIRY

M. Sage (ed., *Warfare in Ancient Greece: A Sourcebook* [London 1996]) has recently provided a collection of primary sources that concern Greek warfare. There is also a brief collection of translated ancient testimony on the Greeks at war in S. Spyridakis and B. Nystrom, *Ancient Greece: Documentary Perspectives* (Dubuque 1997). For a review of secondary work by classical scholars, see most recently P. Ducrey, "Aspects de l'histoire de la guerre en Grèce ancienne, 1945–1996," in P. Brulé and J. Oulhen, eds., *Esclavage, guerre, économie en Grèce ancienne: Hommages à Yvon Garlan* (Paris 1997), which updates the more comprehensive survey of R. Lonis, "La guerre en Grèce, années de recherche 1968–1983," *Révue des Etudes Grecques* 98 (1985), 321–79. In the spring 1999 issue of the *Journal of Military History* I have written a review essay on the status of secondary scholarship concerning Greek and Roman military history, "The Status of Ancient Military History: Traditional Work, Recent Research, and On-going Controversies," *JMH* 63 (April 1999) 379–419.

P. Krentz and E. Wheeler have provided a wonderful Greek text and translation (but no commentary) of Polyaenus' *Stratagems of War* (Chicago 1994), which replaces R. Shepherd's unreliable 1793 edition (dedicated to Lord Cornwallis). J. DeVoto has also edited and translated Flavius Arrianus' *Tactical Handbook* (Chicago 1993), which heretofore had been nearly impossible to find in English. See now, too, A. M. Devine's new English translation of *Aelian's Manual of Military Tactics* in *Ancient World* 19.1–2 (1989), 31–64.

Peter Hunt's *Slaves, Warfare, and Ideology in the Greek Historians* (Cambridge 1998) discusses the underappreciation of slaves in infantry and sea battles, and attributes the neglect of their contribution to the class outlook and ideology of the Greek historians.

CHAPTER 6. THE BURDEN OF HOPLITE ARMS AND ARMOR

E. Jarva's recent *Archaiologica on Archaic Greek Body Armor* (Rovaniemi 1996) confirms the earlier findings of *The Western Way of War* concerning weight, price, durability, and difficulty of arms. The value of Jarva's work is his interest in the practical, as he explores how hoplite armor was worn, how much it weighed, how it was built—and for whom. There are fine photographs and drawings of hoplite equipment in A. Yalouris and N. Yalouris, *Olympia: A Guide to the Museum and Sanctuary* (Athens 1987).

A brief review of the offensive weapons of the hoplite is found in J. K. Anderson, "Hoplite Weapons and Offensive Arms," in V. Hanson, ed., *Hoplites: The Ancient Greek Battle Experience* (London 1991), 15–37. For a discussion of the refinements of hoplite weapons and armor—the buttspike, the backplate, and the concavity of the shield—see V. Hanson, "Hoplite Technology in Phalanx Battle," in V. Hanson, ed., *Hoplites: The Ancient Greek Battle Experience* (London 1991), 63–84. The diffusion of greaves beyond the Greek world is noted by E. R. Knauer, *"Knemides* in the East? Some Observations on the Impact of Greek Body Armor on 'Barbarian' Tribes," in R. Rosen and J. Farrell, eds., *Nomodeiktes: Greek Studies in Honor of Martin Ostwald* (Ann Arbor 1993), 235–54.

There is an original discussion of Persian and Lydian arms and armor that illustrates just how different such equipment was from Greek models in C. Greenwalt, "Arms and Weapons at Sardis in the Mid-Sixth Century B.C.," *Arkeoloji Ve Sanat* 19.79 (1997), 2–20. For the ubiquity of Greek arms in the southern Balkans, see M. Hockey et al., "An Illyrian Helmet in the British Museum," *Annual of the British School at Athens* 87 (1992), 281–91.

CHAPTER 7. THE OLD MEN

During the fourth century B.C., citizen militias may have had less need to call up men well over fifty for frontline service as traditionally had been done in the early polis—perhaps because of the increasing availability of mercenary troops on the open market. Questions of age and military service, demographic trends, and age-class systems are discussed now in Robert Sallares, *The Ecology of the Ancient Greek World* (Ithaca 1991), 176–80. On the

steady displacement of militias by professional armies, see L. Mari-
novich, *Le mercenariat grec au IVe siècle avant notre ère et la crise de la
polis,* trans. J. Garlan and Y. Garlan (Paris 1988); and P. McKech-
nie, *Outsiders in the Greek City-States during the Fourth Century B.C.*
(Cambridge 1989).

CHAPTER 8. THE DREAD OF MASSED ATTACK

There is a growing body of work now on combat duress and battle shock under the conditions of massed fighting—often drawing loosely on the experience of Vietnam veterans. See most
prominently, Jonathan Shay, *Achilles in Viet-Nam* (New York 1994).
D. Grossman, *On Killing: The Psychological Cost of Learning to Kill
in War and Society* (New York 1995), has extensive discussions of
firsthand accounts of soldiers' reactions to killing and the fear
of battle.

The prebattle sacrifice is reviewed by M. Jameson, "Sacrifice
before Battle," in V. Hanson, ed., *Hoplites: The Ancient Greek Battle
Experience* (London 1991), 197–227. There are fine discussions
of war's imagery in the Greek poets and philosophers in N.
Spiegel's *War and Peace in Classical Greek Literature* (Jerusalem
1990).

CHAPTER 9. A SOLDIER'S GENERAL

The idea of a Greek general fighting alongside his men, urging
them on before and during battle, and sharing in their dangers
firsthand has not been refuted. Everett Wheeler ("The Hoplite
as General," in V. Hanson, ed., *Hoplites: The Ancient Greek Battle
Experience* [London 1991], 121–71) has questioned my notion that
the hoplite general usually fought alongside his troops in the first
rank. His objections have been systematically answered by W. K.
Pritchett, "The General on the Battlefield," in his *Essays in Greek
History* (Amsterdam 1994), 111–44, and *Studies in Ancient Greek
Topography,* part 8 (Amsterdam 1992), 62. Pritchett reaffirms the
traditional view that Greek generals in the age of the city-state

usually fought as hoplites in or near the front rank, and thereby often perished.

For the idea that Greek generals really did address their troops before battle (*contra* M. H. Hansen, "The Battle Exhortation in Ancient Historiography," *Historia* 42 [1993], 161–80), consult, again, W. K. Pritchett, "The General's Exhortation in Greek Warfare," in his *Essays in Greek History* (Amsterdam 1994), 27–109. For the extraordinary degree to which generals were under civilian audit and control at Athens, see now also D. Hamel, *Athenian Generals: Military Authority in the Classical Period* (Leiden 1998).

The increasing (and often incompetent) use of ruse and pre-battle planning by generals in the late fifth and fourth century is discussed by J. Roisman, *The General Demosthenes and His Use of Military Surprise* (Stuttgart 1993).

CHAPTER 10. UNIT SPIRIT AND MORALE: THE ORIGINS OF THE REGIMENTAL SYSTEM

N. Jones, *Public Organization in Ancient Greece: A Documentary Study* (Philadelphia 1987), demonstrates the uniformity of tribal organization throughout the Greek world; the regimental nature of hoplite musters clearly was a Panhellenic phenomenon. For the value of the unit in ancient military practice, see F. W. Smith, "The Fighting Unit: An Essay in Structural Military History," *L'Antiquité* 59 (1990), 149–65.

For the specifics of the Theban Sacred Band, see now J. G. De Voto, "The Theban Sacred Band," *Ancient World* 23 (1992), 3–19; and D. Ogden, "Homosexuality and Warfare in Ancient Greece," in A. B. Lloyd, ed., *Battle in Antiquity* (London 1996), 107–68. On specialized units during the fourth century at Athens, see L. Trittle, "*Epilektoi* at Athens in the Fourth Century," *Ancient History Bulletin* 3 (1989), 54–55.

CHAPTER 11. DRINK

D. Whitehead (*Aineias the Tactician: How to Survive under Siege* [Oxford 1990], 141) has questioned my interpretation that in Xenophon, *Hellenica* 6.4.8, the Spartans drank too much before battle, on the grounds Xenophon wrote that it was "expressly moderate." Whitehead misses the flavor of the passage *hypopinontôn kai ton oinon paroxunai ti autous.* When troops have drunk moderately, such activity merits no mention. But at Leuktra, Xenophon is expressly seeking to explain the disorder of the Spartan advance—and the use of wine is brought up as one reason for their confusion and lethargy. The explicit acknowledgment of "having a little to drink" and "the wine exciting them a little," in both ancient Greek and modern English, is often a euphemistic way of conceding that one has in fact had something *more than a little* to drink—or at least enough alcohol to affect one's behavior noticeably.

CHAPTER 12. THE CHARGE

J. Lazenby (*The Defence of Greece* [Warminister 1989], 66–68) reaffirms the commonly held view that the Greeks at Marathon broke into "a run" during the last two hundred yards to avoid missile attack. For the charge, and the need to avoid Persian missiles, see also A. Santosuosso, *Soldiers, Citizens, and the Symbols of War: From Classical Greece to Republican Rome* (Boulder 1997), 33–35.

CHAPTER 13. A COLLISION OF MEN

J. Lazenby ("The Killing Zone," in V. Hanson, ed., *Hoplites: The Ancient Greek Battle Experience* [London 1991], 87–109) has doubted that the spears of the front rank were often broken. But the phenomenon was captured not only in literature but in ceramic painting as well. See, for example, the incidents of hoplite fighting painted on an unguent vase from the early sixth century B.C. (J. Lazenby, "Hoplite Warfare," in J. Hackett, ed., *A History of War in the Ancient World* [London 1989], 75). Of some eleven combat episodes portrayed, in at least six scenes spears are shown broken. Early hoplites may have carried two spears because of the frequency of breakage; see J. K. Anderson, "Hoplite Weapons and Offensive Arms," in V. Hanson, ed., *Hoplites: The Ancient Greek Battle Experience* (London 1991), 15–37, especially 20–23.

CHAPTER 14. TEARS AND GAPS

S. Hornblower (*A Commentary on Thucydides*, 2 vols. [Oxford 1992–96], 303–8) has some pertinent comments on hoplite collisions concerning the battle of Delion. Peter Krentz ("The Strategic Culture of Periclean Athens," in C. Hamilton and P. Krentz, eds., *Polis and Polemos* [Claremont 1997], 55–72) has questioned whether the sequence of hoplite battle and its protocols were either all that dominant in classical Greek warfare or even reflections of preexisting social, economic, and cultural interests. I have briefly addressed his objections in the revised edition of *Warfare and Agriculture in Classical Greece* (Berkeley and Los Angeles 1998), 204–5, and hope to state the case more fully in an upcoming article. Whatever we may think about the actual extent of hoplite protocols, there is an undeniable ethical and reactionary vein in Greek literature—found in Plato, Aristotle, Demosthenes, Polybius, Xenophon, and Plutarch—that sees hoplite battle as somehow more formal, fair, and honorable (and inexpensive) than what followed.

CHAPTER 15. THE PUSH AND COLLAPSE

I am not convinced by recent attempts to reargue that hoplite battle was fluid and that literal pushing did not normally occur. See, for example, G. L. Cawkwell, "Orthodoxy and Hoplites," *Classical Quarterly* 39 (1989), 375–89; P. Krentz, "Continuing the *Othismos* on *Othismos*," *Ancient History Bulletin* 8.2 (1994), 45–49; and a promised forthcoming article by A. Goldsworthy, "The *Othismos*, Myths and Heresies: The Nature of Hoplite Battle," in *War in History* (cf. A. Goldsworthy, *The Roman Army at War, 100 B.C.–200 A.D.* [Oxford 1996], 206–9). See instead now the definitive article by R. Luginbill ("*Othismos:* The Importance of the

Mass-Shove in Hoplite Warfare," *Phoenix* 48 [1994], 51–61), who points out that hoplites may well have been pushing on the shoulder rather than the back of the man in front.

For the growing importance of horsemen in the late fifth and fourth century for pursuit after hoplite battles, see in general L. Worley, *Hippeis: The Cavalry of Ancient Greece* (Boulder 1994); I. G. Spence, *The Cavalry of Classical Greece: A Social and Military History* (Oxford 1993); and G. Bugh, *The Horsemen of Athens* (Princeton 1988).

CHAPTER 16. CONFUSION, MISDIRECTION, AND MOB VIOLENCE

On the confused nature of hoplite battle, see J. Lazenby, "The Killing Zone," in V. Hanson, ed., *Hoplites: The Ancient Greek Battle Experience* (London 1991), 95–97. Peter Krentz ("The *Salpinx* in Greek Warfare," in V. Hanson, ed., *Hoplites: The Ancient Greek Battle Experience* [London 1991], 110–20) points out that after the initial trumpet call to battle, the *salpinx* was not used to command troops—understandable, given the confusion of the mêlée and the brief duration of hoplite battle.

CHAPTER 17. THE KILLING FIELD

For replacement of the fallen and some figures on casualties in Greek battles, see N. G. L. Hammond, "Casualties and Reinforcements of Citizen Soldiers in Greece and Macedonia," *Journal of Hellenic Studies* 109 (1989), 56–68. There are also statistics on casualties in major Greek battles in R. Gabriel and K. Metz's *From Sumer to Rome: The Military Capabilities of Ancient Armies* (Westport 1991), 84–95. For the identification of the hoplite dead after battle, see P. Vaughn, "The Identification and Retrieval of the Hoplite Battle-Dead," in V. Hanson, ed., *Hoplites: The Ancient Greek Battle Experience* (London 1991), 38–62. For commemoration of the fallen, see now E. Rice, "The Glorious Dead: Commemoration of the Fallen and Portrayal of Victory in the Late Classical and Hellenistic World," in J. Rich and G. Shipley, eds., *War and Society in the Greek World* (London 1993), 224–57.

CHAPTER 18. THE WOUNDED

There is an intriguing diagnosis of the cause of Alexander the Great's death, which illustrates how modern medicine can shed light on ancient disease and trauma, by R. Richard, E. Borza, and R. Benitez, "A Mysterious Death," *New England Journal of Medicine* 338 (June 11, 1998), 1764–69. P. Prioreschi ("Skull Trauma in Egyptian and Hippocratic Medicine," *Gesnerus* 50 [1993], 167–78) points out how much more effective Greek medicine was in treating head wounds than its counterparts elsewhere in the Mediterranean.

CHAPTER 19. EPILOGUE

On the cultural and social background to the change from hoplite warfare to the more dynamic infantry practice of Philip and Alexander, see V. D. Hanson, *The Wars of the Ancient Greeks* (London 1999). The influence of capital in Greek warmaking and the evolution away from hoplite warfare is discussed by L. Kallet-Marx, *Money, Expense, and Naval Power in Thucydides' History 1–5.24* (Berkeley and Los Angeles 1993); and by V. Gabrielsen, *Financing the Athenian Fleet* (Baltimore 1994). The theme that hoplites were supplemented by a variety of forces as part of a larger transformation in Greek society that saw greater roles for capital and technology is taken up implicitly in a number of recent works. See especially M. Munn, *The Defense of Attica* (Berkeley and Los Angeles 1993); and L. Burckhardt, *Bürger und Soldaten* (Stuttgart 1996). In regard to these changes at Athens, see C. Meier, "Die Rolle des Krieges im klassischen Athen," *Historische Zeitschrift* 251 (1990), 555–605. There are two helpful essays in J. Rich and G. Shipley, eds., *War and Society in the Greek World* (London 1993), that show how warfare from the fourth century onward had a deleterious effect on the average citizen, and was used for the aims of a rather small elite: see P. Millett, "Warfare, Economy, and Democracy in Classical Athens" (177–96); and M. Austin, "Alexander and the Macedonian Invasion of Asia: Aspects of the Historiography of War and Empire in Antiquity" (197–223). These changes in fourth-century warfare are now summarized in Y. Garlan's "Warfare," in D. Lewis et al., *Cambridge Ancient History*, 2d ed., vol. 6, *The Fourth Century B.C.* (Cambridge 1994), 678–92.

Index

Index Locorum

Permissions Acknowledgments

A Note About the Author

Victor Hanson was educated at the University of California at Santa Cruz, the American School of Classical Studies (Athens), and Stanford University, where he received his Ph.D. in Classics in 1980. The author of *Warfare and Agriculture in Classical Greece* and other books on Greek history, he is currently professor of Classical Languages and coordinator of the Classical Studies Program at California State University, Fresno. With his wife and three children, he lives and works on his family's small farm near Selma, California, where he was born in 1953.

Also by Victor Davis Hanson:

Warfare and Agriculture in Classical Greece (1983, 1998)

Hoplites: The Ancient Greek Battle Experience (editor, 1991)

The Other Greeks: The Agrarian Roots of Western Civilization (1995)

Fields Without Dreams: Defending the Agrarian Idea (1996)

Who Killed Homer? Greek Wisdom and the Demise of Classical Education (with John Heath, 1998)

The Wars of the Ancient Greeks (1999)

The Soul of Battle (1999)

The Land Was Everything: Letters From an American Farmer (2000)